Research and Development in Expert Systems III

THE BRITISH COMPUTER SOCIETY WORKSHOP SERIES

Editor: P. HAMMERSLEY

The BCS Workshop Series aims to report developments of an advanced technical standard undertaken by members of The British Computer Society through the Society's study groups and conference organizations. The series should be compulsive reading for all whose work or interest involves computing technology and for both undergraduate and post-graduate students. Volumes in this Series will mirror the quality of papers published in the BCS's technical periodical *The Computer Journal* and range widely across topics in computer hardware, software, applications and management.

Some current titles:

Current Perspectives in Health Computing
Ed. B. Kostrewski

Research and Development in Information Retrieval
Ed. C. J. van Rijsbergen

Proceedings of the Third British National Conference on Databases (BNCOD3)
Ed. J. Longstaff

Research and Development in Expert Systems
Ed. M. A. Bramer

Proceedings of the Fourth British National Conference on Databases (BNCOD4)
Ed. A. F. Grundy

People and Computers: Designing the Interface
Eds. P. Johnson and S. Cook

Expert Systems 85
(Research and Development in Expert Systems II)
Ed. M. Merry

Text Processing and Information Retrieval
Ed. J. C. van Vliet

Proceedings of the Fifth British National Conference on Databases (BNCOD5)
Ed. E. A. Oxborrow

People and Computers: Designing for Usability
Eds. M. D. Harrison and A. F. Monk

Research and Development in Expert Systems III
Ed. M. A. Bramer

Research and Development in Expert Systems III

Proceedings of Expert Systems '86, the Sixth Annual Technical Conference
of the British Computer Society Specialist Group on Expert Systems,
Brighton, 15 - 18 December 1986

Edited by M. A. BRAMER

*Head of the School of Computing and Information Technology,
Thames Polytechnic*

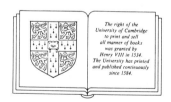

Published by
CAMBRIDGE UNIVERSITY PRESS
on behalf of
THE BRITISH COMPUTER SOCIETY
Cambridge
London   New York   New Rochelle
Melbourne   Sydney

Published by the Press Syndicate of the University of Cambridge
The Pitt Building, Trumpington Street, Cambridge CB3 1RP
32 East 57th Street, New York, NY 10022, USA
10 Stamford Road, Oakleigh, Melbourne, Australia

First published 1987

Printed in Great Britain at the University Press, Cambridge

Library of Congress cataloging in publication data available

British Library cataloguing in publication data

British Computer Society. *Specialist Group on Expert Systems. Technical Conference (6th:1986 Metropole Hotel, Brighton)*
Research and development in expert systems III: proceedings of Expert Systems '86, the Sixth Annual Technical Conference of the British Computer Society Specialist Group on Expert Systems, Metropole Hotel, Brighton, 15-18 December 1986.---(The British Computer Society workshop series)

1. Expert systems (Computer science)
I. Title II. Bramer, M.A. III. Series
006.3'3 QA76.76.E95

ISBN 0 521 34145 X

Contents

Preface

The papers in this volume are those presented at Expert Systems '86, the sixth annual conference of the British Computer Society Specialist Group on Expert Systems, held at the Metropole Hotel, Brighton from December 15th-18th 1986.

There are 21 refereed papers, plus invited papers by Professor Brian Gaines, Dr Luc Steels and Professor Tom Stanier.

On behalf of the Programme Committee, I should like to thank all those who took part in the refereeing of papers this year. Their names are listed below.

Special thanks are also due to Professor Tom Addis, for his support and encouragement as overall Conference Chairman for Expert Systems '86, and to Conference Clearway for all their excellent work in administering the conference and not least for their help in the preparation of this volume.

Max Bramer
Programme Chairman, Expert Systems '86

Programme Committee

Max Bramer (Chairman)	Martin Merry
Bernard Kelly	Richard Young

Referees (in addition to Programme Committee members)

Alan Bundy	Chris Mellish
Michael Clarke	Stuart Moralee
Bill Clocksin	Alan Rector
Alison Kidd	Peter Ross
John Lumley	Bill Sharpe
Abe Mamdani	John Tait

EXPERT SYSTEMS IN BRITAIN: PROGRESS AND PROSPECTS

M.A.Bramer
School of Computing and Information Technology
Thames Polytechnic
Wellington Street
London SE18 6PF

Abstract

It is now five years since the first major Expert Systems conference was
held in Britain. This paper reviews progress in the field in those
intervening five years and considers the prospects for future development,
including the social issues that will inevitably arise as Expert Systems
grows into a large worldwide industry.

1. Expert Systems in Britain 1981-86

The fifth anniversary of the first major Expert Systems conference in
Britain, Expert Systems '81, organised in London in December 1981 by the
British Computer Society Specialist Group on Expert Systems, seems an
appropriate time (or at least provides a reasonable excuse) to review
progess in this increasingly important field.

Although the earliest Expert System- Dendral- has its origins as long ago
as 1965, interest in Expert Systems took a long time to develop in
Britain, as in the rest of the world.

In retrospect the inauguration by Professor Donald Michie (then Professor
of Machine Intelligence at Edinburgh University) in the Summer of 1980 of
a new specialist group of the British Computer Society, to cover the then
little-known topic of Expert Systems appears to have been a landmark event.

Although the inaugural meeting itself was well attended, the suspicion
persisted for some time afterwards that the field in question was one that
barely existed, and that the number of active participants in this country
could easily be counted on the fingers of one hand.

From that relatively humble beginning, the British Expert Systems
community has experienced an explosive period of growth. Virtually every
University and Polytechnic now seems to have its Expert Systems projects
and the list of commercial companies (from the very large down to the very
small) actively involved in the field is both long and impressive.

The availability of both hardware and software tools for Expert Systems
and its parent field of Artificial Intelligence (which in 1981 was limited
to little more than the languages Lisp and Prolog and computers such as
the DecSystem-10/20 and the Vax) has changed out of all recognition, with
dozens of products now competing for attention, including powerful
programming languages, Expert System shells and Artificial Intelligence
development environments, running on a variety of mainframes, personal
computers and workstations. Pre-packaged Expert Systems are also becoming
available (for applications such as interpreting the Statutory Sick Pay

legislation), although not yet in large numbers.

The BCS Specialist Group on Expert Systems (SGES) has served as a focus for much of this activity. Its membership has risen to over 1200 (presumably only a small proportion of those involved in the field at all levels) and is still rising rapidly. The group has run an annual series of major technical conferences- Expert Systems '81 to '86- with large attendances.

The first conference, in 1981, consisted principally of presentations of well-established systems from the USA (notably PROSPECTOR and R1), plus a number of projects at a much earlier stage of development in Britain. Many of the papers were on topics such as 'Finding uses for Expert Systems', 'What Expert Systems can Offer Software Engineering', 'The Potential of Expert Systems in Engineering' or 'How Banks Might Use Expert Systems'.

At the 1983 conference, held at Churchill College, Cambridge, many of the presentations concerned initial results and experience gained from building prototype systems using a variety of fairly rudimentary shells.

By the 1986 conference, the content and emphasis of the annual conference had changed markedly from 1981, with a strong emphasis on significant practical systems (most of them developed or under development in Britain) for applications such as Medical Image Interpretation, Taxation, Continuous Evolutionary Process Control, Brickwork Design and Surface Classification, developed using a wide range of increasingly sophisticated hardware and software. To support the technical content of the conference, there was also a substantial programme of invited company presentations, panel sessions, exhibits by both hardware and software suppliers and other 'fringe' events.

Although these conferences rightly reflect the substantial advances that have been made in the last five years, a study of the corresponding Proceedings also reveals that advances in the basic theory have been very much harder to achieve (see Section 3 below).

To complement the SGES events, there is a seemingly never-ending stream of commercial conferences, workshops, management tutorials etc. of all kinds, and in recent months a plethora of new magazines and journals. Although the number of books on Expert Systems has increased considerably, the literature of the field remains surprisingly unsatisfactory, with very few recommendable textbooks at either introductory or advanced level.

Typically, conferences (and books) precede journals as indicators of evolving subfields. Just as Expert Systems conferences emerged with a separate identity from Artificial Intelligence, so do recent conferences on topics such as 'Expert Systems in Computer-Aided Design', 'Expert Systems for Structural Design' and 'Expert Database Systems' show the ways in which the field is likely to develop in the next few years. The recent formation of a joint subgroup of the Northern branches of the SGES and the BCS Human-Computer Interface (HCI) specialist group, resulting in joint meetings and conferences, etc. of the two fields and their associated communities may also be a significant pointer to the future.

The huge upsurge of interest and activity in Britain is not an isolated phenomenon- similar upsurges have occurred in the United States and in much of Western Europe. The common cause is easy to trace: the announcement towards the end of 1981 of the major Japanese initiative to produce so-called "fifth-generation" computers in which it was asserted that "Intelligence will be greatly improved to approach that of a human being" (JIPDEC, 1981).

As yet, all this activity has resulted in very few applications systems in regular practical use. However, this is likely to be no more than a function of the timescales involved, and the European market for Expert Systems has been predicted to be growing to a value of several billions of pounds per annum by the early 1990s. In the United States, where industrial applications projects started somewhat earlier than in Britain, a recent report indicates that there are at least a thousand major (i.e. million-dollar) projects currently in progress, mostly scheduled for completion in 1987-88, and covering a wide range of applications in a variety of industries (Hewett, 1986).

As well as the traditional application areas for Expert Systems, such as medicine, attention is increasingly becoming focussed in Britain and elsewhere on forming links between Expert Systems and the conventional problems of Data Processing and commercial computing, including the interface between Expert Systems and Database Management Systems, the development of Intelligent Front Ends to complex software packages and information retrieval systems, applications in real-time process control and embedding expert modules in otherwise standard Data Processing software. In the current economic climate in Britain, it is not surprising that a great deal of attention is also turning to Expert Systems for financial applications.

2. The Alvey Programme

In Britain the direct catalyst to action following the Japanese announcement of its Fifth Generation Computer Systems (FGCS) programme in 1981 was the launching of the Alvey Programme for Advanced Information Technology. The establishment of this programme was the principal recommendation of a high-powered committee chaired by Mr. John Alvey, then Senior Director for Technology at British Telecom, which was established by the Department of Industry (now the Department of Trade and Industry) in March 1982 and reported seven months later.

In the Alvey Report (Department of Industry, 1982), Intelligent Knowledge-Based Systems (abbreviated to IKBS) was identified as a major area in need of development. The term IKBS was chosen as a euphemism for 'Artificial Intelligence', a field which had been discredited by the publication of the influential- but also naive and misguided- Lighthill Report to the (then) Science Research Council nine years before (Science Research Council, 1973).

The Alvey Programme as eventually established is a collaboration between the Department of Trade and Industry, the Science and Engineering Research Council (SERC), the Ministry of Defence and industry. The entire programme is worth around 350 million over five years (around 200 million from government, the rest from industry) for 'pre-competitive' research in four principal areas including IKBS.

In the climate of the time when the Alvey Programme was set up, IKBS was widely taken to mean only Expert Systems, but the significance of other aspects of Artificial Intelligence (such as speech recognition and computer vision) soon became generally apparent.

The Alvey Programme has been involved in stimulating and financing numerous developments in all aspects of Artificial Intelligence, including the funding of many collaborative research and development projects, the initiation of 'community clubs' of companies with common interests (such as insurance companies) to develop Expert Systems, and the organisation of a large number of workshops.

One of the greatest benefits of the Programme has undoubtedly been the bridge it has helped to forge between workers in industry and academe. This has not always been achieved without difficulty, but has been both necessary and desirable for both sides- to industry because of its continuing shortage of the relevant technical expertise, and to academe as a source of practical projects (and- not unimportantly- of finance in a climate of unrelenting hostility to the entire education system in government circles).

Unfortunately, the difficulties involved in any collaboration (not least between those who have little experience in working together, such as industry and academe in many cases) seem to have been seriously underrated by the funding bodies concerned at the start of the programme.

Although a strong emphasis on collaborative projects was a major feature of the Alvey Programme, the 'management overhead' involved in both setting up projects and running them once established proved to be very high in many cases- a problem exacerbated by Alvey's policy of financing only 50% of the costs of the industrial partner and the severe restrictions on charging for management time, secretarial costs etc. traditionally imposed by SERC, the body through which academic collaborators on Alvey projects were funded.

The most severe drawback of the Alvey Programme has certainly been the diversion of leading researchers away from research on to organisation (and fund-raising). It is hard to avoid the conclusion that leading British researchers in Expert Systems and related technical areas now spend considerably less time on fundamental research than they did five years ago. The value of fundamental research does not seem fully to have been understood, the belief apparently being held that a huge worldwide Expert Systems industry can be built on the basis of an unreliable underlying theory.

Although the Alvey Programme is not much more than halfway through its five-year life, it is in the nature of such programmes that the great majority of its funds are already committed to projects currently in progress. Discussions about a possible successor are already well advanced and at the time of writing (September 1986) a committee chaired by Sir Austin Bide- known as the Information Technology (1986) Committee- is preparing a report to the Minister of State for Industry and Information Technology on a possible 'After Alvey' programme.

As an input to this, the Engineering Board of SERC decided in April 1985 to establish an 'After Alvey' Working Party under the chairmanship of Professor Eric Ash to consider the involvement of the academic sector in any follow-on programme. The working party's report appeared in March 1986 (Science and Engineering Research Council, 1986) and recommended a follow-on programme closely integrated with European activities in which the academic sector would have an indispensable role. It was proposed that the national funding of the academic component of the programme would be around 25 million per annum and that the University Grants Committee and the National Advisory Body (roughly the equivalent of the UGC for Polytechnics and colleges) should participate from the outset in the planning of the programme.

In considering the progress to date of the Alvey Programme, the After Alvey Working Party commented "... few substantial results have yet been achieved as is only to be expected. It is quite evident that although after the scheduled five years for the first phase of Alvey, the present trickle of results will have turned into a flood, much will remain to be done. It is inconceivable for example that we will have adequate understanding of many of the fundamental concepts of IKBS in that time. Indeed in the Alvey Report IKBS was envisaged anyway as a ten year programme .... to break off after five years will fail to reap the benefits of the investment already made. Nor is it reasonable to suggest that these subjects will have reached a degree of maturity such that all future funding could be undertaken by industry. This is most obviously true in IKBS ...".

Unfortunately, at the present time the prospects for a second phase of the Alvey Programme do not seem good. If the Programme is extended, which seems improbable, it is likely to be in a very different form (thus incurring a high 'startup overhead' for a second time), with more emphasis on applications. This latter aspect would be particularly alarming in view of the lack of impact of the Alvey Programme itself on fundamental (and crucial) technical issues.

3. Technical Issues

Although the Expert systems "industry" has increased enormously in the last five years, as has the field's commercial recognition, it is important to realise that the theoretical basis of the subject has advanced very little. In all the euphoria, difficult theoretical and methodological issues have been forgotten or ignored but not solved.

Alongside the growing volume of good research and development work currently in progress are a number of activities of little value and with only a nominal relationship to Expert Systems, but which operate under the Expert Systems umbrella and may bring the field into disrepute if not controlled. The current position is reminiscent of the early days of databases, when anyone with a program using a sequential file- or better still a random-access file- felt free to reclassify himself as a database administrator (with a corresponding rise in status and perhaps salary). Many of the Expert Systems commonly demonstrated are nothing of the sort, but straightforward rule-based programs performing tasks which could perfectly well have been achieved in numerous other but less fashionable ways.

Many of the technical problems involved in building Expert Systems have been known for a long time, for example the problems of reasoning with uncertain information, consistency maintenance and missing knowledge which were referred to by Bramer (1985).

Although progress with such problems is inevitably slow, one area where progress is being made is that of reasoning with uncertainty, where the probabilistic methods of MYCIN, PROSPECTOR, etc. are being replaced by methods more akin to human reasoning such as the use of formal definitions of linguistic concepts of certainty, such as 'X is likely' or 'X is suspected' (see, for example, Ellam and Maisey (1986) for an example of inexact reasoning in a medical domain). An alternative approach being pursued in a number of centres is to develop non-standard logics, e.g. for 'default reasoning'.

Alongside such long-standing theoretical issues, new research areas are growing up, looking at 'human-centred' questions relevant to Expert Systems, such as the types of advice required by the users of an Expert System and the appropriateness of the explanation facilities frequently provided (see, for example, Kidd (1985) and Hughes (1986)). Other research is concerned with the crucial problem of eliciting knowledge from experts (see, for example, Gammack and Young (1985)).

Although there are individuals and research groups actively considering such theoretical and methodological matters, the need for a satisfactory methodology for all aspects of the development and maintenance of Expert Systems and the importance of placing consistency maintenance, reasoning with uncertainty etc. on a sound theoretical basis seems little appreciated by most of those developing systems 'in the field'- as indeed was the need for properly founded development methodologies for conventional Data Processing systems not long ago.

When Expert Systems first entered the spotlight, the idea of using rules as a representation for knowledge seems to have struck many with the force of revelation. So much so, that some have not fully realised the need for more complex representations for some (probably most) domains. Such more complex representations were, in fact, used in most of the original (and now 'classic') Expert Systems, even in MYCIN, but this was not fully appreciated at first.

This misconception is now dissolving as more and more practical systems are being developed. The use of simple shells (which use a fixed representation regardless of the domain in question) is giving way to the use of sophisticated Artificial Intelligence 'development environments' combining several representations (for example, LOOPS combines the features of four different programming paradigms).

The use of the term 'Deep Knowledge Based Systems' (DKBS) reflects the new awareness that rules alone are often insufficient as a representation for expert knowledge.

Steels (1986) uses the term 'second generation' Expert Systems to denote those that combine heuristic reasoning based on rules with deep reasoning based on a model of the problem domain, as opposed to 'first generation' systems which rely purely on heuristic knowledge in the form of rules.

With the coming of the second generation, it would seem that Expert Systems is in the process of rejoining its parent field of Artificial Intelligence, as indeed is necessary if its full potential is to be achieved.

4. Social Issues

Even when Expert Systems eventually develop a firm theoretical and methodological basis, the field will not cease to be a focus for discussion and probably controversy.

Expert Systems development, along with most other areas of technological change, cannot be viewed in isolation from the social and political context in which it takes place.

It is often pointed out that all technology has the potential for both positive and negative uses, as if this is a justification for neglecting any further analysis. This argument is particularly inadequate in the case of Expert Systems.

What is fundamentally different about Expert Systems, in contrast to technological developments such as, say, telephones, cars, computerised stock control systems or bank cash dispensers, all of which have their negative side but are fundamentally helpful, is that Expert Systems are frequently (although not always) concerned with the judgements made by highly-skilled experts who collectively comprise the leaders of society.

The inherent suspicion that Expert Systems may take major decisions out of the hands of people and place computers in charge of tasks such as diagnosing their illnesses, handling their legal problems, running the financial affairs of the companies in which they work and controlling weapons systems may be expressed far more often by the 'outsider' to the field than by those on the inside, but (however far removed from current practice or possibility) it surely deserves consideration and answer, rather than the dismissive response it often receives.

The most sensitive uses to which Expert Systems are likely to be put are in military applications. The possibilities for signal interpretation systems and for command and control systems (to name only two areas of application) are already clear. The Expert Systems community would seem to include all shades of opinion on the desirability of such uses, from those who are directly involved in them and regard them as self-evidently right to those who see them as self-evidently wrong and immoral.

Not very long ago, even the most powerful and malicious of tyrants could affect no more than a relatively small part of the world. Now an increasing number of individuals can destroy or ruin a high proportion of the world and its entire population of humans and other animals with a single action, and the chance of this happening by accident seems to be already uncomfortably high. (The cynic might argue that putting an Expert System in charge of nuclear weapons does not seem so dangerous when one considers the humans that currently perform the task. A highly-intelligent Expert System might contain only one (heuristic) rule: 'For all situations S and Weapons W, do not use W in situation S'. However, it would not be wise to rely on this argument.)

The danger with applying any new technology in the military area and perhaps most of all with incorporating human judgement or expertise into computer programs for military applications is that it may act as a destabilizing factor by introducing ever more complexity into a world-wide system of defence/offence that is already precariously balanced and barely controllable.

If successful, the incorporation of human judgement might also act as a stabilizing factor, of course, but the notorious problems and failures of the computer industry even with entirely deterministic and routine tasks such as payroll (hardware errors, software bugs, difficulties of maintenance etc.) do not inspire confidence. To these must be added the rudimentary state of the knowledge engineer's art and the embryonic nature of the development methodology currently employed for building Expert Systems.

An associated problem is the growing involvement of the military in the funding of academic research. This is happening but is not yet a cause for serious alarm in Britain, but is certainly becoming so in the U.S.A. not least as the pressure grows for academic institutions to become involved in the U.S. government's 'Strategic Defence Initiative' (SDI), popularly known as 'Star Wars'. The risk is, of course, that those who disapprove of such programmes or regard them as unsound or excessively dangerous will be forced to smother their concerns or abandon research altogether.

An alarming recent development, which it is hoped is not symptomatic of future trends is the abrupt cancellation of the publication of a book by Richard Ennals, a British Artificial Intelligence researcher and former member of the Alvey Directorate, entitled 'Star Wars: A Question of Initiative', scheduled for publication in September 1986 and widely publicized by the publishers in the customary glowing terms.

However, the Guardian of September 19th 1986 reported: 'Exactly a month ago, the British subsidiary of the US-based publisher, John Wiley and Sons, issued a press release urging the media to attend a press conference to launch what promised to be a lively and controversial book on Star Wars. It quoted flattering comments by Denis Healey, David Steel and Shirley Williams .... But those in search of enlightenment were disappointed. Last Friday night, Ennals was told that the book had been abruptly withdrawn by the publishers. He was not given a reason for the decision....[the book] asks a number of leading questions- what restrictions will be imposed on academic freedom by participation in SDI; what impact will it have on other international research projects; what is going to be the impact of public expenditure on civil research programmes?'.

The Guardian concludes that for the moment, Ennals cannot ask these questions in a book and itself asks 'Who needs the Official Secrets Act?'.

The implications of this report are unmistakable. It would be pleasing to report that the publishers had produced a complete rebuttal of all suspicions and accusations and a full explanation of their actions, but at the time of writing this had not appeared.

Another part of the impact that Expert Systems may come to make on

society, where the applications domains are not themselves open to
suspicion or criticism, is in the 'deskilling' of expert tasks, where the
availability of Expert Systems may enable expert-level decisions to be
made by those with considerably less expertise (or none at all) themselves.

To take a medical example, it may be possible for the General Practitioner
to operate at the level of skill of a top consultant in some specialised
area.

Paradoxically, it is possible that this will operate in a detrimental way,
by fostering an increasing reliance on relatively junior members of staff.
It would be easy to use the availability of Expert Systems as an excuse
for dispensing with access to consultants altogether for the large
majority of patients (for example, those making use of the British
National Health Service), rather than making more of the consultants' time
available to deal with the most difficult cases.

A further problem which cannot be neglected indefinitely is that of
accountability for the actions, decisions or recommendations of Expert
Systems.

In a paper first presented at Expert Systems '82, Cendrowska and Bramer
(1984) present a 'rational reconstruction' of the MYCIN medical
consultation system, known as RMYCIN. Their system makes use of part of
the knowledge base of the original MYCIN system and the authors included
the following disclaimer in their paper: "It would be very unwise and
possibly dangerous to assume that a consultation with RMYCIN was of any
medical value whatsoever .... [RMYCIN has goals] which do not include
medical reliability.".

In this case, the likelihood of anyone suffering injury from using the
system was extremely small, if only because of the unavailability of the
programming language (Wonderpop- a variant of POP-2) in which the system
was written. However, as the number of pre-packaged Expert Systems
increases, the potential for their mis-use (not to mention errors
resulting from bugs in the systems) increases correspondingly.

Most individuals would not even consider taking on for themselves the role
of a highly-skilled professional such as a solicitor, a doctor or an
accountant (even assuming it were always legal to do so), without
possessing the necessary technical knowledge and experience. However, it
is perfectly possible for anyone to make use of books incorporating the
expertise of such experts, as the readily available medical textbooks and
the recent 'Do your own house conveyancing' books illustrate.
Incorporating knowledge of this kind in Expert Systems makes its
accessibility still greater, potentially giving almost anyone access to
(e.g) medical or legal advice of the highest quality and thus enabling
them to perform as their own professional experts and advisors, should
they choose to do so.

While the supply of such software is restricted to software houses with
considerable skill and high integrity and their users are appropriately
chosen, this might be regarded as highly desirable, indeed a way of
breaking down the 'power of the priesthood' in a number of professions.

Unfortunately, the reality is likely to be very different. It is easy to predict a flood of low-cost software produced for the hobbyist/home-computer market. No-one who has followed the progress of this market could feel confident that low-cost will not lead to low-quality and low-reliability. The dangers of giving even good information to those without the ability to interpret it correctly are also well-known. This would be bad enough if all the systems were completely deterministic ones, but many will inevitably include heuristics, inexact reasoning etc. and will unavoidably make errors on occasions (just like human experts), not to mention the possibly more major errors resulting from poor programming, use of low-grade 'experts' to build the systems and so on.

It is by no means self-evident that disclaimers on software of this kind will have any legal force. Equally, it is notoriously difficult to successfully (and usefully) take legal action against very small companies or private individuals.

It is difficult to see how the proliferation of low-grade Expert System software could possibly be stopped if it took hold amongst computer hobbyists. Although not a problem now, this could easily become one. It has recently been suggested that AISB (the Society for the Study of Artificial Intelligence and the Simulation of Behaviour) should introduce a code of conduct for its members, but it is unlikely that this approach would work, since AISB would have considerable difficulties in validating Expert Systems and no effective powers against transgressors (who could simply choose not to be members). Without the associated powers, a code of conduct could even prove counter-productive as companies could point to their membership of the society as evidence of their 'good credentials'.

Of course, this is little different from the position in the computer industry as a whole. The essential difference is the much greater risk involved in giving a large number of individuals access to professional-level expertise which is in fact erroneous, or possibly correct but misleading. Compared with this, the risk of a games program containing a bug or a word processing program occasionally losing a line of text is quite insignificant.

5. The Broader Perspective: Is the Brain a Computer?

The question of whether the human brain is no more than a computer is not a new one, but so far does not seem to have impinged much on the public consciousness. This may be going to change. A recent book by Simons (1986) even has the alarming title 'Is Man a Robot?' and suggests that there is a sense in which the answer is 'yes'. Not long ago, for such a book to emerge from outside the wilder side of the research community would have been unthinkable. Today it emanates from the Chief Editor of the (British) National Computing Centre.

One of the earliest areas of application of the techniques of Artificial Intelligence was to the programming of computers to play chess. One of the pioneers in this field was the Soviet chess grandmaster Mikhail Botvinnik, one of the strongest human chess players of all time, a celebrated electrical engineer and a man usually noted for the temperate nature of his views.

In a lecture in the Russian town of Vladimir in July 1968, Botvinnik is quoted as making the astonishing remark: "We have set our sights on solving a very great problem....the creation of an artificial intellect-an electronic machine capable of playing chess.... What will it mean ... if this work is successfully completed? ....When an electronic machine has started playing chess and played it successfully this will be such a momentous event that every schoolboy will want to know about it. In world history, it will perhaps fall not far short in importance of the discovery of fire." (Botvinnik,1968).

It is a measure of the progress that has been made that we do now have computers that play chess at master level, and it is not inconceivable that the world championship (usually regarded as a supreme intellectual achievement) may come within reach of computer programs in the next few years.

The momentous consequences predicted by Botvinnik have not come to pass, but this may yet occur. Suppose that 'started playing chess and played it successfully' were replaced by 'eclipsed the performance of internationally renowned experts in medicine, the law, economics, mathematics, logic, engineering and passed every known test of human intelligence' in the penultimate sentence, it is surely probable that the impact would be at least as great as Botvinnik suggests.

It need hardly be said that Expert Systems cannot yet even remotely claim the levels of performance mentioned above. However, it is perfectly possible that the production of a series of Expert Systems with far less substantial expertise than those may catalyse a widespread change in public perception and the general acceptance of the view that the brain is no more than a computer- an opinion which today commands only slight support.

Note that such changes of belief are not a matter of obtaining incontrovertible evidence or of persuading the leading philosophers to adopt a different point of view. (The consensus view that humans are descended from apes is not based on a deep understanding of the works of Charles Darwin. It is much more likely to be based on a visit to the monkey house in the zoo.)

It is already well understood that the human body behaves like a machine in many ways. The next step may be the acceptance that the human brain is no more than another form of machine, with all the implications for the cherished ideas of 'consciousness' and even 'being alive' that this may entail.

It is perfectly possible that we shall live to see this change of belief (it is no more unlikely than a widespread belief in the evolution of humans from animals was in 1800). If it does occur, the impact on humanity's view both of itself and of the legitimate role of Expert Systems in society may be considerable indeed.

References

Botvinnik, M.M. (1968). M.M.Botvinnik declares... . Chess, 34, nos.563-4, pp.3-8. [Summary of lecture in English translation]

Bramer, M.A. (1985). Expert systems: the vision and the reality. In Research and development in expert systems, ed. M.A.Bramer, pp.1-12. Cambridge: Cambridge University Press.

Cendrowska, J. and Bramer, M.A. (1984). A rational reconstruction of the MYCIN consultation system. Int. J. Man-Machine Studies, 20, pp.229-317.

Department of Industry (1982). A programme for advanced information technology: the report of the Alvey Committee. London: Her Majesty's Stationery Office.

Ellam, S.V. and Maisey, M.N. (1986). A knowledge based system to assist in medical image interpretation: design and evaluation methodology. In Research and development in expert systems III, ed. M.A.Bramer. Cambridge: Cambridge University Press. [This volume.]

Gammack, J.G. and Young, R.M. (1985). Psychological techniques for eliciting expert knowledge. In Research and development in expert systems, ed. M.A.Bramer, pp.105-112. Cambridge: Cambridge University Press.

Hewett, J. (1986). Commercial expert systems in North America. In Proceedings of the Sixth International Workshop on Expert Systems and Their Applications, Avignon, France, April 1986, pp.35-41.

Hughes, S. (1986). Question classification in rule-based systems. In Research and development in expert systems III, ed. M.A.Bramer. Cambridge: Cambridge University Press. [This volume.]

JIPDEC (1981). Preliminary report on study and research on fifth-generation computers 1979-1980. Japan Information Processing Development Center.

Kidd, A. (1985). What do users ask?- some thoughts on diagnostic advice. In Expert Systems 85, ed. M.Merry, pp.9-19. Cambridge: Cambridge University Press.

Science and Engineering Research Council (1986). After the Alvey programme: academic research in information technology.

Science Research Council (1973). Artificial Intelligence: a paper symposium.

Simons,G. (1986). Is man a robot?. Chichester: J.Wiley and Sons Ltd.

Steels, L. (1986). In Research and development in expert systems III, ed. M.A.Bramer. Cambridge: Cambridge University Press. [This volume.]

FOUNDATIONS OF KNOWLEDGE ENGINEERING

Brian R Gaines
Dept. Computer Science, University of Calgary, Alberta, Canada T2N 1N4

Abstract
An anticipatory system formulation of human cognitive psychology is presented which provides scientific foundations for knowledge engineering. The formulation gives an operational model of the notion of expertise and the role it plays in our society. It suggests that the basic cognitive system that should be considered is a social organization, rather than an individual. Computational models of inductive inference already developed can be applied directly to the social model. One practical consequence of the model is a hierarchy of knowledge transfer methodologies which defines the areas of application of the knowledge engineering techniques already in use. This analysis clarifies some of the problems of expertise transfer noted in the literature, in particular, what forms of knowledge are accessible through what methodologies. The model is being used as a framework within which to extend and develop a family of knowledge support systems to expedite the development of expert system applications.

1. Introduction

The term *knowledge engineering* was coined by Feigenbaum (1980) to encompass the process of reducing a large body of knowledge to a precise set of facts and rules. Knowledge engineering is now recognized as a fundamental problem in expert system applications, and it is generally seen as a major bottleneck impeding applications to new domains. Guidelines about knowledge engineering techniques have been published (Hayes-Roth, Waterman & Lenat 1983) and the psychological problems of knowledge transfer have been analysed (Welbank 1983). However, no scientific framework for knowledge engineering has been established, and present techniques are based on intuition, experience and empirical results rather than deep foundations.

This weakness is not unreasonable at this stage of the rapid growth of a new technology, but lack of scientific foundations is an impediment to the development of sound engineering principles supporting the application of expert systems. Empirical studies of knowledge engineering raise doubts about the possibility of eliciting expert knowledge using available techniques (Collins, Green & Draper 1985). Collins (1985) studied knowledge transfer processes among scientists and suggests that some knowledge may not be accessible through the expert, not only because he cannot express it, but also because he may not be aware of its significance to his activity. In an earlier study Hawkins (1983) emphasized the severe limitations of expertise and its dependence on critical assumptions which are often implicit.

Much human activity is not accessible to awareness (Dixon 1981), and the problem of knowledge elicitation from a skilled person is well-documented (Nisbett & Wilson 1977, Broadbent, Fitzgerald and Broadbent 1986). Bainbridge (1979, 1986) notes that there is no necessary correlation between verbal reports and mental behavior, and that many psychologists feel that verbal data are useless. However, this remark must be taken in the context of experimental psychologists working within a positivist, behavioral paradigm. Other schools of psychology see the problem not as methodological but as psychological and resulting from cognitive defences that impede internal communication for a variety of reasons (Freud 1914, Kelly 1955, Rogers 1967). Clinical psychologists in particular have developed techniques for making use of verbal interaction to identify underlying cognitive processes, for example through structured interviewing techniques. These can be used to by-pass cognitive defences, including those resulting from automization of skilled behavior.

However, knowledge engineering is an important aspect of advanced computer technology, and neither the pragmatic development of interviewing methods nor the importation of techniques from clinical psychology will in themselves be regarded as satisfactory foundations for an engineering discipline. We need to be eclectic in acquiring knowledge engineering techniques from all possible sources, but we also need to complement our pragmatism with effort to develop scientific foundations for our activities. We cannot be satisfied until we have a precise understanding of the processes underlying expertise, its operation, acquisition and transfer. This is not a simple requirement since it entails understanding the nature of knowledge, its dynamics and application. The foundations of computer technology in the physical sciences are no longer adequate and need extension into the humanities. The philosophy, psychology and sociology of knowledge processes are highly significant to future computing, and we have to operationalize theories and obtain precise answers to questions that have long been regarded as certainly controversial and possibly intractable.

This paper presents a model of knowledge processes in human society that is based on a systemic model of knowledge acquisition with strong mathematical foundations (Gaines & Shaw 1984b, 1985), gives an operational formulation of expertise as an essential component of the inductive process (Gaines 1977), and models the dynamics of knowledge transfer in a way that encompasses both human social processes (Shaw 1985) and the application of technology (Shaw & Gaines 1986a).

2. The Knowledge Acquisition Process

The systemic principle behind a cognitive psychological model that provides adequate foundations for knowledge engineering is that the human species is uniquely characterized as a highly anticipatory system, modeling the world so as to increase its probability of survival. This is is the basis of Kelly's (1955) personal construct psychology, and the modeling principle involved can be given strong formal foundations. Klir (1976, 1985) proposed an *epistemological hierarchy* accounting for the main components of any modeling systems and their inter-relations. Gaines (1977) gave a mathematical formulation of the general problem of modeling as a relation between order relations at different levels of the hierarchy. Gaines & Shaw (1981) gave a general interpretation of this hierarchy as generated by *levels of distinction* and showed how it was instantiated in psychological terms. The hierarchy has proved a valuable conceptual tool in analyzing a wide variety of modeling systems both in terms of their ontological presuppositions and their epistemological processes.

The notion of a *distinction* is a basic concept underlying the representation of knowledge (Gaines & Shaw 1984b, 1985). It is sufficient primitive to give foundations for systems theory including that of a system itself (Gaines 1980). In psychological form, as a *personal construct* (Kelly 1955, Shaw 1980), the notion has been used to derive very effective techniques for knowledge transfer from experts to expert systems (Shaw & Gaines 1983a, Boose 1985). Its foundational role in knowledge acquisition is evident in the hierarchical representation of distinctions in a modeling system shown in Figure 1. The levels of the hierarchy itself are the results of distinctions that we make so that no additional primitives are introduced—in Klir's (1976) terminology:
• The *source system* is distinguished as those distinctions made by a particular modeling system—it is a distinction about distinctions defining a construct system;
• The *data system* is distinguished as those distinctions that have been made about a particular event—a distinction about distinctions defining an event.
• The *generative system* is distinguished as a set of distinctions that also defines an event—these are model-generated rather than event-generated—it is the match between the model-generated and event-generated distinctions that determines the degree of approximation of the model to the world—this is a distinction about distinctions among distinctions that defines goodness of fit;

- The *structure system* is distinguished as a set of distinctions that compare models—it is the order relation of simplicity/complexity on models that determines the preference for the simplest model that is an adequate approximation to the world—this is a distinction about distinctions that defines our preference for simple models;
- The *meta system* is distinguished as a set of distinctions that specify the basis of these comparisons.
- The *meta-meta system*, and higher levels, are distinguished as sets of distinctions that specify further relations among the distinctions on the level below.

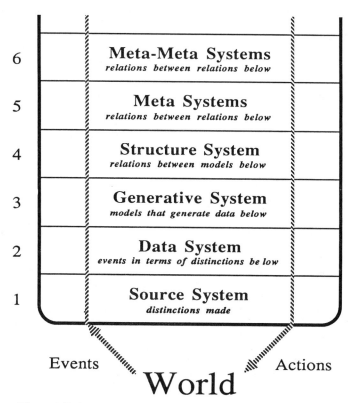

6	**Meta-Meta Systems** *relations between relations below*
5	**Meta Systems** *relations between relations below*
4	**Structure System** *relations between models below*
3	**Generative System** *models that generate data below*
2	**Data System** *events in terms of distinctions be low*
1	**Source System** *distinctions made*

Events   World   Actions

Figure 1 Epistemological hierarchy of a system modeling a world

Note that the upper levels of modeling are totally dependent on the system of distinctions used to express experience through the source system.

Distinctions are not just static partitions of experience. They may be operations: actions in psychological terms; processes in computational terms. Whether a system finds a distinction in the world, imposes it passively as a view of the world, or imposes it actively as a change in the world, is irrelevant to the basic modeling theory. It makes no difference to the theory whether distinctions are instantiated through sensation or action. In knowledge engineering we have to incorporate both the expert's prediction and control processes.

3 Learning in the Hierarchy

The hierarchy of Figure 1 accounts for knowledge acquisition as the modeling of events enabling adequate prediction and action. A modeling schema results from distinctions about distinctions at each level in the hierarchy. In prediction the key distinction is to what degree a level accounts for the information flowing through it and hence this distinction may be termed one of *surprise* (Gaines 1977), in the sense used by the economist Shackle (1955). Surprise goes in opposition to the degree of membership (Zadeh 1965, Gaines 1983) of a predicted event to an actual event and the expected surprise is a form of entropy. Surprise at the lowest level of the hierarchy corresponds to distinctions being inadequate to capture events; surprise at the next level to inadequate variety to experience events; at the next level to inadequate approximation to predict events; at the next level to inadequate simplicity to explain events; at the next level to inadequate comprehensiveness.to account for events.

The formal theory of modeling is one in which models are selected at each level down the hierarchy to minimize the rate at which surprise is passing up the hierarchy. The criteria for model selection independent of the data are generally thought of as being ones of *simplicity/complexity*: of two models which fit the data equally well choose the simplest. However, notions of simplicity/complexity are not well-defined nor intrinsic to the class of models. The simplicity/complexity ordering is arbitrary and in its most general form is just one of *preference*. Hence the general modeling schema is one in which surprise flows up the hierarchy and preference flows down. In situations that are mathematically well-defined, such as determining the structure of a stochastic automaton from its behavior, such a model schema gives the correct results (Gaines 1977). Conversely, the success of the schema in stabilizing with regard to a given world defines the characteristics of that world.

Thus the basic modeling schema for learning from experience is one in which surprise flows up the hierarchy and preferences flow down. In primitive organisms only the lower levels of the hierarchy are developed, surprise is generated from experience and preference is genetically encoded. In higher organisms the modeling process generalizes both surprise and preference to cope with novel environments. Human life has developed the upper levels of the hierarchy and detached surprise from experience and preference from its genetic roots. Surprise can flow up from a level without flowing into it from below because the processes *at* that level have generated novelty. Preference can be generated at a high level detached from both experience and genetic origins and flow down to affect the relations of the organism to the world.

4 Psychological Interpretation of the Hierarchy

The loop in Figure 1 from events through distinctions up through the modeling hierarchy and then down again to predictions and actions characterizes what Shaw (1980) has termed the *personal scientist*. The systemic hierarchy of Figure 1 has a psychological analog as shown in Figure 2:
• The source level is one of *constructs*, distinctions made in interacting with the world;
• The data level is one of *experiences*, events which happen to us, and we make happen, in terms of the distinctions already made;
• The generative level is one of *hypotheses* which are rationalizations of experience;
• The structure level is one of *analogies* which are correspondences between these rationalizations;
• The meta level is one of *abstractions* which are foundations of analogies;
• The meta-meta level is one of *transcendencies* which are accounts of abstractions.
Interaction with the world is, therefore, mediated through the construct system to produce experience which is modeled through the higher levels and leads to predictions, decisions and actions again mediated through the construct system.

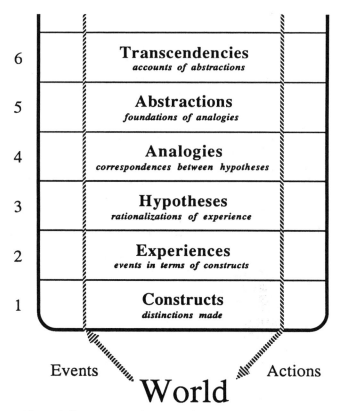

Figure 2 Construction hierarchy of a person modeling a world

5 Roles, Groups and Societies as Cross-Sections of the Hierarchy

The anticipatory processes of the modeling hierarchy may be extended to the operation of society by viewing groups of people as larger cross-sections comprising multiple individuals (Shaw & Gaines 1981). This concept may be given deeper significance by considering the *inductive inference* process underlying knowledge acquisition and modeled in the hierarchy. Whereas the deductive logical inference that underlies the operation of conventional computers is well-understood and well-founded, the inductive inference that underlies human learning is not. Deduction guarantees to take us from valid data to valid inferences, but the inferences are thereby part of the data—no new knowledge is generated. Induction takes us from valid data to models of that data that go beyond it—by predicting data we have not yet observed, and by giving explanations of the data in terms of concepts that are unobservable. Induction generates new knowledge but, as Hume (1739) pointed out over 200 years ago, the process is not deductively valid and it is a circular argument to claim that it is inductively valid.

Philosophers have continued to debate Hume's arguments and search for justification of the inductive process. Goodman (1973) proposed that we accept the circularity but note that it involves a dynamic equilibrium between data and inference rules as shown in Figure 3: "A rule is amended if it yields an inference we are unwilling to accept; an inference is rejected if it violates a rule we are unwilling to amend." Rawls (1971) in his theory of justice terms this a *reflective equilibrium*. Recently Stich and Nisbett (1984) noted flaws in Goodman's argument and repaired them by proposing that the equilibrium is social not individual: "a rule of inference is justified if it captures the reflective practice not of the person using it but of the appropriate experts in our society." This argument arose in the context of the explanation of the authority of *experts* in society, but it is also significant in suggesting that the basic system underlying knowledge acquisition is a society rather than an individual.

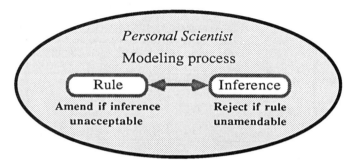

Figure 3 Reflective equilibrium in inductive inference

The extension of the modeling hierarchy to social processes is simple since Figure 1 presents a general modeling schema and applies as much to groups of people, companies and societies as it does to the roles of a person. The epistemological hierarchy of a person is a cross-section of the epistemological hierarchy of the society generating their life-world. Pask's (1975) concept of *P-Individuals* as the basic units of psycho-socio-processes allows roles, people, groups, organizations and societies to be treated in a uniform framework (Shaw & Gaines 1981, 1986a). An individual is defined in cognitive terms as a psychological process (Pask 1980) and more complex psychological and social structures may be defined similarly by taking into account the possibilities of timesharing, process switching and distributed processing with psychological processors. For example, one person may assume many psychological roles (process switching), whereas a group of people working together may act as a single goal-seeking entity and hence behave as one process (distributed processing).

6 Representation of Expert Skills in the Hierarchy

In the analysis of expertise the *skills* to achieve goals in the world are the crucial capabilities of the modeling system, and hierarchical models of skills (Powers 1973, Rasmussen 1983) are naturally subsumed within the modeling formulation. Figure 4 shows the basis for action at different levels in the modeling hierarchy.
- At level one, the activation of a construct may be linked directly to a primitive act, another construct. This corresponds to reflex actions and stimulus-response connections. In system-theoretic terms this level might be implemented by conditional probability calculations giving confirmation-theoretic inductive inference.
- At level two, constellations of experience may be linked to complete action sequences through rules derived from similar experience. In system-theoretic terms this level might be implemented by fuzzy production rules giving generalization-based inductive inference. These constellations may be regarded as prototypical schema, or frame-like structures in computational terms.

- At level three, a generative model of experience, may be used to compute an optimal action sequence. In system-theoretic terms this level might be implemented by a state-based modeling scheme giving model-based inductive inference.
- At level four, a variety of alternative models may be compared as a basis for selecting one appropriate to the required goals. In system-theoretic terms this level might be implemented by a category-theoretic functional analysis scheme giving analogical inductive inference.
- At level five, generalized abstract models may be used as templets from which to instantiate one appropriate to the required goals. In system-theoretic terms this level might be implemented by a category-theoretic factoring scheme abstracting the mathematical form of an analogy and giving abstractional inductive inference.
- At level six, the entire process described may be transcended through a recognition that it is based on distinctions being made at various level, and an attempt to rationalize these distinctions and create new ones. In system-theoretic terms this level might be implemented by a distinction-based analysis scheme giving what might be termed transcendental inductive inference.

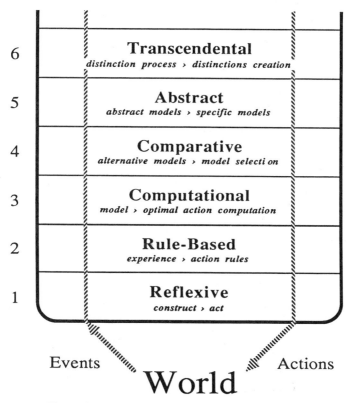

Figure 4 Action hierarchy of system modeling a world

It is an interesting comment on the state of the art in computer science that it has proceeds "middle-outward" in its representation of the knowledge involved in skills at different levels of the hierarchy. Information technology has been primarily concerned with level three activities, and is only now beginning through expert system developments to emulate level two activities.

7 Language and Culture in Knowledge Acquisition

The creation of new knowledge takes place through the surprise/preference flows within the hierarchy and it is these processes that determine the rate of technological invention and product innovation. The human capability for an entire society to act as a distributed knowledge acquisition system is dependent on the role of communication processes in coordinating activity at a given level of the hierarchy across different people. This communication process whereby each person does not have to undertake all aspects of the inductive process but can share the results of such processing by others supports what is generally termed the *culture* of a society (Vanderburg 1985). People use language for much of this communication but they also have in common with other animals the capability to communicate cultural information without the use of language. Mimicry is an important mechanism for knowledge acquisition as is reinforcement through reward and punishment.

The human development of language enables coordination to take place in a rich and subtle fashion that greatly enhances, but does not replace, the more basic mechanisms in common with other species. It is particularly important at the upper levels of the hierarchy where direct expression is difficult. From an individual point of view, language is a way of by-passing the normal modeling procedures and interacting directly with the system at any level. In particular it can directly affect the preference system. Much skilled activity is not directly accessible through language, but even when language cannot mediate the direct transmission of knowledge it may be used to achieve the same effect by the indirect support of other mechanisms. For example, one can describe a good learning environment, or a behavior in sufficient detail for mimicry. Language is essential to much of human learning, and our interaction with the knowledge construct (Wojciechowski 1983, Gaines & Shaw 1983b) is just as important as our interaction with the world (Shaw & Gaines 1983b, 1984, Gaines & Shaw 1984a). The evolutionary pressures would be very strong in selecting genes giving the capability for a species to act as a single distributed individual, combining autonomy and cohesion through linguistic communication. Linguistic transfer of knowledge is the most important process for the dissemination of information, for example in technology transfer.

Figure 5 shows the cultural support for knowledge acquisition at different levels in the modeling hierarchy.
- The reflexive knowledge at level one has no verbal component and comes directly from experience, often that of mimicking the behavior of others. This level has been termed *informal* to correspond to Hall's (1959) definition of cultural transmission of behavior of this type.
- The rule-based knowledge at level two is usually transmitted by reinforcement of behavior, verbal rules, or is induced from the patterns of knowledge at level 1. This level has been termed *formal* to correspond to Hall's definition of cultural transmission of behavior of this type.
- The computational knowledge at level three is usually transmitted by technical explanation, or is induced from the patterns of knowledge at level two. This level has been termed *technical* to correspond to Hall's definition of cultural transmission of behavior of this type.
- The comparative knowledge at level four is usually transmitted by simile and metaphorical analysis, or is induced from the patterns of knowledge at level three. Hall does give a name to this level but the term *comparative* captures his own activity of highlighting the features of one culture by contrasting it with others.
- The *abstract* knowledge at level five is usually transmitted through mathematical representation, or is induced from the patterns of knowledge at level four.

- The *transcendental* knowledge at level six is usually transmitted by general system-theoretic analysis, or is induced from the patterns of knowledge at level five. Many mystical and consciousness-raising techniques may be seen as attempts to communicate knowledge at this level when formal analysis is impossible. It involves moving outside the framework established at the lower levels. Pope (1984) has given examples of this process in a wide range of cultures.

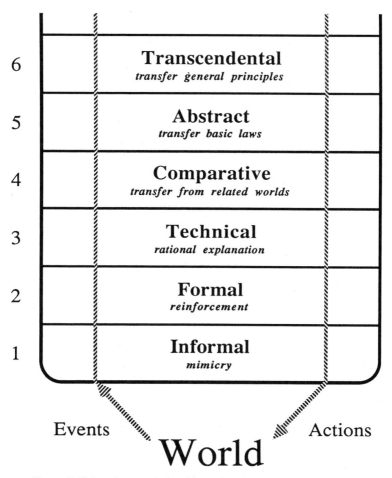

Figure 5 Cultural transmission hierarchy of people modeling a world

8. Conclusions

The anticipatory system formulation of human cognitive psychology outlined in this paper provides scientific foundations for knowledge engineering that lead to some interesting conclusions:-

1. It gives an operational model of the notion of expertise and the role it plays in our society, and hence provides formal foundations for expert systems;
2. Computational models of inductive inference already developed can be applied directly to the social model;
3. It suggests that the basic cognitive system that should be considered is a social organization, rather than an individual;
4. It suggestss that we should consider groups of experts rather than individual experts in developing expert systems;
5. One practical consequence of the model is to define a hierarchy of knowledge transfer methodologies as shown in Figure 6;
6. The hierarchy indicates the areas of application of the knowledge engineering techniques already in use.

This analysis clarifies some of the problems of expertise transfer noted in the literature, in particular, what forms of knowledge are accessible through what methodologies. The model is being used as a framework within which to extend and develop a family of knowledge support systems to expedite the development of expert system applications.

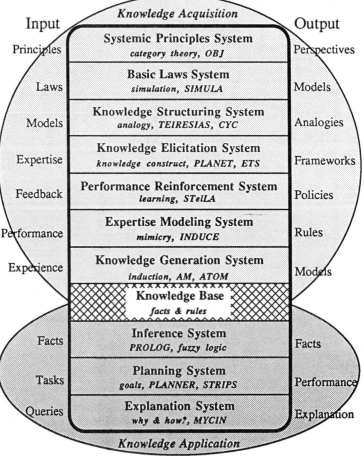

Figure 6 Knowledge engineering hierarchy for expert systems

Acknowledgements

Financial assistance for this work has been made available by the National Sciences and Engineering Research Council of Canada.

References

Bainbridge, L. (1979). Verbal reports as evidence of the process operator's knowledge. International Journal of Man-Machine Studies, 11(4), 411-436 (July).

Bainbridge, L. (1986). Asking questions and accessing knowledge. Future Computing Systems 1, in press.

Boose, J.H. (1985). A knowledge acquisition program for expert systems based on personal construct psychology. International Journal of Man-Machine Studies 20(1), 21-43 (January).

Broadbent, D.E., FitzGerald, P. & Broadbent, M.H.P. (1986). Implicit and explicit knowledge in the control of complex systems. British Journal of Psychology 77, 33-50.

Collins, H.M. (1985). Changing Order: Replication and Induction in Scientific Practice. London: SAGE.

Collins, H.M., Green, R.H. & Draper, R.C. (1985). Where's the expertise?: expert systems as mediums of knowledge transfer. Merry, M., Ed. Expert Systems 85, pp. 323-334. Cambridge University Press.

Dixon, N. (1981). Preconscious Processing. Chichester: Wiley.

Feigenbaum, E.A. (1980). Knowledge Engineering: the Applied Side of Artificial Intelligence. Report STAN-CS-80-812. Dept. Computer Science, Stanford University.

Freud, S. (1914). Psychopathology of Everyday Life. London: Benn.

Gaines, B.R. (1977). System identification, approximation and complexity. International Journal of General Systems, 3, 145-174.

Gaines, B.R. (1980). General systems research: quo vadis ?. Gaines, B.R., Ed. General Systems 1979. Vol. 24, pp. 1-9. Kentucky: Society for General Systems Research.

Gaines, B.R. (1983). Precise past—fuzzy future. International Journal of Man-Machine Studies, 19(1), 117-134 (July).

Gaines, B.R. & Shaw, M.L.G. (1981). A programme for the development of a systems methodology of knowledge and action. Reckmeyer, W.J., Ed. General Systems Research & Design: Precursors and Futures. pp. 255-264. Society for General Systems Research.

Gaines, B.R. & Shaw, M.L.G. (1983). Is there a knowledge environment?. Lasker, G., Ed. The Relation Between Major World Problems and Systems Learning. pp. 27-34. Society for General Systems Research (May).

Gaines, B.R. & Shaw, M.L.G. (1984a). The Art of Computer Conversation: A New Medium for Communication. Englewood Cliffs, New Jersey: Prentice Hall.

Gaines, B.R. & Shaw, M.L.G. (1984b). Hierarchies of distinctions as generators of system theories. Smith, A.W., Ed. Proceedings of the Society for General Systems Research International Conference. pp. 559-566. California: Intersystems.

Gaines, B.R. & Shaw, M.L.G. (1985). Three world views and system philosophies. Banathy, B.H., Ed. Proceedings of the Society for General Systems Research International Conference. pp. 387-396. California: Intersystems.

Goodman, N. (1973). Fact, Fiction and Forecast. Indianapolis: Bobbs-Merrill.

Hall, E.T. (1959). The Silent Language. New York: Doubleday.

Hawkins, D. (1983). An analysis of expert thinking. International Journal of Man-Machine Studies, 18(1), 1-47 (January).

Hayes-Roth, F., Waterman, D.A. & Lenat, D.B., Eds. (1983). Building Expert Systems. Reading, Massachusetts: Addison-Wesley.

Hume, D. (1739). A Treatise of Human Nature. London: John Noon.

Kelly, G.A. (1955). The Psychology of Personal Constructs. New York: Norton.

Klir, G.J. (1976). Identification of generative structures in empirical data. International Journal of General Systems, 3, 89-104.

Klir, G.J. (1985). Architecture of Systems Problem Solving, New York: Plenum Press.

Nisbett, R.E. & Wilson, T.D.. (1977). Telling more than we can know: verbal reports on mental processes. Psychological Review 84, 231-259.

Pask, G. (1975). Conversation, Cognition and Learning. Amsterdam: Elsevier.

Pask, G. (1980). Developments in conversation theory—Part I. International Journal of Man-Machine Studies, 13(4), 357-411 (November).

Pope, S. (1984). Conceptual synthesis: beating at the ivory gate?. Smith, W., Ed. Systems Methodologies and Isomorphies. pp. 31-40. California: Intersystems.

Powers, W.T. (1973). Behavior: The Control of Perception. New York: Aldine.

Rasmussen, J. (1983). Skills, rules and knowledge; signals, signs and symbols, and other distinctions in human performance models. IEEE Transactions on Systems, Man & Cybernetics, SMC-13(3), 257-266 (May/June).

Rawls, J. (1971). A Theory of Justice. Massachusetts: Harvard University Press.

Rogers, C.R. (1967). On Becoming a Person: A Therapist's View of Psychotherapy. London: Constable.

Shackle, G.L.S. (1955). Uncertainty in Economics. Cambridge University Press.

Shaw, M.L.G. (1980). On Becoming a Personal Scientist: Interactive Computer Elicitation of Personal Models of the World. London: Academic Press.

Shaw, M.L.G. (1985). Communities of knowledge. Epting, F. & Landfield, A.W., Eds. Anticipating Personal Construct Psychology. pp. 25-35. University of Nebraska Press.

Shaw, M.L.G. & Gaines, B.R. (1981). The personal scientist in the community of science. Reckmeyer, W.J., Ed. General Systems Research and Design: Precursors and Futures. pp. 59-68. Society for General Systems Research (January).

Shaw, M.L.G. & Gaines, B.R. (1983a). A computer aid to knowledge engineering. Proceedings of Expert Systems 83. pp. 263-271. London: British Computer Society.

Shaw, M.L.G. & Gaines, B.R. (1983b). Computer systems in the knowledge environment: a new medium. Lasker, G., Ed. The Relation Between Major World Problems and Systems Learning. pp. 35-41. Society for General Systems Research.

Shaw, M.L.G. & Gaines, B.R. (1984). Fifth generation computers as the next stage of a new medium. AFIPS Proceedings of National Computer Conference. Vol. 53, pp. 445-451. Arlington, Virginia: AFIPS Press.

Shaw, M.L.G. & Gaines, B.R. (1986a). A framework for knowledge-based systems unifying expert systems and simulation. Luker, P.A. & Adelsberger, H.H., Eds. Intelligent Simulation Environments, 38-43 (January). La Jolla, California: Society for Computer Simulation.

Shaw, M.L.G. & Gaines, B.R. (1986b). Interactive elicitation of knowledge from experts. Future Computing Systems, 1(2), to appear.

Shaw, M.L.G. & Gaines, B.R. (1986c). An interactive knowledge elicitation technique using personal construct technology. Kidd, A., Ed. Knowledge Eliciation for Expert Systems: A Practical Handbook. To appear. Plenum Press.

Stich, S.P. & Nisbett, R.E. (1984). Expertise, justification and the psychology of inductive reasoning. Haskell, T.L., Ed. The Authority of Experts. pp. 226-241. Bloomington, Indiana: Indiana University Press.

Vanderburg, W.H. (1985). The Growth of Minds and Cultures: A Unified Theory of the Structure of Human Experience. Toronto: University Press.

Welbank, M. (1983). A Review of Knowledge Acquisition Techniques for Expert Systems. BTRL, Ipswich: Martlesham Consultancy Services.

Wojciechowski, J.A. (1983). The impact of knowledge on man: the ecology of knowledge. Hommage a Francois Meyer. pp. 161-175. Marseille: Laffitte.

Zadeh, L.A. (1965). Fuzzy sets. Information and Control, 8, 338-353.

LEARNING DECISION RULES IN NOISY DOMAINS

Tim Niblett, Ivan Bratko
The Turing Institute, University of Strathclyde

Abstract

The ID3 algorithm, originally developed by Ross Quinlan, and its derivatives have formed the basis for several practical learning systems. The work of Kononenko and Bratko, and of Quinlan himself, has shown that the ID3 algorithm performs poorly in noisy domains. Both the accuracy and the compactness - hence explanatory power, of the induced rules can be severely degraded. Different modifications based on the idea of tree pruning have been suggested to overcome this problem. These modifications are of an *ad hoc* nature. This paper tries to analyse these approaches in a mathematical way. The analysis considers two different approaches to tree pruning. The first approach constructs an exact probabilistic test for significance. The second approach provides the basis for formulating an optimisation criterion for selecting the most promising decision tree among all upper subtrees of a decision tree. This leads to an efficient algorithm for determining the optimal such upper subtree, relative to an estimate of the prior probabilities of the different decision classes. We believe that this offers a new approach to the problem of coping with noisy domains.

1. Introduction

Since its introduction by Quinlan (Quinlan 1979) the ID3 algorithm and its derivatives (ACLS, Niblett and Paterson 1982), Structured Induction (Shapiro and Niblett 1982), Assistant (Kononenko et al. 1984)) has been used as the basis for many practical learning systems. The original algorithm was developed to solve problems in the domain of chess endgames, where no noise or uncertainty is inherent. Many, if not most, domains to which expert systems can be applied contain noise or uncertainty. Both Quinlan (1983) and Kononenko et al. (1984) have developed versions of ID3 which attempt to deal with noisy domains. We discuss these approaches, in particular that of Quinlan, and suggest two alternative modifications to the basic algorithm. We compare the performance of the original ID3 algorithm with both suggested alternatives on a medical domain. We also study the performance of Assistant on this domain. We show that the new modifications classify more accurately, and produce shorter rules, than the original ID3 algorithm.

1.1 Outline of paper

Section 2 describes the original ID3 algorithm, and explains why its performance deteriorates in the presence of noise. The approach of Quinlan (1983), where a χ^2 significance test is applied to prune decision trees is described. Section 3 presents an alternative to Quinlan's approach where an exact test of probabilities is used to decide termination. We see that that this exact criterion can be used both to guide and terminate search. We show that as the number of examples dealt with approaches infinity this criterion approaches Quinlan's original entropy formulation. Section 4 considers another approach which uses an exact estimate of the classification error at each stage to terminate search. Section 5 describes the experimental results obtained by running the various algorithms considered on a concrete medical domain. In section 6 the results are discussed and we conclude that the effect of pruning decision trees

†Address for correspondence: *The Turing Institute, George House, 36 North Hanover St., GLASGOW G1 2AD. Ivan Bratko is on leave from Faculty of Electrical Engineering, Trzaska 25, Ljubljana, Yugoslavia*

is to significantly decrease the size of the decision tree produced, while maintaining its classificational accuracy. The technique of error estimation appears to produce considerably smaller trees than the other approaches.

2. ID3 and approaches to noise

The ID3 algorithm produces classification rules in the form of decision trees. The basic aim of the system is to construct a rule for classifying objects in some domain of interest from a presentation of examples in a *training set* whose classes are given. The hope is that rules constructed in this manner will perform well when asked to classify further previously unseen examples. For the sake of convenience we shall assume in what follows that there are two classes in which objects may fall, c and $\overline{c}$. Each example presented to the learning system is characterised by a set of attribute values, together with a class value (c or $\overline{c}$). Each attribute a_i can take one of a finite number of values $v_{i1}, \cdots, v_{in_i}$. A *decision tree* has on each interior node a test of an attribute a_j with one subtree for each value the attribute may take $(v_{j1}, \cdots, v_{jn_j})$. Leaves of the decision tree are labelled with a single class value, which signals the outcome of the classification rule. ID3 constructs a decision tree recursively from a set of examples E, according to the following algorithm:

(1)   Set the current examples C to E

(2)   If C satisfies the termination condition $TE(C)$ halt

(3)   For each attribute a_i determine the value of the (real) function IDM(C, a_i). With the attribute a_j that has the largest value of this function divide the set C into subsets by attribute values $(v_{j1}, \cdots, v_{jn_j})$. For each such subset of examples $E_k, (k \leq n_j)$ recursively re-enter at step (1) with E set to E_k. Set the subtrees of the current node to be the subtrees thus produced. Notice that this procedure relies on a termination condition TE and an "evaluation function" IDM. The termination condition for ID3 is simply that all the examples have the same class. The evaluation function is an information-theoretic measure based on the entropy of the set E. Let E be composed of n_1 examples with class c and n_2 examples with class $\overline{c}$. The entropy of the distribution is $-(p_1\ln p_1 + p_2\ln p_2)$, where $p_1 = n_1/(n_1+n_2)$ etc. Now we can estimate the decrease in entropy by subtracting this figure from the value of the entropy after splitting by the chosen attribute. We will generalise to k classes and l attribute values, and call the number of examples in the ith class with the j value of the attribute n_{ij}. Similarly call the probability of an example falling into the ith class with the jth attribute value p_{ij} and the probability of an example falling into the ith class p_i. The entropy decrease then simplifies as follows,
Entropy before:

$$-\sum_i p_i\ln p_i$$

Entropy after:

$$-\sum_{ij}\ln p_{ij}$$

Difference:

$$\sum_i\sum_j p_{ij}\ln(p_{ij}/p_i)$$

We have chosen to present the algorithm in this rather cumbersome way because all the variants of the algorithm we shall consider are different in respect of the termination criterion and evaluation function. One variation of the basis algorithm that we use for the testing described below, produces only binary splits at each node. It does this by considering all possible divisions of the attribute values into 2 sets, and then computes the entropy measure (*IDM*) for a split of one set against the other. Work with Assistant (Kononenko et al. 1984) has shown that binary splitting in this way improves the classificational accuracy of the induced trees. It should be noted however that Assistant uses a heuristic approach to the problem of finding the optimal binary split, rather than the complete search used in our tests. We shall refer to this version of the ID3 algorithm as $ID3_2$. When there is noise, arising from errors in the description of attributes or classes, or some inherent uncertainty in the domain these functions are not adequate. It may be the case for example that two examples share the same attribute values and have different class values. Clearly no rule can correctly classify these examples. From now on we shall be investigating modifications that allow us to classify successfully in the presence of noise.

2.1 Quinlan's approach to noise

Quinlan (1983) has investigated the problem of learning from noisy data with the ID3 algorithm. His algorithm leaves unchanged the evaluation function and substitutes a new termination criterion based on a χ^2 test. Consider a set E consisting of n examples. For any attribute a with attribute values $v_1,...,v_m$ we consider the null hypothesis that the sub-populations of examples created when we split E are drawn from the same population as E. To test the null hypothesis consider the number of examples n_{ij} with class c_i and attribute value v_j. The expected number of examples e_{ij} under the null hypothesis is $(\sum_j n_{ij} \times \sum_i n_{ij})/n$. The statistic $\sum_{ij}(n_{ij}-e_{ij})^2/e_{ij}$ is approximately chi-squared with $n-1$ degrees of freedom. Quinlan's termination criterion is to halt if no attribute has a value for this statistic that is significant at the 99% level (the choice of 99% as the significance level is arbitrary). There is one drawback with this method of termination, which is that the above statistic is not distributed like χ^2 when the e_{ij} are small. This could be serious when we are dealing with small training sets (Quinlan used a set of several hundred), and means that the technique may well be inapplicable when smaller training sets are used. We discuss a solution to this problem in the next section. More recently Quinlan (Quinlan et al 1986) and colleagues have investigated the post-pruning of already formed decision trees using an optimisation criterion that offsets the complexity of the tree against its observed classificational accuracy on the training examples. We shall discuss this approach in more detail later. Our interest in this paper is to see how the performance of the learning algorithm improves when it is adapted for noise. This improvement can occur in 2 ways, as a decrease in the size of rule and as an improvement in the classificational accuracy of the rules. We shall take up this problem later, after considering another approach to noise handling.

3. An exact test for significance

In this section we present a significance test for the same null hypothesis considered by Quinlan in the previous section, which is exact and can be used for any sized data whatsoever. We shall describe the test and show that in the limit, as the number of test examples goes to infinity, the numerical value obtained for the probabilities considered tends towards the information theoretic criterion described above. In the following we shall be concerned with problems having 2-valued attributes and two classes. This leads to a 2×2 contingency table when evaluating attributes. As we have seen the drawback of Quinlan's approach to noise estimation is that the statistic he uses ($\sum_{ij}(O_{ij}-E_{ij})^2/(E_{ij})$) is not distributed like χ^2 when the E_{ij} are small. Unfortunately this situation arises all the time when a tree is being created. In the 2×2 case we can calculate exactly the probability that the χ^2 test is trying to estimate. Consider the following 2×2 table.

Table		
	c_1	c_2
v_1	n_{11}	n_{12}
v_2	n_{21}	n_{22}

We consider the marginal totals to be fixed and ask, *what is the probability of getting such an extreme distribution by chance given the null hypothesis that $p(c_i|v_1) = p(c_i|v_2)$?*.

We can calculate the exact probability of observing the above totals, when the 4 marginal totals are regarded as fixed. It is:

$$ p = \frac{\binom{n_{11}+n_{21}}{n_{11}}\binom{n_{12}+n_{22}}{n_{12}}}{\binom{n}{n_{11}+n_{12}}} $$

This simplifies to:

$$ p = \frac{(n_{11}+n_{12})!(n_{21}+n_{22})!(n_{11}+n_{21})!(n_{12}+n_{22})!}{n!n_{11}!n_{12}!n_{21}!n_{22}!} $$

To calculate the probability of this distribution or one more extreme we also need to calculate the probabilities of more extreme distributions. Consider Table 1 again. Let us assume, without loss of generality, that n_{11} is the largest entry. More extreme tables will be those with entries

$$ \begin{bmatrix} n_{11}+k & n_{12}-k \\ n_{21}-k & n_{22}+k \end{bmatrix} $$

where k is a positive integer, and no entry is negative. The sum of the probabilities of all such tables is equal to the probability of this or a more extreme result. This probability is the one estimated by the χ^2 test. It is perfectly practical to implement this test for values of n up to about 150, and we have done this. To use the computed value in deciding termination of the tree expansion inside ID3 we merely agree to terminate search when the probability is greater than 0.05 (for a 95% confidence limit).

4. Error estimation

An alternative to the above approach and closer in flavour to that taken by Assistant is to try and estimate the error at any given node in the decision if we were to base our evaluation on the test examples on that node. Given an estimate for the error at any given node we can guess whether it is worth continuing the search by looking at the expected error of the tree expanded by testing one more attribute.

4.1 Estimation in the 2×2 case

We assume for convenience that we are in the 2×2 case considered above, with 2 classes and 2 attribute values (v_1 and v_2).
If we denote the error of node N as $e(N)$ then we would decide to terminate search if

$e(N) \leq p(v_1)e(E_1) + p(v_2)e(E_2)$, where we are associating error estimates with the observed example populations E_i. Let us consider the error at node N. We assume that we have two classes c and $\bar{c}$ with probabilities of occurrence p_c and $p_{\bar{c}}$ $(=1-p_c)$. We observe n examples, n_c of which fall into class c. We can assume without loss of generality that $n_c \geq n_{\bar{c}}$. What is the expected error in assigning a new example to class c?. We shall write $pd(A|B)$ for the probability density function of A given B. The expected error rate $=$

$$\int_0^1 (1-x)pd(p_c=x|n_c)dx$$

$$= \int_0^1 \frac{(1-x)p(n_c|p_c=x)pd(p_c=x)}{\int_0^1 d(n_c|p_c=x)pd(p_c=x)dx} dx$$

We assume that we have a prior distribution for p_c so that $pd(p_c=x)=1$

$$= \frac{\int_0^1 (1-x)p(n_c|p_c=x)dx}{\int_0^1 p(n_c|p_c=x)dx} \qquad (I)$$

Now $p(n_c|p_c=x) = \dfrac{n!}{n_c!(1-n_c)!}x^{n_c}(1-x)^{n-n_c}$. So the previous equation (I) reduces to

$$\frac{\int_0^1 (1-x)x^{n_c}(1-x)^{n-n_c}dx}{\int_0^1 x^{n_c}(1-x)^{n-n_c}dx}$$

$$= \frac{\displaystyle\sum_{i=0}^{n-n_c+1} \frac{(-1)^i\binom{n-n_c+1}{i}}{n_c+i+2}}{\displaystyle\sum_{i=0}^{n-n_c} \frac{(-1)^i\binom{n-n_c}{i}}{n_c+i+1}} \qquad (II)$$

We get this sum since

$$\int_0^1 x^m (1-x)^n dx = \int_0^1 \sum_{i=0}^n \binom{n}{i}(-1)^i x^{m+i} = \sum_{i=0}^n (-1)^i\binom{n}{i}\int_0^1 x^{m+i}dx = \sum_{i=0}^n \frac{(-1)^i\binom{n}{i}}{m+i+1}$$

The expression of equation (II) above can be simplified by observing that

$$\sum_{i=0}^n \frac{(-1)^i\binom{n}{i}}{\alpha+i} = \frac{n!}{\displaystyle\prod_{i=0}^n (\alpha+i)}$$

Equation (II) then simplifies to $(n-n_c+1)/(n+2)$, and can be used as the basic of a simple test to determine whether to prune or not. Donald Michie has pointed out to us that this is a generalisation of Laplace's law of succession which states that if an event of unknown probability occurs n times running, the best estimate of the probability of its occurrence at the $n+1$st trial is $(n+1)/(n+2)$.

4.2 Estimation in the general case

The above result can be extended to the case where there are multiple classes. In this case if there are k classes and the prior distribution for each class is uniform (with constant value $1/k$), then the expected error assuming that n_c examples from n are observed with class c is $(n-n_c+k-1)/(n+k)$. One possible drawback with this approach is that it may not be appropriate to use the uniform prior distribution, since the examples at an interior node in the tree have been selected from a biased population. We can evaluate this effect by considering the chance that a given example at a specified node in a decision tree will be 'selected' to go down a branch, corresponding to a particular attribute value. We will assume that the attribute in question has only 2 values, although the extension to multiple values is straightforward. Let the event that an example has class c be denoted by c, and that it is 'selected' by an attribute value be s. The prior distribution of classes over examples is given by the above equation (II) for the examples at some node *Node*. Let the number of examples at node *Node* be R, r of which have class c. Let the number of examples that are selected by the attribute value be N, n of which have class c Then the following holds:

$$p(c) = (r+1)/(R+k)$$

$$\overline{p(c)} = (R-r+k-1)/(R+k)$$

$$p(s|c) = (n+1)/(r+2)$$

$$p(s|\overline{c}) = (N-n+1)/(R-r+2)$$

$$p(c.s) = p(s|c)p(c)$$

$$p(\overline{c}.s) = p(s|\overline{c})p(\overline{c})$$

$$p(c|s) = (n+1)(r+1)/(n+1)(r+1)+ \quad \frac{(r+2)(N-n+1)(R-r+k-1)}{R-r+2}$$

This approximates to $(n+1)/(N+2)$ as r and R tend to infinity, which is the previous result (equation II).

4.3 Using the error estimates for pruning

One method of using the above error estimates for pruning the decision tree is in the evaluation of the termination condition *TE*. A more interesting approach, and the one taken here, is to use ID3 to create a complete tree and then prune the entire tree, getting an upper subtree with the same root, but optimal in classificational power with respect to the above error estimate. The algorithm used is defined by procedure *prunetree(Tree, Error)*, where *Tree* is the tree to be pruned and *Error* is the error value returned.

Procedure *prunetree*

(1) Set N to be the root of $Tree$

(2) Calculate the error E of N

(3) If N is a leaf return pruned $Tree = N$ and $Error = E$

(4) For each subtree rooted at N apply *prunetree* to get a pruned subtree and an error estimate. Calculate the expected error Es if we split at N and use the subtrees to classify (based on the error estimate for the subtrees).

(5) If Es is greater than E let pruned $Tree = N$ and $Error = E$. Otherwise let pruned $Tree$ = the tree rooted at N with subtrees being the pruned subtrees from step (4). Let $Error = Es$.

5. Testing the algorithms and Conclusions

With the exception of the ASSISTANT program, written in PASCAL at the University of Ljubljana all the algorithms described in this section are implemented in Quintus Prolog and run on SUN-2 machines. Tests were conducted on a medical database, obtained from the AI group at the University of Ljubljana. The data relate to lymphatic cancers. The relevant characteristics of the database of examples is shown below.

Property of Domain	Property Value
domain name	lymphography
number of attributes	18
no. of possible values per attribute	between 2 & 8 (average 3.3)
number of classes	4
total number of examples	148
distribution of examples amongst classes	
(number of examples in $C_1, \cdots, C_4$)	2,81,61,4
% used for induction (training)	50% (randomly chosen)
% used to test induced rules (testing)	50% (those remaining)

The experimental procedure involved the following programs.

- ID3
- $ID3_2$ (ID3 with binary splitting of attributes).
- ID3 with exact probability cutoff standard evaluation function.
- ID3 with the error estimate post-pruning of an ID3 or $ID3_2$ tree.
- ASSISTANT

For a description of the advantages gained by using binary splits see (Kononenko et al. 1984). As mentioned above our experiments were conducted using a complete search of all possible binary splits. Two sets of experiments were performed, the first to evaluate the exact probability cutoff in 2×2 cases (binary splitting and two classes), the second to evaluate the merits of the error estimate post-pruning procedure in the general and 2×k case (where k is the number of classes).

5.1 The 2×2 experiment

To create the 2×2 situation in the lymphography domain we chose classes *malignantlymphoma* (81 examples from 148) and *other*, lumping three classes into the category *other*. The following programs were run:

- $ID3_2$
- $ID3_2$ with the exact probability cutoff (95%)
- $ID3_2$ with error estimate post-pruning. The error estimate used was that given by equation (II) of Section 4, not using the correction for the prior distribution.

The results in the table below were obtained by running each of the programs 10 times on a randomly selected set of training data, comprising approximately half of the 148 examples. The resulting trees were tested on the remaining examples.

Algorithm	Results	
	% correct on test examples	average rule size
$ID3_2$	73.0	8.0
$ID3_2$ with cutoff	72.5	6.6
$ID3_2$ post-prune	73.0	4.2

Predictive power of algorithms (percentage of correct predictions)

These results indicate that the pruning techniques do not affect the classificational error, but they do improve the quality of the induced rules.

5.2 The general experiment.

In this experiment the algorithms were tested over all 4 of the classes in the domain. The testing procedure was the same as the previous case, with each algorithm being tested 10 times on randomly chosen examples, consisting of approximately half the entire database and being tested on the rest of the examples. The following table shows the results. The algorithms tested were:

- ID3 - the raw ID3 algorithm
- $ID3_2$
- ID3 with error post-pruning
- $ID3_2$ with error post-pruning
- Assistant - an $ID3_2$-like algorithm with pruning, using another pruning criterion, see (Kononenko et al. 1984).
- NAIVE - a naive algorithm that predicts the most common class in the training set. This shows the default accuracy below which an algorithm should not fall. It should be noted that this naive algorithm was run on the 10 randomly generated training sets, rather than having its accuracy estimated from the class totals given above.

The results need some qualification in that they differ somewhat from those obtained with Assistant (under slightly different conditions). These differences are largely explained by the fact that Assistant was trained on 70% of the domain examples, giving a higher classificational accuracy and larger decision trees.

Algorithm	Results	
	% correct on test examples	average rule size
ID3	67.7	44.6
ID3$_2$	71.1	29.8
ID3 post-prune	72.4	13.2
ID3$_2$ post-prune	73.8	7.2
ASSISTANT	74	29
NAIVE	55.7	-

Predictive power of algorithms (percentage of correct predictions)

5.3 Conclusions

The results of our investigation show that the use of an error estimate to prune an already-created decision tree can create rules that are both simple and highly predictive. Preliminary results indicate that this procedure is more effective than using a 'run-time' estimate based on an exact test of significance. The post-pruned rules in the multi-class binary-split case are less than a third the size of the rules produced by ASSISTANT which uses an ad-hoc measure to prune a tree at 'rule creation' time. These results show that the efficient and robust ID3 algorithm, which has had considerable success in noiseless domains can be successfully used to provide high quality induced rules in noisy real-world domains. Approaches which involves the post-pruning of decision has been described by Breiman et al. (1984) and by Quinlan et al. (1986). Both these approaches combine an error estimate at tree leaves with a 'badness' function that penalises more complex trees. Both approaches use the observed accuracy of classification at leaves as an estimate of their error. Thus a leaf with a single example has a zero error estimate, and no pruning can take place without some form of 'badness' estimate. The difference with our approach is that with the 'Laplacian' error estimate we can attempt to optimise the error estimate alone. It may be useful to combine the two approaches.

Acknowledgements

The medical data used for experiments was originally obtained from the University Medical Center, Ljubljana; provided by G. Klanjscek and M. Soklic. The development and production of comparison results for assistant was done by I. Kononenko in Ljubljans and P. Clarke at the Turing Institute. Assistant was ported to Unix by B. Cestnik. We are grateful for useful comment and advice from J. Zhengping and D. Michie. This work was partly supported by the Office of Naval Research under contract N00014-85-G-0243.

REFERENCES

Breiman, L, Friedman, JH, Olshen, RA & Stone CJ (1984) **Classification and Regression Trees** Belmont: Wadsworth.

Kononenko, I, Bratko, I & Roskar E (1984) Experiments in automatic learning of medical diagnostic rules. **Technical Report,** Jozef Stefan Institute, Ljubljana, Yugoslavia

Niblett, T. & Paterson, A. (1982) ACLS MANUAL. **Edinburgh, UK and Champaign, USA:**

Intelligent Terminals Ltd.

Quinlan, JR (1979) Discovering rules by induction from large collections of examples. In **Introductory Readings in Expert Systems** (ed. D Michie) pp 33-46. London: Gordon and Breach

Quinlan, JR, Compton, PJ, Horn KA & Lazarus, L (1986) Inductive knowledge acquisition: a case study. in **Proceedings of the second Australian conference on application of Expert Systems** Sydney: New South Wales Institute of Technology.

Quinlan, JR (1983) Learning from noisy data. In **Proceedings of the International Machine Learning Workshop** University of Illinois at Urbana Champaign, pp 58-64

Shapiro, A. & Niblett, T, (1982) Automatic induction of classification rules for a chess end-game. In **Advances in Computer Chess 3** (ed. MRB Clarke) pp 73-92. Oxford: Pergamon.

Probabilistic Induction by Dynamic Path Generation in
Virtual Trees

Dr. A.P. White,
Centre for Computing and Computer Science,
University of Birmingham,
P.O. Box 363,
Birmingham,
B15 2TT,
United Kingdom.

Abstract

An alternative approach to uncertain inference in
expert systems is described, which could be regarded as a
synthesis of techniques from the domains of artificial
intelligence and mathematical statistics. It utilises a type of
automatic induction but, unlike conventional induction
algorithms, it can function with noisy data (i.e. when clashes
are found in the training set). Furthermore, it circumvents the
combinatorial explosion inherent in generating large
classification trees by only generating the particular path
required on each occasion. It uses a stepwise approach in which,
at each stage, that attribute providing the greatest additional
discriminating power between classes (above that already
obtained) is chosen to form the next node in the actual path
being formed in the virtual tree. As each new attribute is used,
its interactions with all the attributes already utilised are
fully taken into account, thus avoiding reliance on the
assumption of conditional independence. A rudimentary system
(PREDICTOR) which operates according to these principles has
been written. Various adaptations to deal with missing or
uncertain evidence are described, as are additional features
such as a window, a facility for focusing discrimination on a
subset of classes chosen by the user and a modification to deal
with subjective data.

1. Orthodox rule-based systems

Traditional rule-based systems suffer from a number of
serious deficiencies when attempts are made to incorporate
mechanisms for dealing with uncertainty. The present author has
attempted to illustrate these shortcomings elsewhere (White,
1985). Perhaps the most serious flaw is the assumption of
conditional independence in circumstances where it is not
justified. This particular topic has also been discussed by
Szolovits and Pauker (1978). It has also been admitted by
members of the PROSPECTOR team in their final report (Duda et
al, 1979). Other difficulties relate to the peculiarities
arising from the use of fuzzy logic for combining probabilities.
This has been criticised both by myself (White, 1985) and by

Quinlan (1983a). Further problems are caused by inconsistencies in the parameters built into such systems as a consequence of their being subjective estimates. Attempts to avoid these problems by not using formal probability theory have fallen victim to exactly the same difficulties, as shown by Adams (1976) in his discussion of the MYCIN system.

2. Automatic induction

Another approach to the task of constructing rules is that known as automatic induction, in which data on past cases are fed to some induction algorithm which yields rules which may then be applied to new cases. A common approach taken by induction algorithms has been described by Quinlan (1986) as the "Top Down Induction of Decision Trees" (leading to the acronym "TDIDT"). In essence, this involves constructing decision trees for classification purposes. The trees are constructed by beginning at the root and proceeding downwards to the leaves. The ancestor of many TDIDT programs is CLS (Hunt, Marin and Stone, 1966). More recent systems of the same type include ID3 (Quinlan 1979, 1983b), ACLS (Patterson and Niblett, 1983) and ASSISTANT (Kononenko, Bratko and Roskar, 1984).

However, one drawback of typical induction algorithms is that they cannot handle noisy data. If a given attribute profile corresponds to different classes for different cases, then a "clash" is said to have occurred. This will cause the induction algorithm to halt and possibly request further attributes which could be used to discriminate between the offending cases.

Such a state of affairs is acceptable in a situation where the entire set of cases is finite (and not too large), e.g. simple chess endgame analysis. In these circumstances, we know that there is no real uncertainty in the problem and that clashes should not occur. By contrast, there are other domains (e.g. some areas of medical diagnosis) where, for all practical purposes, it is reasonable to regard some level of uncertainty as intrinsic to the nature of the problem. In such a domain, it may be more appropriate to regard a given attribute profile as imperfectly indicative of more than one class.

3. Probabilistic induction

Another approach to the problem of uncertain inference in expert systems might loosely be described as a synthesis of ideas from artificial intelligence and mathematical statistics. It is essentially an extension of automatic induction to enable it to deal with uncertainty. The basic method has something in common with the discriminant function for categorical data described by Sturt (1981) and also with the statistical classification technique outlined by Mabbett et al (1980). It is also closely related to the techniques described by Hart (1985) and Quinlan (1986). However, it differs from these approaches (and from statistical techniques in general) in that no model or classification tree is constructed for predictive purposes - instead each new case is matched against past data on a subset of attributes, by a process about to be described. Other differences are that the system is capable of providing more of the customary features of expert systems than can usually be found in orthodox statistical approaches.

Suppose that we are concerned with some problem domain in which each case possesses values on n binary attributes, A_i, $i = 1,n$. Let us further suppose that each case falls into one and only one of the k classes, H_j, $j = 1,k$ and that these classes are mutually exclusive and jointly exhaustive. Let us use the notation a_i to represent a particular value of A_i and h to represent a particular value of H. Let us also represent the sequence of values a_i, $i = 1,n$ by the vector **a**. Thus a general case can be represented as (h,**a**) and the frequency count of such a case by the notation f(h,**a**). The first thing to do is to form a frequency table of cases in which the values of such frequencies are known. Such a table would consist (conceptually) of a series of records, each containing an attribute vector, **a**, and a set of corresponding frequencies for each of the classes, $f(H_j|\mathbf{a})$, $j = 1,k$. As the number of possible attribute vectors becomes large, the table would be expected to become increasingly sparse (i.e. would have an increasingly large proportion of evidence patterns with all class frequencies zero). Therefore, from a computational point of view, the <u>actual</u> storage mechanism would probably be of some type that did not require such patterns to be stored at all.

If we now consider a new case, in which **a** is known, but h is not, then the computation of probabilities for classifying this case proceeds along the following lines. Ideally, we need the k conditional probabilities $p(H_j|\mathbf{a})$, $j = 1,k$. Of course, with sufficient data, these conditional probabilities can be obtained simply from the various frequencies $f(H_j|\mathbf{a})$. However, with sparse data this technique will result either in poor estimates due to small frequencies and overfitting (White and Reed, 1986) or undefined quantities due to dividing zero by zero. Thus some other procedure is required.

The conditional probabilities described in the previous paragraph are, of course, probabilities which are conditional on the full set of attributes. The technique about to be described here depends on conditioning upon some subset of the attributes, proceeding in a stepwise fashion dealing with one attribute at a time. The first step is to find that attribute which is the most powerful discriminator between the k classes of H, among the past cases. The way that this is done in PREDICTOR is to form a k x 2 class by attribute value contingency table of $f(H_j|a_i)$ for each of the n attributes and to choose as the best discriminator that particular A_i showing the strongest interaction with class, as measured by the χ^2 test statistic for the table. Let us call this attribute A_{max}. The entire frequency table for the past cases is then conditioned upon that value of A_{max} found in the new case, thereby forming a sub-table.

This process is repeated, discriminating upon successive attributes in turn, until no further steps can be taken. This occurs either when none of the remaining attributes can yield a statistically significant χ^2 value when crossed with H, or when further conditioning would cause too many cases to be lost from the current sub-table. The final step is straightforward. The entire remaining sub-table is collapsed into k cells (one for each value of H) and the probabilities for class membership formed from these in the obvious manner (along with their confidence intervals, if required).

It should be noted that when each new attribute is conditioned upon, its interactions with those attributes that have already been used are automatically taken into account by the very nature of the process employed. Thus there is no need to make the customary assumption of conditional independence between attributes, which is so often violated in conventional expert systems.

Some thought needs to be given to the level of statistical significance chosen to define the cutoff value for χ^2. In discussing a similar scheme, Quinlan (1986) suggests a probability level of 0.01 but some work by the present author (as yet unpublished) indicates that this might be too stringent and that a level of 0.05 would be preferable. A more thorough (though time-consuming) approach is to use cross-validation to select an optimal level of significance.

4. Dynamic path generation in virtual trees

This process might be more intelligible to computing scientists if viewed in tree form. To aid the explanation, consider a simple example. Suppose we are dealing with a domain characterised by three classes (H_1, H_2 and H_3) and three binary attributes (A_1, A_2 and A_3) and suppose that we also have available the set of training data shown in Table 1. The resulting complete induction tree is shown in Figure 1.

The process of classifying a new case proceeds by following a path through the tree from the root down to the appropriate leaf node, where the estimated probabilities of class membership are located. Of course, if the whole tree were derived beforehand, then the process of derivation would fall victim to the combinatorial explosion, with the expected derivation time increasing exponentially with n, the number of attributes. Furthermore, with a large tree, only a small proportion of the paths would ever be used during the lifetime of the system! The procedure used here is to generate nothing more than the path required to classify the case currently under consideration, i.e. training and use are collapsed into a single operational phase. Thus the tree portrayed in Figure 1 is intended to be a virtual tree. Hence all the paths in it except

$f(H_1)$	$f(H_2)$	$f(H_3)$	A_1	A_2	A_3
30	15	10	0	0	0
70	10	15	0	0	1
10	20	65	0	1	0
10	20	55	0	1	1
60	10	15	1	0	0
60	5	20	1	0	1
10	55	45	1	1	0
10	45	55	1	1	1

Table 1.   An example of a set of training cases.

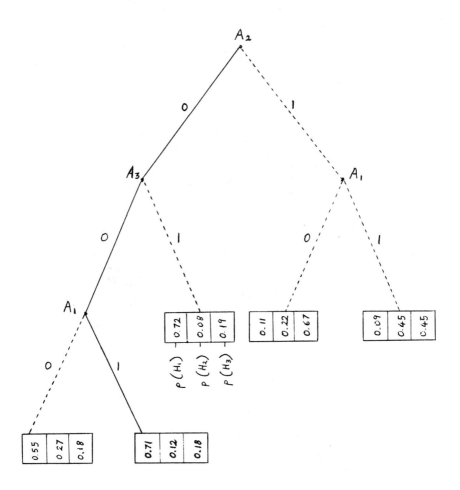

Figure 1. The complete probabilistic induction tree generated from the data in Table 1. The solid line represents the classification of a new case. A cutoff value of 3.84 was used for χ^2 (corresponding to a significance level of 0.05).

one are represented by broken lines to indicate that they have
not been generated, but could be. The single path indicated by
the solid line represents the classification of a new case of
unknown class membership.

This path is generated dynamically, as follows. At
each node on the path, the algorithm determines which attribute
would provide most information concerning class membership of
the case under consideration, given the values of the attributes
further up the path. If the algorithm is operating
interactively, the user is then interrogated concerning the
value of that attribute and the resulting information enables
the next segment of the path to be generated. The process is
repeated at each subsequent node on the path until either no
further attributes remain or until no further statistically
significant discrimination can be made by any of the remaining
attributes. At this point, the current node becomes a leaf node,
yielding the estimated probabilities of class membership.

There remain a number of features which require
further attention. Some of these are statistical refinements and
others are features which expert systems normally provide but
which tend not to be found in statistical software. First of
all, there is the issue of discrete attributes which are not
binary. These are dealt with in PREDICTOR by a very simple
mechanism. Each such attribute is recast as binary on a case by
case basis in the process of constructing the dynamic path. The
value taken by a given case depends on whether that case has the
same value for the attribute as the new case (when it will take
the value 1), or some other value (when it will take the value
0). Of course, this is actually only done dynamically when
forming the k x 2 tables for such attributes and when branching
upon them.

The following sections deal with features relating to
missing or uncertain evidence.

5. Missing value techniques

Missing values in attributes of new cases can be dealt
with quite simply. As these attributes can never be branched
upon when dealing with the new case in question, they must be
collapsed over at the final stage. To save execution time, they
can be flagged for this operation to be performed at the leaf
node.

In terms of the tree structure, this means that the
paths are now strictly dynamic. Whereas hitherto the entire tree
could have been generated, this is now impossible - at least
without advance knowledge concerning which attributes are
missing. Thus the adoption of dynamic path generation in virtual
trees in combination with missing attribute values means that we
are now considering not just paths from a single tree but paths
from a large number of trees - a very flexible approach. If the
algorithm is extended to deal with this feature, it operates as
follows. At each node on the path, the algorithm establishes a

rank order for the conditional importance of the statistically significant attributes not already branched on, using the same technique as described previously. As before, it interrogates the user concerning the value of the most important attribute at that node. If the user indicates a missing value for that attribute, then it cannot be branched on and the algorithm tries again with the second candidate on the list. This process continues until either a node is established (allowing the process to continue) or until the list of candidates is exhausted, at which point a leaf node is formed.

Turning to the problem of missing values in the set of training cases, the solution is to use an extra level for each of the attributes, regarding them as ternary. This extra level is dealt with quite simply in the various stages by the following rules:

(1) When <u>branching</u> upon an attribute, cases in the database with missing values for that attribute are always <u>excluded</u> from further consideration.

(2) A missing value for a particular attribute in the new case is <u>not</u> regarded as matching missing values on the same attributes in the training set.

6. The <u>strategy</u> <u>for</u> <u>uncertain</u> <u>evidence</u>

If the user is completely uncertain concerning the value of a particular attribute, then it should assume its prior value and be dealt with as a missing value, as described in the previous section.

However, for intermediate levels of uncertainty, some other strategy is required. If an attribute, A_i, that has uncertainty associated with it is not branched upon, then no further special action need be taken because the final sub-table will be collapsed over this attribute. On the other hand, if A_i is one of those attributes that are branched upon, then further steps are required, as follows. The technique is straightforward. Essentially, it uses <u>both</u> sub-trees that result from conditioning upon an uncertain attribute, followed (at the end of the branching process) by collapse of both sub-tables and the computation of <u>two</u> sets of conditional probabilities, one based on $A_i = 1$ and the other on $A_i = 0$. Each final conditional probability is then computed as the weighted sum of the two appropriate conditional probabilities, where the weights are the subjective probabilities of $A_i = 1$ and $A_i = 0$. A similar technique is used for two or more uncertain attributes. In the general case, for n uncertain attributes, each of the k final conditional probabilities is estimated as the weighted sum of 2^n terms. The weights concerned are the probabilities of conjunctions of attribute values. As the events corresponding to these values are not independent (in general), products of the simple event probabilities will not give the correct weights. However, the correlation information for these attributes can be obtained from information in the database which enables the correct conjunctive probabilities to be calculated.

From a computational point of view, an equivalent result can be obtained in a simpler manner. Because conditioning upon a number of attributes is a commutative process, conditioning upon the uncertain attributes can be left until last. In this scheme, uncertain attributes are flagged for postponed conditioning, rather than being conditioned upon immediately. Thus uncertain attributes are branched on last in the tree structure. This can save a considerable amount of execution time.

It should be noted that this approach is probabilistically correct, unlike the "dog-leg" interpolation functions found in many expert systems, such as PROSPECTOR and MYCIN.

7. Further features

One of the features judged to be important in conventional expert systems is the presence of a "window", i.e. the user should be able to see how the system got to its present state. The approach outlined earlier can certainly be supplied with a "window" in much the same way as any other stepwise statistical procedure. It is quite easy to program the system to report at each stage which attribute it is branching upon and, if required, what the k final conditional probabilities would be if the current sub-table was collapsed without further conditioning, i.e. if a leaf node was formed at that point of the tree. PREDICTOR already has part of such a "window" in place.

This idea prompts a further one concerning the focus of discrimination. At any given stage in the branching process, the user might wish to shift the focus of discrimination away from a global consideration of all k classes to a particular subset - perhaps two or three - which seem more likely to be relevant. This feature could be implemented simply by altering the x^2 test used at each stage of the conditioning process, so that the test statistic would be based on the appropriate subset of classes.

In passing, it is also worth mentioning the topic of user intervention. Allowing the user the power to override the automatic branching process so that it takes place on attributes selected by the user is obviously easy to build into the system, although the advantage of such a feature is not immediately obvious, as it reduces the effectiveness of the discrimination process.

8. Subjective data

Finally, the issue of subjective data should be tackled. As PREDICTOR was conceived, it was intended to operate on objective (i.e. actual) data from past cases. However, it has recently occurred to the author that it might be feasible to use the same scheme to operate on subjective data. These data might be elicited from the domain expert, as follows. He would be asked to imagine some large number of cases (e.g. one hundred thousand) and would then be asked to specify how he would expect these cases to be distributed over the various attribute vectors and classes in the imaginary database. The intention is that the expert should pick out those combinations of class and attribute which are relatively common and also those which are relatively rare and attempt to estimate their frequencies. Having estimated these "peaks" and "troughs" in the multivariate frequency distribution, the remaining cases would be spread evenly over the database. Such a method of eliciting subjective data neatly circumvents problems arising from getting the expert to estimate impossibly complicated likelihood ratios and ensures consistency in the estimates - thereby avoiding the problem of inconsistent priors (White, 1985).

However, one problem with this approach remains. The statistical sensitivity (or "power" in statistical terminology) depends on the number of imaginary cases that are used. If this number is too small, the system will be of little use because it will make few inference steps (or perhaps none at all) before coming to an automatic halt. If the number is too large then the system will possess a spurious degree of precision. Thus it is clear that employing frequencies in this subjective way makes nonsense of the idea of using a significance test as a stopping rule for the stepwise discrimination process. It seems that, in these circumstances, the only strategy open to us is to examine the <u>magnitude</u> of discrimination effects, rather than their level of <u>significance</u>, in order to decide when to cease the conditioning process.

9. Concluding remarks

A final comment is needed concerning the nature of the database. With conventional inductive systems, it is necessary to ensure that unusual or "difficult" cases are included in the training set. With probabilistic induction, there is an additional requirement that the database represents an unbiased sample from the population of cases that it is intended to represent. If it does not, then the algorithm cannot be guaranteed to operate correctly because it may be "misled" by various incorrect probabilities formed from the data.

The system outlined in the previous sections seems to offer most of the features of a conventional expert system but suffers from none of the statistical deficiencies desribed elsewhere (White, 1985). An expert system (PREDICTOR) which works on these lines is currently in operation and is being further developed.

References

Adams, J.B. (1976). A probability model of medical reasoning and the MYCIN model. Mathematical Biosciences, *32*, 177-186.

Duda, R.O., Hart, P.E., Konolige, K. & Reboh, R. (1979). A computer based consultant for mineral exploration. Final Report, SRI Projects 5821 and 6415, SRI International, Menlo Park, California.

Hart, A.E. (1985). Experience in the use of an inductive system in knowledge engineering. In Research and Development in Expert Systems, ed. M.A. Bramer, pp. 117-126. Cambridge: Cambridge University Press.

Hunt, E.B., Marin, J. & Stone, P.J. (1966). Experiments in Induction. New York: Academic Press.

Kononenko, I., Bratko, I. & Roskar (1984). Experiments in automatic learning of medical diagnostic rules. Technical Report. Jozef Stefan Institute, Ljubjana, Yugoslavia.

Mabbett, A., Stone, M. & Washbrook, J. (1980). Cross-validatory selection of binary variables in differential diagnosis. Applied Statistics, *29*, 198-204.

Patterson, A. & Niblett, T. (1983). ACLS User Manual. Glasgow: Intelligent Terminals Ltd.

Quinlan, J.R. (1979). Discovering rules by induction from large collections of examples. In Expert Systems in the Micro Electronic Age, ed. D. Michie, pp. 168-201.

Quinlan, J.R. (1983a). Inferno: a cautious approach to uncertain inference. The Computer Journal, *26*, 255-269.

Quinlan, J.R. (1983b). Learning efficient classification procedures and their application to chess endgames. In Machine Learning: An Artificial Intelligence Approach, eds. R.S. Michalski, J.G. Carbonell & T.M. Mitchell. Palo Alto: Tioga Publishing Company.

Quinlan, J.R. (1986). Induction of decision trees. Machine Learning, *1*, 81-106.

Sturt, E. (1981). Computerized construction in Fortran of a discriminant function for categorical data. Applied Statistics, *30*, 213-222.

Szolovits, P. and Pauker, S.G. (1978). Categorical and probabilistic reasoning in medical diagnosis. Artificial Intelligence, *11*, 115-144.

White, A.P. (1985). Inference deficiencies in rule-based expert systems. In Research and Development in Expert Systems, ed. M.A. Bramer, pp. 39-50. Cambridge: Cambridge University Press.

White, A.P. & Reed (1986). Some predictive difficulties in automatic induction. In Proceedings of the International Meeting on Advances in Learning, Les Arcs, eds. Y. Kodratoff & R.S. Michalski, pp. 132-139. Paris: Universite de Paris Sud.

ON THE VALIDITY AND APPLICABILITY OF THE INFERNO SYSTEM

X. LIU, A. GAMMERMAN
Department of Computer Science
Heriot-Watt University
79 Grassmarket
Edinburgh EH1 2HJ

Abstract

Quinlan's INFERNO is a system for probabilistic inference that has some advantages over some other existing techniques, such as Bayesian inference which is employed, for example, in PROSPECTOR. However, the method used for the termination of the algorithm in INFERNO may lead to incorrect outcome of inferences; and further, the INFERNO system cannot cope with the numerical information that is often entailed in real world problems. This paper investigates the termination problem in some detail and analyses the existing approaches to it. A more feasible solution is proposed, implemented and evaluated. Finally, the considerations for extending INFERNO's capability of handling numerical information are described; the difficulties arising are shown; and possible areas of future research are suggested.

1. Introduction

Recently, much attention has been centered on the area of inexact reasoning. A variety of different methods have been proposed, such as the Bayesian approach based on probability theory (Duda etc 1979), certainty factors based on the confirmation model (Buchanan 1984), the Dempster-Shafer method based on the theory of evidence (Shafer 1976), approximate reasoning based on possibility theory (Zadeh 1978), and non-numeric approach based on the theory of endorsements (Cohen 1983) etc. Probability theory, the classical formalism for dealing with uncertainty, has been extensively employed in knowledge-based systems, for example, PROSPECTOR (Duda etc 1979) and AL/X (Reiter 1980). However, the techniques used in most of those systems have been derived by considerably weakening the theoretical foundations of their origin for real application (Mamdani etc 1985). In particular White (1984) describes the principal deficiencies of these systems like PROSPECTOR: violation of the assumption of conditional independence, the difficulties in combining evidences, the problems of inconsistent prior information, and the general difficulties arising from the use of the subjective estimates of probabilities.

Quinlan's INFERNO (1983) is a recent probabilistic inference system that solves some of the problems of earlier systems such as the first three listed above. Moreover, INFERNO can make inferences in a cyclic way, a desirable but unaccomplished feature in systems like PROSPECTOR and AL/X in which only acyclic inference (from questions to goal hypotheses) can be performed in the network so that the flexibility of inference is seriously limited (Blake 1984). Another uncommon feature of INFERNO is its ability to deal with inconsistent information in the sense that if the information provided to the system is inconsistent, INFERNO can make this fact evident along with some alternative ways that the information could be made consistent. However, the appropriateness of this feature is open to question (Cheeseman 1985; Mamdani 1985).

Since INFERNO can make inferences in a cyclic way, ideally information should be able to propagate in the network until a consistent state is reached. INFERNO, however, allows only a very limited degree of propagation of information in the sense that propagation is allowed only once along each arc in the network, as a precaution against the non-termination of the inference process. Thus, INFERNO can not make full use of the information given by users, resulting in the imprecise (Quinlan 1983) and, in some cases, incorrect results, which will be shown in this paper. Blake (1984) tackles this problem by applying a linear optimisation procedure. His system allows free propagation of information. Unfortunately, some attractive features of INFERNO have been lost.

Also, the current INFERNO system can only deal with unquantified (logical) propositions and relations among them. But the real world tasks often entail numerical (quantified) but non-probabilistic information, as pointed out by Quinlan himself (1983). It would therefore be useful to develop a mechanism in INFERNO that can deal with quantified propositions and the relations between them, such as plus, minus, multiply and divide etc; and also the relations between unquantified and quantified propositions, like range etc employed in (Cox & Broughton).

This paper describes the termination problem of INFERNO. A linear optimisation approach is analysed, and a relaxed method of the INFERNO algorithm is proposed, followed by a comparative study between this method and the one employed in INFERNO. Finally, the considerations for extending INFERNO's capability of handling numerical information are described; and some difficulties arising are shown.

2. INFERNO

In INFERNO, knowledge is represented as a fixed set of propositions and relations between them. We shall use single capital letters like A, B, C to represent propositions and the same notations that have been used in (Quinlan 1983) for the relations between them, such as conjoins, disconjoins etc.

Given a proposition A, INFERNO uses a two-value scheme to represent its belief by two lower bounds $t(A)$ and $f(A)$, where

$$t(A) \leq p(A) \qquad \&$$
$$f(A) \leq p(\text{not } A)$$

That is, $t(A)$ is a lower bound on the probability of A, $p(A)$, derived from the evidence for A, and $f(A)$ is a lower bound on the probability of not(A), $p(\neg A)$, derived from the evidence against A. Therefore, the probability $p(A)$ of proposition A lies in the interval $[t(A), 1-f(A)]$.

Logical relations are represented as inequalities constraints, which we shall refer to as probabilistic constraints in the following parts, derived from the definitions of $t(A)$, $f(A)$ and from some basic definitions of probability theory (see Appendix A for an example).

The way INFERNO works is as follows: initially, trivial bounds $t(A)=0$ and $f(A)=0$ are assigned to each proposition A. These bounds are then increased either by the information provided from users or by inferences made from other propositions, obeying the propagation control strategy expressed in the production rule:

```
If    the previous value of the bound on the left-hand side of
      a constraint is less than the value of the right-hand side
Then  the bound is increased to this new value
```

to ensure all the propagation constraints are satisfied until the consistent state of the network is reached.

3. INFERNO Termination

To get the correct consequences of the inference process, as indicated above, information should be allowed to propagate in the network until all the constraints have been satisfied. Thus ideally, there should be no artificial termination condition for the propagation algorithm. In practice, however, to ensure that the inference process terminates, only a limited degree of propagation is allowed in the inference net.

3.1. The Termination Condition of INFERNO

An example, taken from (Quinlan 1983), is given in Appendix B, illustrating the case where an endless propagation chain with positive increase bounds can arise, if the information about a proposition is inconsistent. Also, Shapiro showed an example in which the same problem can arise even when the data are consistent (Quinlan 1983). INFERNO takes a conservative approach to this kind of problems. Basically, it prohibits changes propagating back to the original source during the inference process. In another words, propagation is allowed only once along each arc in the inference net (Blake 1984).

The consequence of this early artificial action is that the termination of the propagation is always guaranteed, but the outcome of inference may not be as precise as we can infer from the data (Quinlan 1983), and may even be incorrect, as illustrated below.

3.2. The 'order' Problem

It turns out that the outcome of inference in INFERNO depends on the order in which the user's pieces of information are supplied. Figure 1 is a small network illustrating this case: there are five propositions labelled A to E and two relations between them. A is the conjunction of B and C, and these are known to be independent. B is the conjunction of D and E; they are also independent. The notation used in Appendix A for such a relation, A conjoins-independent { B, C }, is abbreviated to { A: B, C } in the following parts. So the two relations here are referred to as { A: B, C } and { B: D, E }. Suppose that the information is provided for three of the propositions, C, D, E, in the network:

```
t(C)=0.8,  f(C)=0.2,  &
t(D)=0.6,  f(D)=0.4,  &
t(E)=0.5,  f(E)=0.5.
```

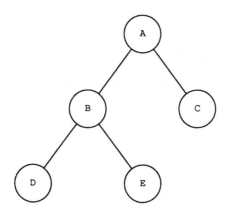

```
A   conjoins-independent  { B, C }
B   conjoins-independent  { D, E }
```

Figure 1

That means the probability of C, p(C), lies in the interval [0.8,0.8], i,e: p(C)=0.8, the same for p(D)=0.6, p(E)=0.5. So according to probability theory, the correct results for propositions B and A should be p(B)=0.3, p(A)=0.24 respectively. It means that the results for B and A from INFERNO should also be t(B)=0.3, f(B)=0.7, t(A)=0.24 and f(A)=0.76.

Suppose, now, the users supply the relation { A: B, C } preceding relation { B: D, E }. At the beginning, t(A), f(A), t(B) and f(B) are instantiated to 0 according to the algorithm, and the values for C, D, E are as illustrated above. The results for A from propagating the constraints for relation { A: B, C }, as in Appendix A, are: t(A)=0 from constraint (1); and f(A)=0.2 from constraint (2), next the constraints for relation { B: D, E } are propagated and B is instantiated to t(B)=0.3 and f(B)=0.7. Now the constraints for the relation { A: B, C } should be propagated again to get the correct answer t(A)=0.24 and f(A)=0.76 since the values for B have been changed, ie, the constraints for the relation | A: B, C | are not satisfied any longer. But INFERNO forbids this since the constraints for | A: B, C | have been propagated once already. Therefore, the final outcome for A is the interval [0, 0.8], an obviously incorrect estimate.

But the correct results for A can be obtained if the users supply the relation | A: B, C | following relation | B: D, E |. The constraints for | B: D, E | are first propagated and B is instantiated to t(B)=0.3 and f(B)=0.7. Then, the constraints for the relation | A: B, C | are propagated, and the correct answer t(A)=0.24 and f(A)=0.76 is obtained in the end.

3.3. Consequences of the Order Problem

It might be argued that the order problem could disappear if the information supplied to the system is well organised. For example, it can easily be shown in the PROSPECTOR-like systems in which only acyclic inference can be performed that the information could be arranged in a "perfect" order, from questions to goal hypotheses, so that all the constraints only need to propagate once, as in the second case of the above example. However, in the systems such as INFERNO in which cyclic inference is expected, there is no way of supplying information in a "perfect" order, as in acyclic inference systems, thus resulting in the impossibility of propagating all the corresponding constraints only once. Therefore, the termination condition in INFERNO can be a serious problem, as the outcome of inference could be incorrect.

4. Optimisation Approach

An optimisation procedure, proposed by Hinton (1978), is employed by Blake (1984) to allow unlimited propagation in the inference network. Termination is assured by a convergent algorithm to perform the optimisation. The resulting system can make better use of information provided by users than INFERNO. Unfortunately, this benefit is at the expense of calling back several serious problems that INFERNO tries to avoid in its initial goal. These are the single probability value for propositions, the need for prior probability and the inability to deal with non-linear constraints, which are brought about by the need to satisfy the conditions of the linear optimisation procedure employed. Also, the system is more computationally expensive than INFERNO because of the relaxation method used.

The need to improve this approach or propose another solution arises from the side-effects resulting from this optimisation approach, which are discussed in the following sections.

4.1. Single Probability Value for Propositions

Several problems can arise when a single probability value represents the state of belief for an event. As pointed out in (Quinlan 1983), the first problem is that nothing can be known from the single value about its precision. The second is that the single value combines the evidence for and against a proposition without indicating how much there is of each. It is easy to see that the belief in a particular proposition is, often, not necessarily the complement of the disbelief in the same proposition. The third is the difficulty in dealing with inconsistent information, as put in (Quinlan 1983):

> It is only in systems using a two-valued approach where the values are probabilities that there is a firm basis for detecting general inconsistency.

That does not mean that the systems using the single-value approaches can not detect inconsistency. It is just more difficult, more computationally expensive perhaps in systems employing single-value approaches, say Blake's system, than in those using two-valued approaches.

4.2. The Need of Prior Probability

The estimation of prior probabilities for many of the propositions being dealt with is tedious. Also, it is difficult to assign the prior probabilities in advance to some particular propositions for a certain application area. Also, it seems impossible at the moment to guarantee that all the prior probabilities could be chosen consistently, especially for a large knowledge base. But it has been found (Cheeseman 1985; Quinlan 1983) that supplying the prior probability can lead to more precise results, if it can indeed be known in advance, for example, in application areas such as poker.

4.3. Inability to Deal With Non-linear Constraints

The inability to handle non-linear constraints excludes the possibility of asserting common relationships such as independence between propositions since their corresponding constraints are non-linear. The consequence of this is that the result can not be precise when the relations like independence between propositions are indeed known.

5. A Relaxed Method of INFERNO Approach

This section is devoted to a proposal of another termination method, a relaxation of the INFERNO method. It is possible to allow information to be propagated back to the original source so that more information could be made use of than in INFERNO. This results in correct consequences of the inference process, provided that no positive feedback loop, such as the one in Appendix B, occurs in the network. Also little extra computational expense is needed.

Initially, it works in exactly the same way as INFERNO. However, when some changes are found to propagate back to the source, instead of stopping there like INFERNO, the information is allowed to propagate through the network (probably the same arc a few times) as it should. There are two termination conditions for it:

1. When the network reaches the consistent state, ie, the values of every proposition in the network are stable. This happens when the t-values and f-values of all the propositions in the system have not changed in one complete propagation cycle.

2. When the positive feedback loop occurs in the network. This happens when the sum of the corresponding pair $f(A)$ and $t(A)$ is more than 1, where A is the proposition appearing in the left-hand side of a constraint.

It is not difficult to see that the above method should be correct as long as the algorithm can terminate, since it is only the termination condition in INFERNO that prevents propagation from going back to the original source. It can be shown that the termination of the algorithm of INFERNO can be guaranteed by the above termination conditions. In INFERNO, the value of the left-hand side of any particular constraint, say $t(A)$ or $f(A)$, can only be increased starting from 0 (see section 2). So one of two cases should occur: either when $t(A)+f(A) > 1$, whose corresponding propagation process will meet the second condition above; or when $t(A)+f(A) \leq 1$, whose inference process will settle down on the first condition owing to the positive increase nature of the control strategy for $t(A)$ and $f(A)$.

6. Comparative Study of Two Methods

Two versions of INFERNO have been written in PROLOG running on VAX under Unix. One is the exact INFERNO system. Another uses the relaxed termination method. Various examples have been tested in the two systems. The results, discussed in the following sections, show that:

(1) when there is no possible positive loop happening inside the network, and the information about some particular relations can be propagated more than once, the inference outcomes from the new termination conditions are always correct, unlike INFERNO's termination condition from which the consequences of inference depend on the order in which user's information is supplied;

(2) the information about any relations in the network only need to propagate once, the results of the two methods are exactly the same;

(3) when there is a positive loop inside the network, there is no theoretical ground on which a comparison of two methods is possible, since an inconsistency may be involved.

For the first case where there is no possible positive loop in the network, ie, no danger of non-termination for the the algorithm, and the information about some particular relations could be propagated more than once, the right thing to do is to let it propagate through the network to get the correct results.

In section 3.2, it has been shown that the outcome of the inference process may depend on the order in which the information is supplied to the system owing to the termination condition of INFERNO. The same example is taken here to show how the new termination conditions overcome that dependence problem and lead to correct consequences of inference process. For the first case where the users supply the relation { A: B, C { preceding relation { B: D, E {, the termination condition in INFERNO forbids propagation back to the relation { A: B, C {, resulting in the incorrect answer for A. The new termination conditions make this back-propagation possible, therefore the correct answer for A, t(A)=0.24 and f(A)=0.76 can be obtained for the example above. Moreover, the inference process eventually settles down on the first of new termination conditions, since no t-value or f-value of any propositions will be changed during the next propagation cycle after t(A)=0.24 and f(A)=0.76 have been gained for A. The second case in that example, in which the users supply the relation { A: B, C { following relation { B: D, E {, can be subsumed into the second case here where the information about any relations in the system only need to propagate once. It will be shown next that correct results can be obtained by the new termination conditions for this case as well.

For the second case where the information about any relations in the system only need to propagate once, therefore no positive loop problem involved the results of the two system are the same. Take the above example, if users supply { B: D, E { preceding { A: B, C {, first the values for B are changed to t(B)=0.3 and f(B)=0.7, then the values for A are changed to t(A)=0.24 and f(A)=0.76. There is no need to propagate constraints for those two relations after the second cycle under the new termination conditions, since the values of none of the propositions can be changed in the second cycle. It has been shown in section 3.2 that the termination condition in INFERNO will also stop after the second cycle in this case.

In summary, the major contribution of new termination conditions is that the outcome of inference in INFERNO no longer depends on the order in which the information is supplied to the system. Therefore, the validity of the inferences is guaranteed not only for acyclic inference, but also for cyclic inference.

7. The Considerations and Difficulties in Marrying Numerical and Probabilistic Constraints

The principal consideration of marrying numerical and probabilistic constraints has been to handle numerical constraints in a similar way as INFERNO does for probabilistic constraints, so that all the relations in the system can be treated in a uniform way. In general, the following three points should be taken into account: representation scheme for numerical propositions, constraints that can be derived from numerical relations, and the control strategy for propagating these constraints.

7.1. Representation Scheme and Corresponding Constraints

Based on the above considerations, the decision for choosing the proper representation scheme for quantified propositions is very much inspired by the INFERNO system. As stated above, INFERNO uses a two-value scheme to represent the degree of belief about an event. To be able to marry quantified and unquantified propositions naturally in INFERNO, we adopt the two-value scheme for quantified propositions as well. Given v(A) as the value for a numerical proposition A, there are two values l(A) and u(A) to characterise it, where

$$l(A) \leq v(A) \leq u(A) \qquad (1)$$

I.e, l(A) is the lower bound of v(A), and u(A) is the upper bound.

The relations among numerical propositions or between quantified and unquantified propositions considered here are most of those appearing in (Cox & Broughton): plus, minus, multiply, divide, range. These relations and their interpretation are given in Table 1.

```
-------------------------------------------------------------------
Table 1.   The augmented relations and their interpretation
RELATION                                    INTERPRETATION
A   plus    | B, C |                v(A) = v(B) + v(C)
A   minus   | B, C |                v(A) = v(B) - v(C)
A   multiply | B, C |               v(A) = v(B) * v(C)
A   divide  | B, C' |               v(A) = v(B) / v(C)
A   range   | B, LB, UB |                      0        v(B) ≤ LB
                                          [ 1        v(B) ≥ UB
                                 p(A) =       v(B)-LB
                                          [ -------        else
                                            UB-LB
-------------------------------------------------------------------
```

Where LB and UB are the lower and upper bounds of "range" respectively (see (Cox & Broughton) for the detail); others, such as A, B, C are numerical propositions.

As in the case of logical propositions, it is obvious that two-value schemes give the user a better chance to express his belief about some numerical propositions than single-value schemes. For example, if the user is uncertain about some numerical propositions, a single-value scheme would force him to make the best guess he can, while a two-value scheme allows the user to express this uncertainty using the interval; if some numerical propositions are indeed known to be certain, the user can still express it using the formalism:

$$l(A) = v(A) = u(A)$$

which is equivalent to a single-value scheme.

The corresponding constraints are derived from (1) above and the rules of arithmetic calculation, listed in Table 2.

```
-------------------------------------------------------------------
Table 2.        The numerical constraints

A plus          | B, C |
                l(A) = l(B)+l(C)
                u(A) = u(B)+u(C)

A minus         | B, C |
                l(A) = l(B)-u(C)
                u(A) = u(B)-l(C)

A multiply      | B, C |
                l(A) = l(B)*l(C)
                u(A) = u(B)*u(C)

A divide        | B, C |
                l(A) = l(B)/u(C)
                u(A) = u(B)/l(C)
```

```
A range          | B,  LB,  UB |
                 t(A) = 0,  f(A) = 1      when  v(B) < LB;
                 t(A) = 1,  f(A) = 0            v(B) > UB;

                 0 ≤ t(A)                       else
                         v(B)-LB
                 t(A) ≤  -------
                         UB - LB
                         UB-v(B)
                 f(A) ≤  -------
                         UB - LB
```

7.2. Propagation

It has been found (Liu 1986) that some difficulties can arise when the control strategy for propagating probabilistic constraints in INFERNO attempts to serve as a way of propagating numerical constraints. Here is one of them.

As stated in section 2, each logical proposition A in INFERNO initially has the bounds t(A)=0 and f(A)=0. That means that the probability for A lies in the interval [0, 1]. Then the information about some propositions is provided by the users, and propagated in the inference network. As information is provided or inferred, the range within which the probability p(A) of proposition A is known to lie can only become smaller (Quinlan 1983), which is compatible with the positive increase scheme of the control strategy in INFERNO.

However, in the case of numerical propositions, there is no reason that, given a numerical proposition A, the corresponding l(A) and u(A) can not be decreased during the propagation process. So a suitable method for propagating numerical information needs to be explored.

8. Conclusion

The optimisation approach to the termination problem of INFERNO is difficult to apply to real problems since it is at the expense of losing some very useful features of INFERNO. The proposed approach improves INFERNO in the sense that it allows more propagation in the network with little additional computational effort, thereby making both cyclic and acyclic inference valid.

It has turned out that the control strategy for propagating probabilistic constraints in INFERNO seems no longer suitable for propagating numerical constraints. The work is being carried out in the hope that a new control strategy can be discovered to propagate numerical constraints correctly and effectively.

REFERENCES

Blake, A. (1984).
Probabilistic Inference By Linear Optimisation
Proc. of the 4th Annual Technical Conference of the British
Computer Society Specialist Group on Expert System.

Buchanan, B.G. & Shortliffe, E.H. (1984).
Rule-Based Expert Systems: Addison-Wesley.

Cheeseman, P. (1985)
In Defence of Probability: Proc. of 9th IJCAI, vol 2, p1002-1009

Cohen, P.R. & Grinberg, M.R. (1983).
A Theory of Heuristic Reasoning about Uncertainty
The AI Magazine, Summer-Fall.

Cox, P.R. & Broughton, R.K.
Micro Expert Users Manual Version 2.1, ISIS Systems Ltd.

Duda, R.O., Gaschnig, J. & Hart, P.E. (1979)
Model Design in the Prospector Consultant System for Mineral
Exploration, in Expert Systems in the Micro Electronic Age,
ed D.Michie, Edinburgh University Press.

Hinton, G.H. (1978).
Relaxation and Its Role in Vision, Ph.D thesis, Edinburgh University.

Liu, X. (1986)
Issues around Marrying Numerical and Probabilistic Constraints in
INFERNO, Internal Report, Computer Science Dept, Heriot-Watt Univ.

Abe Mamdani, Janet Efstathiou & Dominic Pang. (1985).
Inference under Uncertainty
Proc. of the 5th Annual Technical Conference of the British
computer Society Specialist Group on Expert System.

Quinlan, J.R. (1983).
INFERNO: A Cautious Approach to Uncertain Inference
The Computer Journal Vol 26, No 3.

Reiter, J. (1980).
AL/X: An Expert System Using Plausible Inference
Intelligent Terminals Ltd., Oxford.

Shafer, G. (1976).
A Mathematical Theory of Evidence, Princeton Univ. Press,
Princeton, N.J.

White, A.P. (1984).
Inference Deficiencies in Rule-Based Expert System
Proc. of the 4th Annual Technical Conference of the British
Computer Society Specialist Group on Expert System.

Zadeh, L.A. (1978).
Fuzzy Sets as a Basis for a Theory of Possibility
Fuzzy Sets and Systems, 1, 3-28.

APPENDIX

A. Derivation of Constraints for a Logical Relation

Here is an example to show how the propagation constraints are derived for one particular relation. We call this relation A conjoins-independent { B, C }, where A, B, C are propositions, A is the conjunction of B and C, and B and C are independent.

The corresponding constraints are derived from the straightforward manipulation of some relations in probability theory, using the identities:

$$p(X) + p(^-X) = 1 \qquad\qquad (a)$$
$$t(X) \leq p(X) \leq 1 - f(X) \qquad\qquad (b)$$

for any proposition X.

According to the rule for combining the probabilities of independent events in probability theory, we have

$$p(A) = p(B)*p(C) \qquad (c) \quad giving$$

$$p(A) \geq t(B)*t(C) \qquad (1')$$
$$p(\tilde{}A) = 1-p(A) = 1-(1-p(\tilde{}B))*(1-p(\tilde{}C))$$
$$\geq 1-(1-f(B))*(1-f(C)) \qquad (2')$$

Rewriting (c) as

$$p(B) = p(A)/p(C) \geq t(A)/(1-p(\tilde{}C))$$
$$\geq t(A)/(1-f(C)) \qquad (3.1')$$

the same for C:

$$p(C) \geq t(A)/(1-f(B)) \qquad (3.2')$$

Since

$$p(\tilde{}B) = 1-p(B) = 1-p(A)/p(C)$$
$$= 1-(1-p(\tilde{}A))/p(C)$$
$$\geq 1-(1-f(A))/p(C)$$
$$\geq 1-(1-f(A))/t(C) \qquad (4.1')$$

the same for C:

$$p(\tilde{}C) \geq 1-(1-f(A))/t(B) \qquad (4.2')$$

So the constraints corresponding to the relation A conjoins-independent $\{$ B, C $\}$ are:

$$t(A) \geq t(B)*t(C) \qquad (1)$$
$$f(A) \geq 1-(1-f(B))*(1-f(C)) \qquad (2)$$
$$t(B) \geq t(A)/(1-f(C)) \qquad (3.1)$$
$$t(C) \geq t(A)/(1-f(B)) \qquad (3.2)$$
$$f(B) \geq 1-(1-f(A))/t(C) \qquad (4.1)$$
$$f(C) \geq 1-(1-f(A))/t(B) \qquad (4.2)$$

B. An Example of Positive Feedback Loop

An example is taken from (Quinlan 1983) to show that a propagation chain with ever-increasing bounds can arise if the information about propositions is not consistent.

Consider the relation A conjoins-independent $\{$ B, C $\}$ above and suppose the bound t(B) is increased to a value X. By propagation constraint (1) above, t(A) must be increased to X*t(C), and substituting this value in constraint (3.1),

$$t(B) \geq X*t(C)/(1-f(C))$$

If t(C)+f(C)>1, this would require t(B) to be greater than X, so there is a positive feedback loop and the propagation process can never terminate.

MODELLING ANALOGICAL REASONING FOR LEGAL APPLICATIONS

Alison E. Adam* and Andrew D. Taylor
Department of Systems, Gillow House,
University of Lancaster, Lancaster LA1 4YX
*Current address: Department of Computation,
UMIST, P.O. Box 88, Manchester M60 1QD

Abstract

In the Alvey DHSS Large Demonstrator Project, we have been developing an approach to expert systems and the law, which attempts to acknowledge the richness of the legal decision making process in the significance of appeals to case law and reasoning by analogy, and the importance of interpretation of legislative rules.

The paper describes how the DHSS Adjudication Officer (AO), for whom a prototype computer system has been developed, may be viewed as a legal decision maker, and then goes on to discuss the problem of analogical reasoning in a legal context with an example from the AO domain. Material derived from the philosophy of science on scientific analogy is explored in the construction of a conceptual model of analogy which is then applied to the problem of the Adjudication Officer. The implementation of this model in the computer system is described with reference to an example case.

1. Introduction

Work in the area of expert systems and the law has traditionally focused on the representation of legislation by use of rule-based systems or logic programming (Sergot 1985). Recent work in the field of jurisprudence argues against such an approach by describing the impossibility of defining the law in terms of clear rules and thereby making a case for the limitations of logic programming in the representation of the legal process (Leith 1985).

In the Alvey DHSS Large Demonstrator project we have been developing an approach which attempts to acknowledge the richness of the legal decision making process while maintaining that this process can be supported by knowledge based systems. This work is driven by two considerations; firstly, the significance of appeals to case law and reasoning by analogy; secondly, the importance of _interpretation_ of legislative rules and the fact that a particular case is always open to reinterpretation, highlighting different features of the case and invoking separate parts of the legislation.

A computer system which can directly reason by analogy from the current case to previous case law was felt to be both overambitious and not necessarily of value in supporting legal decision makers. Rather, we believe that the construction of _models_ of significant parts of case law can act as a forceful representation of knowledge and can support the process of reasoning by analogy by suggesting a variety of interpretations for a particular case. The development of these ideas has most usefully been fed by work on models and analogy from the philosophy of science.

        This paper describes the particular problem domain of the
Demonstrator project, the legal context in which the problems reside and
how the work from philosophy of science has directed our system
development. Subsequently we describe the functions of the system
developed and our future areas of exploration.

2. Adjudication Officer Decision Making

        A prototype computer system has been designed and
implemented within the project, as a potential aid to the decision
making process of the DHSS Adjudication Officer (AO) on the condition of
"incapacity for work", which is the central test for Sickness and
Invalidity Benefit.
        Although not in a court of law, AOs are legal decision
makers in that they are bound to make decisions on awarding benefits to
claimants according to Social Security legislation and case law. To aid
this process, AOs are provided with a number of published sources -
copies of the legislation, copies of case law, Neligan's Social Security
Case Law Digest of Commissioners' Decisions and the guidelines for AOs
produced by the Office of the Chief Adjudication Officer. Our analysis
strongly suggests that AOs perform an analogical process in classifying
the present case in accordance with types or categories of past cases,
eg. hospital in-patients, bereaved, nervous illnesses or psychiatric
disorders, deemed incapacity etc. AOs must decide which type of case
they are dealing with and, if necessary, choose between competing
categories of case. It is significant that the AOs' guidelines for
"incapacity for work" for example, include many example or stereotypical
cases to explain and put in context the specific eligibility conditions.
        AO decision making differs from usual legal reasoning
within a court of law in one important sense, in that the presentation of
arguments for and against the case is not present. However, although AOs
are unlikely to explicitly construct arguments for and against
claimants' cases in such an adversarial mode, they must choose between
what are effectively competing analogies from case law (and may choose
more than one) according to their knowledge of the salient features of a
case.
        For example, let us suppose that the AO is dealing with a
claim for Sickness Benefit. The claimant suffers from chronic arthritis
and bronchitis. From time to time he helps in supervisory work, for at
most an hour or two at a time, in the family shop. He is also a
director of a small company. His G.P. encourages him in both these areas
of work for therapeutic reasons. The AO must decide whether to allow or
disallow the claim.
        The conditions for sickness benefit require that the claimant
be "incapable of work". The fact that a claimant is actually doing some
work is evidence that s/he is capable of such work and thus not entitled
to benefit. If the work in question, however, is carried out primarily
for therapeutic purposes then the claimant may be "deemed incapable of
work" under certain circumstances. The AO is required to interpret the
legislative conditions and assess their applicability to particular cases.
        Returning to the example, let us say that the AO has
recognised that this case resembles a case from case law, Commissioners'
Decision R(S) 4/79, where the claimant who suffered from a deep vein
thrombosis in his right leg, occasionally "tinkered" in the family toy

shop business and was encouraged by his doctor in this work (Neligan 1979: Sec. 2.2.8).

But the AO has also spotted a likeness between the present case and case R(S) 5/51, where a claimant crippled by rheumatoid arthritis was the landlord of a butcher's shop, a partner in a smallholding and director of a company. It was held that the unremunerative supervisory work at the butcher's shop could be regarded as negligible, but that the supervision of the other interests for the purposes of remuneration could not be disregarded (Neligan 1979: Sec. 2.2.10).

The general question facing the AO in this case is whether the work should be seen as including a non-negligible component or whether the recommendation of the GP should incline to an assessment of all the work as being therapeutic and therefore permitting an assessment of deemed incapacity.

3. Analogy in Legal Reasoning

Our concern with developing a computer system to aid the process of reasoning by analogy in legal decision making was generated by a recognition of the widespread belief, which Twining and Miers (1983) describe as running through the literature on jurisprudence, that analogical reasoning forms a major part of common law reasoning. Many different positions are possible within this spectrum of belief but two characterisations, detailed below, can help to clarify understanding of the elements of the analogical operation.

Levi (1949) is a representative of the school which sees reasoning by analogy or by example as the fundamental mode of reasoning throughout the law. For him, the law is a dynamic fluid process where legal rules are never clear. The rule of law which is deduced from one case and applied to a second cannot be regarded as fixed as the rule is changed and remade in the process and there are always fundamental ambiguities. The judge in a new case is not bound by a rule of law made by a prior judge but may emphasise other facts in formulating a new and different rule. Levi describes reasoning by example as a three stage process (Levi 1949: pp.1-2; Twining & Miers 1983: p.248)

(a) Case x is like case y
(b) Make a rule for case x
(c) Apply this rule to case y

In contrast, Twining & Miers are exponents of the view that reasoning by example is a two step process where the explicit formulation of a rule is left out.

"Case x resembles case y in respect of A, B and C. Therefore case x should be treated like case y.

The explicit reasoning is from particular to particular without a general rule being articulated at any point. Some interpretation of the rule is implied, but in an indeterminate way, in that any one of an indeterminate number of rule-formulations of differing levels of generality could be selected." (Twining & Miers 1983: p.249)

This process, they argue, is important in case law where opposing sides may employ competing analogies.

> "In case x A, B and C were present and the result was judgment for the plaintiff.

> "In case y, A, B and D were present and the result was judgment for the defendant.

> "In case z (the present case), A, B, C and D are present." (Twining & Miers 1983: p.248)

Twining and Miers suggest that the result of case z will depend on the relative importance of the features of similarity or difference, i.e. factors C and D.

If we return to our example from the previous section, the difficulties can be made apparent. According to Levi, a resemblance can be noted between a past case, R(S) 4/79 and the present case. A rule for case R(S) 4/79 could be made as follows:

If a claimant suffers from a serious chronic illness and the claimant undertakes work which is of a supervisory or negligible nature and the claimant's general practitioner encourages such work for therapeutic reasons, then the claimant should be considered for Sickness Benefit.

Applying this rule in the present case, all three conditions are satisfied and so, according to Levi, it should be treated like case R(S) 4/79.

Equivalently, a rule for case for R(S) 5/51 can be constructed and also applied to the current case – proving equally satisfactory on three conditions.

Under Twining and Miers' representation, the AO could say that in case R(S) 4/79 features (A) chronic serious illness, (B) negligible supervisory work and (C) encouragement by G.P., are present. Case R(S) 5/51 contains the features (A) chronic serious illness (B) negligible supervisory work and (D) other non-negligible work. But the present case has all four elements A, B, C and D and the AO must decide whether it matches best with case R(S) 4/79 with features A, B and C or whether, in fact, case R(S) 5/51 with features A, B and D constitutes a better fit.

Making an anology between cases involves constructing a set of relevant features to describe a case, itself a non-trivial exercise because a decision must be made as to which features are relevant and at what level of generalisation they should be described, out of all the detailed information available for a given case. In this example, the AO decided that the claimant's type of business or occupation was not relevant to the analogy although it might have been a relevant factor in other cases. On the second point, the AO chose to describe the claimant's medical condition as a chronic serious illness but in other circumstances it might have been appropriately described, at a less general level, as bronchitis and arthritis. Furthermore the AO must decide on the relationship between different features where, in practice, the choice of features will not be separate from the decision as to their relationship. In this example, this relates to the expectation that people with chronic serious illnesses may be able to undertake light supervisory work of a negligible nature and that doctors may designate such work as of therapeutic value. The final operation involves matching the present case to a precedent in case law where the past case must also be constructed in terms of a set of relevant features and their corresponding relationship.

Our understanding of the literature on legal reasoning by example or analogy encouraged us to look for a position mid-way between that of Levi and that of Twining and Miers. Levi's characterisation of the process where an explicit intermediate rule is formulated is immediately appealing to the builders of rule based systems. However, to capture the spitit of Levi's work, the computer system would have to reformulate its rules about past cases in the light of each new case presented for consideration, and this does not seem feasible. On the other hand, Twining and Miers' approach may appear to be adequately supported by a browser or other such enquiry system searching case law. To incorporate the essential analogical component, however, the system needs to provide some support for the process of evaluating the relative importance of the features - it has to have some way of representing the knowledge without requiring the user to have to explicitly formulate a general rule.

This analysis therefore encouraged us to look for a better representation of the knowledge used in the process of reasoning by analogy.

4. Scientific Analogy

The theoretical nature of our problem led us to a consideration of work from philosophy of science. There are analogies to be drawn between the construction of scientific theories and the process of legal interpretation. Judges employ a form of analogical reasoning in arguing from an old case to a new case. Scientists reason by analogy from a well-understood theory about a known area of science to a theory about a new and not fully understood scientific area. When the new scientific theory is worked out and well understood, the analogy may no longer be needed. It serves as a device for understanding, explaining and predicting theoretical terms. Hesse's (1970) Models and Analogies in Science gives a full account of the problem of scientific analogy. The following discussion is drawn from one of her examples. Imagine that scientists have observed the properties of sound and have constructed a well-developed theory. Properties of light are now observed and an analogy is made between the properties of light and the properties of sound to aid the explanation and understanding of a theory of light, and also to predict new theoretical terms.

	PROPERTIES OF SOUND	PROPERTIES OF LIGHT
	Echoes	Reflection
	Loudness	Brightness
Causal Relations	Pitch	Colour
	Detected by ear	Detected by eye
	Propagated in air	Propagated in 'ether'

Similarity Relations

Figure 1. Scientific Analogy (Hesse 1970: p.60)

Both the properties of light and sound are theoretical terms which form a model of light and sound respectively. This means that the analogy is drawn between one theoretical term and another, rather than between observables. For instance, we compare echoes with reflection rather than comparing shouting in a cave with shining a beam of light off a mirror.

Hesse's model of scientific analogy is developed in terms of two types of relations. These are horizontal or similarity relations, which are the one-to-one relationships of identity or defference between properties of the analog (sound) and the properties of the explicandum (light) and the vertical or causal relationship between properties, where the same kind of causal relationship exists in the model or analog and the explicandum. Hesse also suggests that analogy provides a justifiable method of hypothesis selection (Hesse 1970: p.77)

5. Models

The significance of Hesse's account of analogy is its relation to the construction of theoretical models. The key feature of these models is that they provide explanation for ill-understood cases/phenomena in terms of something already familiar and intelligible. The model, however, conveys associations and implications which are not completely specifiable. The value of the appeal to analogy is that concepts may be "imported" to the particular or new case which are not present in the data alone and which provide explanations of the case. In the instance of scientific analogy such models can be used to provide theoretical explanations of the data and to lead to predictions concerning additional data. In the context of legal reasoning the model provides an interpretation of the particular case – it establishes the meaning of the available data and its relation to the legislative conditions.

The construction of a theoretical model seems to be dependent on a number of elements. Firstly, it must be decided what is to be included within the model and what is effectively categorised as immaterial. This requires a process of abstraction of significant features. Secondly, the features may be described at various levels of generality or precision. The selection of a particular characterisation of the feature involves a decisive commitment to what is considered an appropriate level of generalised description (Naess 1972). Thirdly, there are the causal relations between or amongst features which implicitly commit us to the material mechanism considered to be at work within the model. It is essentially these three elements which make the reasoning by analogy possible and which supply the explanatory meaning from the model to the particular or new case.

6. The Computer System – Paradigms

The approach taken in our system development is to construct a system which matches features of a current case onto "paradigms" – effectively representing theoretical models of elements of case law. The key feature is that these paradigms "choose themselves" as being relevant rather than allowing the user to specify their own relevance criteria. This is a significant departure from the usual conception of other software developments in the realm of enquiry systems. An enquiry system, in the usual sense, would not help with the AO's problem. This is because an enquiry system would require the AO to know, in advance, which cases are required for retrieval and thereby encourage prejudging the case or jumping to a conclusion. The analogy system merely asks AOs to enter what is known about the claimant and to leave blank anything unknown or patently irrelevant. The system then offers a variety of suggestions as to how the present case may be interpreted in terms of past cases, but offers no actual decision. In presenting a selection of favourable and unfavourable decisions which are like the present case in different ways, the strength of the system lies in its potential to present possibilities which the AO may not have thought of rather than retrieving predetermined data.

The computer system has been developed with a knowledge base of paradigms. These paradigms are computerised theoretical represent- ations of stereotypical cases which model the vertical and horizontal relationships described in the account of scientific analogy. These are derived from case law and other sources such as the AO's guidelines which provide descriptions of appropriate cases (both real and hypothetical). Ultimately, the knowledge base will cover a wide spectrum of the variety of cases which AOs are likely to deal with.

It will be possible to associate items of case law with particular paradigms. It is important, however, that there is potentially a many to many relationship between the paradigms and the case law (although in practice we may only construct two or three paradigms for any one case). This explains, still further, our belief in the importance of paradigms. Case law can be a minefield of irrelevant and distracting detail which, in all examples of its recommended use, is clearly structured and constrained for anything other than highly expert usage. The paradigms can be seen as a way of controlling the usage of, and reference to, case law.

In the computer system, the intention is that an AO should enter details of the present case, i.e. a profile of the claimant, and be presented with paradigms which are analogous to, or like, the claimant profile. Profiles and paradigms have the same overall record structure, implying that the chosen range of fields must be appropriate to cover every contingency, and features which are irrelevant are left blank in both paradigms and profiles.

The next consideration is how the horizontal similarity relations and vertical causal relations derived from the scientific model of analogy are to be applied. In their most basic form, horizontal or similarity relations can be simple matching operations, a familiar concept in many computer systems, eg. where a numerical match is involved or where the system only permits a standard response as with "general state of health", where only "poor", "moderate" or "good" may be entered. Matching is a more difficult problem where AOs are allowed a free format in entering the contents of a field, eg. for occupation or diagnosis, where it would be unreasonable to impose restrictions on what is entered. The system could cope with this in a number of ways. First of all, some forms of general knowledge could be incorporated; an entry of "measles" against the diagnosis field would cause the system to query the user for whether German measles or the ordinary form of measles was intended. An entry of "smallpox" might prompt the system to question whether chicken pox was actually meant, because smallpox is now so rare.

Secondly, as well as general knowledge, the system can have paradigm-specific knowledge, i.e. a paradigm must carry with it certain inferencing mechanisms to help decide whether these difficult free format fields actually match the equivalent field on the input claimant profile. As an example, imagine an AO inputting details into the computer system of a pregnant woman who has been signed off work by her doctor because she is at risk of infection by a disease which could affect her unborn baby. The computer system searches through its knowledge base and comes to a paradigm describing a pregnant children's nurse who was deemed to be incapable of work because of an outbreak of rubella at her place of work (Commissioners' Decision R(S) 1/72 from Neligan 1979: Sec. 2.3.1). Rules applied to the diagnosis field on the paradigm attempt to establish whether the diagnosis on the claimant input profile is of an illness which is known to affect unborn children.

This is a different problem to the smallpox/chicken pox question described as "general knowledge" above. Clearly, the general knowledge capabilities of the system would be required to distinguish between smallpox and chicken pox but it is a piece of knowledge specific to this particular paradigm that German measles may be classified together with other illnesses which are dangerous to pregnant women. If the system cannot establish whether the diagnosis on the profile is in this category of infection, it will query the AO. This mechanism also allows paradigm features to be specified at as general a level as is possible or desirable. For instance, for a given paradigm a diagnosis of "slipped disc" may be required on the claimant's profile for an exact match but on another paradigm the requirement may be the potential to recognise that slipped disc and arthritis of spine both belong to the category of chronic back problems to constitute a match.

Similarly, the computer system must also establish whether the claimant's occupation, entered in the input profile, is one where she is likely to come into contact with children where rubella outbreaks are most common. In this respect, the computer system should be able to detect that lighthousekeeper is not a good match for schoolteacher or children's nurse.

Turning now to vertical or causal relationships and the problem of representing these, Hesse (1970: p.79–81) suggests that, in science, this relationship can be quite different in different circumstances, but the important thing is that there should be no reason to assume that the causal relationships at work in the analog or model

are different from those in the thing to be explained or explicandum.
As we are dealing with a classificatory form of analogy where both
analogs (paradigms) and explicanda (profiles) contain knowledge about
Sickness Benefit claimants then clearly there are certain causal
relationships of the same type. These are the fact that certain illnesses
will cause incapacity for certain occupations for given periods of time.
A gardener who breaks a leg will be incapable of work for several weeks –
there would hardly be any dispute about the undesirability of expecting
gardeners with broken legs to carry out their normal occupation in our
society. So as well as a causal relationship, in the scientific sense,
there is an overtone of a moral or normative relationship. This is seen
most sharply with the "deemed incapacity" paradigms of which the example
relating to rubella is an instance. The nurse could have worked normally,
but we interpret the law to say that she may be deemed incapable of work
because it is morally undesirable that pregnant women should be put at
risk in this way.

In accordance with both Hesse and Twining and Miers, we
recognise the causal relationship but leave it implicit. In other words,
we must specify that some features on a given paradigm are
causally/morally/normatively related but we do not spell out exactly why
or how they are, i.e. we leave implicit the rule that connects them. This
is not to say that a rule may not be implicitly used by the person
defining the paradigm when specifying the paradigm specific knowledge. In
the example of the paradigm concerning deemed incapacity for work due to
a risk of rubella, the crucial or causally related fields and their
contents are occupation and diagnosis (as described above); a response of
"Yes" to the "in employment" field; a period of incapacity less than five
months minus the number of months into pregnancy when the risk commences;
and a response of "Yes" to the "Pregnant" field. The contents of some
fields are ignored, eg. state of health and age. If the claimant input
profile matches in the appropriate ways, as already described, then this
paradigm will be recognised as like or analogous to the profile, and will
be returned to the AO when the computer finishes processing.

In summary, Paradigms are a means of implicitly constructing
a theoretical model without having to explicitly identify a single
general rule. In line with the elements of theoretical models this
involves:

(1) only filling in fields assessed as relevant and using
     descriptive terms which are seen to be appropriate;

(2) specifying if required, classes for fields (either by
     ranges of possible values and/or classification
     networks, glossaries, thesaurus).

(3) identifying causal or normative dependencies between
     fields.

The representation of knowledge in the form of paradigms
provides the "owners" of the system with a mechanism for expressing their
interpretative judgement without having to develop an unrealistic and
misleading set of specific rules. The presentation of the paradigm
leaves the user with the capability of assessing a particular feature in
the context of all its associated information and relevant factors.

7. Alternative Representations

Some alternatives were considered and rejected in designing the system. The most important of these was the possibility of assigning numeric weights to paradigm features and totalling these where a profile feature matched a paradigm feature and then producing a final score for a given paradigm against the profile. To start with, Hesse (1970: p.77) suggests that weighting of similarities between an explicandum and different scientific models does not strengthen the analogical argument. Secondly, under this scheme, because the fields on the paradigm have no sense of a relationship between each other, fortuitous matches between profile fields and their heavily weighted paradigm equivalents could give an artificially high score for a particular paradigm which is, in reality, no more similar to the profile than some other paradigm. We may artificially introduce red herrings. Furthermore, it seems inappropriate to look for a closest or best match; rather, we are looking for arguments which will support the present case.

8. Future Developments – Limiting the Selection

Finally, we must consider, for future development, whether the computer system will flood the user with potentially matching paradigms and whether, under those circumstances, the selection of paradigms should be limited in some way.

It is not clear that it will be necessary to do this. A great deal will be dependent on the knowledge elicitation process – the construction of a new paradigm requires more careful consideration than the addition of single rules. If it becomes apparent that the number of paradigms for certain cases is confusingly high, however, several options are available. As we are unwilling to evaluate paradigms for best matches, it seems more appropriate to develop a classification lattice of paradigms. Certain groups of paradigms may be principally concerned with the general condition of "deemed incapacity", other with "fit for work within limits". We may then either present the level of paradigm which generates most variety amongst paradigms while limiting the number presented.

9. Conclusion

In conclusion, three general points should be made about our work and the expected use of the AO system.

The approach to the design of the AO support system has been driven, overall, by a commitment to providing **support** for the decision making process, rather than an attempt to **replicate** that process. Although many systems proclaim such decision support rather than expert system ambitions, this only manifests itself in the interface design rather than in the underlying representation and inference. The aim of the AO system is to provide a variety of alternative suggestions for how to interpret a case. The system is essentially divergent, and opens up the range of factors to be considered, rather than convergent and focusing on a best decision. This is based on our belief, resulting from analysis, that a considerable danger in AOs' legal interpretation is not to consider a possible and feasible interpretation, and instead jump to a premature solution.

Secondly, we believe that such a system will be of particular relevance to legal decision making, signifying a complementary but distinct type of support to that attempted by rule based representations of legislation. The claim for relevance of representations of legislative rules must depend on the range, volume and complexity of the legislation. Our analysis has not identified this area as being the major difficulty of legal decision making. Rather, we believe that it is in the <u>interpretation</u> of the legislative conditions and deciding when a particular rule is relevant or not, that difficulties arise. The construction of paradigms gives us a knowledge representation for capturing the interpretive expertise of legal authorities.

Finally, we believe that the general approach outlined in this paper is of considerable potential value outside the domain of legal decision making. Much managerial decision making may involve the recognition of a problem as being of a particular type for which there is a known solution. The skill of management is often the <u>interpretation</u> and initial definition of the problem rather than the knowledge of solution strategies or evaluation of complex alternative decision paths. The approach we have adopted should be transferrable to the design and construction of decision support systems in such management areas.

Acknowledgements

This work was carried out as part of the DHSS Large Demonstrator project, supported by the Alvey Directorate of the UK Department of Trade and Industry and the UK Science and Engineering Research Council.

The project collaborators are ICL, Logica, Imperial College, London and the Universities of Lancaster and Surrey. The advice of other project members is gratefully acknowledged. The views expressed here are those of the authors and may not necessarily be shared by other collaborators.

References

Hesse, M.B. (1970). Models and Analogies in Science. Notre Dame, Indiana: University of Notre Dame Press.

Leith, P. (1985). Clear Rules and Legal Expert Systems. 2nd International Conference, Logica, Informatica, Diritto, Florence.

Levi, E.H. (1949). An Introduction to Legal Reasoning. London & Chicago: University of Chicago Press.

Naess, A. (1972). The Pluralist and Possibilist Aspect of the Scientific Enterprise. Oslo: Universitetsforlaget. London: Allen & Unwin.

Neligan, D. (1979). Social Security Case Law Digest of Commissioners' Decisions. London: HMSO. Chapter 2, Sickness Benefit and Invalidity Benefit.

Sergot, M. (1985). Representing Legislation as Logic Programs. Department of Computing, Imperial College, London.

Twining, W. & Miers, D. (1983). How To Do Things With Rules, A Primer of Interpretation. London: Weidenfeld & Nicolson 2nd edition.

PAYE
A TAX EXPERT SYSTEM

Dr I S Torsun
Schools of Studies in Computing
The University of Bradford, BRADFORD, BD7 1DP, UK

Abstract

A Tax Expert System has special characteristics in that its knowledge base is dynamic and changes frequently due to changes in government statutory tax legislation and regulations. Further such an Expert System, to be effective, should access, analyse and make use of existing employee data bases. In this paper the design and development of a Tax Expert System, written in PROLOG, is described; its domain knowledge is PAYE, National Insurance Contribution and Statutory Sick Pay. The Expert System is interfaced to both INGRES relational data base and COBOL data base files. Access and queries to the data bases may be made from within the system. An Explanation sub-component is added to give the user access to the reasoning and decisions made by the system. The paper examines lessons learned, system limitation and the implementation language and concludes by pointing to future research and developments.*

1. Introduction

Personnel Taxation (PT), National Insurance Contribution (NIC) and Statutory Sick Pay (SSP) are operated, in the main, by government tax regulations and legislation which are issued to employers under Income Tax Acts and the Pay As You Earn (PAYE) guidelines and publications. Tax regulations combine many different kinds of reasoning processes: rule-based, case-based, analogical and hypothetical. They have the unique property of being pseudo-formalised in that there exists a large body of formal rules which are used to define and regulate personal taxation. However, these rules are sometimes ambiguous, contradictory and incomplete. Further the rules themselves are in a constant state of change; this is because of changes in government legislation through addition, deletion and updates. Therefore, a Tax Expert System has to be easy to modify and update. It should incorporate case histories and give advice in the face of incomplete or contradictory knowledge. To be effective in its decision making, such an Expert System should access, analyse and update existing employees' data bases which have taken many man-years to design and build. This paper describes the PAYE Tax Expert System, its interface with the INGRES relational data and COBOL data base and the explanation component. The paper also describes limitations of the system and future research work.

2. Principle Features of the Tax Rules

The tax rules have the following form:
if c_1 & c_2 & ... c_n then a_1 & a_2 ... & a_m $(n,m \geqslant 1)$
where c_i is a condition or state and a_j is an action. Typically the average number of conditions in any one rule is 8-10 and the number of actions 1-6. Figure 1

* Acknowledgement: This research has been supported by SERC/ICL co-operative grant GR/C/54555

shows examples of the rules in English text and their equivalent in PROLOG. To a degree the rules are independent and seem to capture self-contained knowledge which may be easily understood by potential users. This degree of independence results in a knowledge base which is easy to modify and whose behaviour is relatively stable in the presence of frequent changes and additions, some of which are large, affecting 100-200 rules at a time. Such changes occur when the government introduces new legislation, for example, those on Statutory Sick Pay, industrial disputes and tax refunds.

An important feature of some tax rules is their time and event dependence (see the tax rule shown in Figure 1(b)). The rule deals with a trade dispute over a period of time. The start, duration and end of the dispute are important factors in determining the tax status of an employee who is involved in the dispute. Currently the PAYE Expert System cannot answer questions involving time and events, except at the superficial level of snapshots at the start and end of the event but not in between. The next version of the system will allow an appropriate treatment of time by defining predicates such as: after, before, end and time. This treatment of time is based upon concepts advocated by Kowalski (1985) and Allen (1984). Another important influence has been the desire to associate time periods with relationships as in Stamper's Legol (1973).

Unlike certain other domains such as mathematics or fault diagnoses, concepts and rules in taxation tend to be open ended; that is, one cannot provide complete or even consistent definitions. Reasoning with unusual cases sometimes depends on past interpretation, usually by court rulings and on occasion by an official tax expert. For example, a person holding shares in a company may receive as dividends further shares rather than cash. Will such be considered as income and therefore liable to income tax? A court ruling in 1965 judged that such dividends are

---

IF	employee is new employee
and	employee is school leaver
and	certificate A of form P46 is completed
and	pay > threshold
and	form P45 not produced
and	employment > 1 week
THEN	enter code for emergency use (200L) on deduction working sheet
and	set cumulative previous week's pay to nil
and	set cumulative previous week's tax to nil
and	send form P46 to tax office
and	calculate tax on cumulative basis using tables A and B
and	issue a coding claim form P15 to employee

----

new-employee (E) :-

   new(E), has-employee(E,P45), school-leaver(E), completed (E,certificate-A), pay(E,PAY), threshold(THRESHOLD), PAY>THRESHOLD, employment (E,WEEK), WEEK>1, dws-tax-code (E,200L), cumulative-prev-pay(E,0), culmulative-prev-tax(E,0), send-tax-office(E,P46), calc-tax-cumulative(E,TAX), issue-form(E,P15).

Figure 1(a)
Tax rule on new employee and its PROLOG equivalent.

IF   employee is entitled to a refund of tax
and   employee has been involved in trade dispute
and   employee is a leaver
and   employee leaves before next April 6
and   employee has not received tax refund
and   trade dispute ended > 42 days
and   unrefunded tax had been paid to tax collector
THEN   complete form P45 with tax due to date as shown in tax tables, excluding
        unrefunded amount

```
trade-dispute(E,-,-,tax-refund,-) :-
        taxrefund(E,REFUND), in-dispute(E,L1), leaver(E), leaves(E,L2,L3),
        not(refund-received(E)), dispute-ended(E,L4), greater(L4,42), tax-
        collector(E,REFUND,Y), Y=='y', process-P45-refund(E,REFUND).
```

Figure 1(b)
Tax rule on trade dispute and tax-refund and the PROLOG equivalent.
L1, L2, L3 represent lists for dates in the form of day, month and year.

IF   employee changes from weekly to monthly paid
and   employee was not contracted out on old scale
and   employee is now contracted out
THEN   set employee pay status to monthly
and   set employee status to contracted out
and   calculate NIC due for total monthly pay at contracted out rate

UNLESS   employee already recieved regular payment at weekly rate
THEN   calculate NIC due for total aggregated pay at contracted out rate
and   subtract NIC already paid for this current tax month
and   amend entries on deduction working sheet accordingly

```
nic-pay-period-change(E,Period1,Period2,Date):-
            current-pay-interval(E,Period1),Period1=='weekly', new-pay-
            interval(E,Period2,Date), Period2=='monthly', contract(E,not-contract-
            out).
nic-pay-period-change-a(E):-
            nic-pay-period-change(E,weekly,monthly,-),
            pay-status(E,monthly), employee-pen-status(E,contract-out), nic-
            calc(E,monthly, contract-out,Y).
nic-pay-period-change-b(E):-
            nic-pay-period-change(E,weekly, monthly, -),
            employee-pay(E,R,regular,weekly), pay-date(E,L1),
            interval(E,L1,coincide), nic-calc(E,total-aggreg,contract-out,Y1), nic-
            payed(E,Y2), Y is (Y1-Y2), nic-dws(E,Y).
```

Figure 1(c)
National Insurance Contribution tax rule and PROLOG equivalent

liable to tax because the extra shares may be translated into cash. A few months later another court overruled this judgement. A tax expert system may have to incorporate both cases and give the two options in its advice. The PAYE Expert System gives all case histories in such situations.

3. The Expert System Structure

The PAYE Expert System is implemented in PROLOG (2) and therefore uses PROLOG theorem proving and backtracking for its inference. It comprises approximately 2000 rules and 500 facts of real knowledge, these exclude information only clauses such as write, read and file handling predicates. The main features of the system are:

(i)   Its domain knowledge is statutory tax rules and regulations, National Insurance Contribution (NIC) and Statutory Sick Pay (SSP).

(ii)   It gives advice on tax regulation, tax codes, tax forms, specific employee tax status, how to operate a PAYE system and general tax information such as what constitutes income liable to tax.

(iii)   It can explain its reasoning and decisions using the commands why, how and explain.

(iv)   It can analyse, update and create employee data records in externally held data files (INGRES and COBOL data base files).

(v)   The PAYE Expert System would complement and/or replace existing manuals and computer procedures.
        . It could act as an "expert" on situations uncommon to the PAYE clerk or expert.
        . It may be used to train personnel who are totally unfamiliar with PAYE, NIC and SSP rules and regulations.

(vi)   The PAYE Expert System could form an important component of an integrated and totally automatic tax system.

The principle components of the system are shown in Figure 2 . These components are described below.

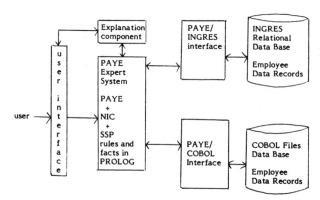

Figure 2
Block diagram of the structure of the PAYE Expert System

3.1 The PAYE Expert System

The PAYE Expert System was developed with a wide range of tasks in the domain of personnel taxation. The knowledge base is made of rules and facts, represented in PROLOG, see Figure 1, which have been extracted from the government Income Tax Act (1970), the official PAYE (1982-5), National Insurance Contribution (1982) and Statutory Sick Pay (1983) guidelines and publications. The knowledge was created by systematically analysing the documentation and when necessary consulting with court rulings and official tax experts from the Inland Revenue.The Expert System initially set out to assist and/or replace the PAYE expert within an organisation and to give information and advice on specific questions. An important design goal is a user interface providing easy and meaningful guidance through the modules and expecting minimum user input. The system gives the user either information of a general nature which applies across the organisation or more usefully on individual employee situations. To give effective advice on a particular situation, the system first tries to deduce the information either from its current data base or from access to external employee data files (INGRES and COBOL data bases). If the information cannot be deduced, then the user is asked to supply it. Logically, from the Expert System point of view, the user is treated as just another kind of external data base. The information about an employee is gathered until all the conditions for the query are satisifed, the set of actions and conclusion are then displayed to the user who has the options to: act upon them, store them in a file for later use, to update the employee data base or discard them. Thus the basic PAYE Expert System is a very large advisory system dealing with both high level general queries and intricate queries relating to complex tax situations. From this basis additional features were developed; the explanation sub-system and more importantly interfaces to both INGRES and COBOL data bases.

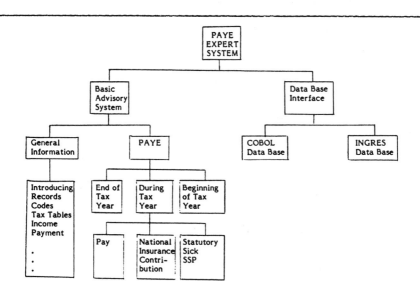

Figure 3(a)
The PAYE top level module architecture

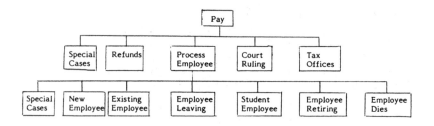

Figure 3(b)
A second level module architecture of the PAYE

System architecture and design strategy

The overall hierarchical and modular nature of the PAYE allowed for a top-down design strategy. The design reflects the near independence of the different knowledge areas that make up the system which are implemented as PROLOG modules. The modules are consulted as and when needed to reduce storage requirements. Because of the modular design, the different modules were created and tested in isolation, top level interfaces and control were added after module developments. Figure 3 shows a block diagram of the architecture of top level modules. The PAYE is split into two logical parts, the basic advisory system which is the core of the whole system within which the user may seek advice about any aspect of PAYE, NIC and SSP. The second part provides the data base interface, currently to INGRES and COBOL data bases, which may be extended to other data bases.

Scripts of a sample interactive session

The following show a simple interactive session with the PAYE Expert System.

[PAYE].

WELCOME TO PAYE EXPERT SYTEM

Please enter today's date:
- day(dd)   15.
- month(mm)   04.
- year(yyyy)   1986.

There are four main areas where the system can give help

for PAY AS YOU EARN 1
for NATIONAL INSURANCE 2
for STATUTORY SICK PAY 3
for QUERIES about data bases 4
to exit from system 99

ITEM? 1.

There are two main areas of PAYE:

GENERAL INFORMATION 1
ADVICE 2

ITEM? 2.

PAYE ADVICE

Please choose the relevant area:

START OF TAX YEAR (BEFORE APRIL 6TH) 1
DURING THE TAX YEAR 2
END OF YEAR (RETURNS) 3
to return to the main menu 9

ITEM? 2.

DURING TAX YEAR

NEW EMPLOYEE 1
SCHOOL LEAVER 2
EXISTING EMPLOYEE 3
LEAVING/LEFT 4
RETIRING/RETIRED 5
DIED IN EMPLOYMENT 6
REFUNDS 7
TAX OFFICE 8
to return to main PAYE menu 9

ITEM? 1.

NEW EMPLOYEE

Please enter National Insurance Number
(format is 2 letter, 6 digits, 1 letter - example ab167342c)

NI No: ax234168b.

Please enter employee name

surname   green.
first initial   i.
second initial   c.

Please enter date of birth

day(dd)   12.
month(mm)   02.
year(yyyy)   1950.

Please enter sex of employee m/f?   m.

Please enter employee payroll number?   501.
If employee is director enter director

Please enter date of employee starting work?

day(dd)   01.
month(mm)   01.
year(yyyy)   1986.

Is the pay interval?

weekly 1
monthly 2
fortnightly 3
4-weekly 4
quarterly 5
half-year 6
yearly 7
irregular 8

ITEM? 1.

What was the employee previous pay interval?
Please choose one of the items listed above

ITEM? 1.

What is employee "green, i.c" weekly gross pay?   120.

Has the tax code suffix H L P T or B?   y.
Please enter tax code?   320H.
Has the employee produced P45?   y.
Is the employee's P45 form relate to the current tax year?   y.
Is the employee on a pension scheme already?   n.
Is employee entitled to a pension?   y.
MY CONCLUSION IS:

1.   PREPARE EMPLOYEE "green, i.c." DEDUCTION WORKING SHEET
       (DWS)
2.   ENTER TAX CODE 320H ON DWS FOR EMPLOYEE "green, i.c"
3.   CALCULATE TAX ON A WEEKLY BASIS
4.   ENTER ON TOP OF PART 3 OF FORM P45
       PENSION 0 WEEK 1 BASIS
5.   DO NOT COMPLETE FORM P45

Do you wish help on any of the above?   n.

Do you wish to assert the above into:

PROLOG data base 1
INGRES data base 2
COBOL data base 3
None of the above 4
ITEM?   4.

3.2 The Data Base Interface

         To be effective in their decision making, Expert Systems should be able
to access, analyse and query existing data bases. While conventional clerical systems
function by amassing and processing large volumes of data algorithmically, Expert
Systems typically address tasks performed by experts and professionals. However,
for Expert Systems to mature into software products for use by a wide spectrum of
users, they have to interface and make use of large data bases that have taken many
man-years to design and build.
         There is a definite urgent need for such an interface, this objective has
been achieved by the PAYE Expert System. An interface has been developed between
the PAYE and the INGRES relataional data base and with the more traditional
COBOL data base files. in both cases it is possible to use the PAYE interactively to:
         . initiate queries and retrieve information (employees' data records) from
         externally held data (INGRES and COBOL data files).
         . update, append and delete externally held data.
         Figure 4 shows a block diagram of the data bases interface. The
interface components are written in PROLOG and they generate the required queries
to INGRES and COBOL data bases. From the user point of view the queries are
treated just like any other predicate in PROLOG, however they are system predicates
and therefore have special purpose and meaning. The predicates provided are: insert,
delete, update, retrieve, select, from and where. These predicates have the usual
meaning to the equivalent operators of the data base. A query is created
interactively, either by the user or the system itself using the above predicates. The
query is then translated into INGRES/QUEL query language (or a COBOL statement)
and then written into an intermediate file, dbquery, used as input to the INGRES (or
COBOL) data base. The result if any, is copied into a result file, dbanswer, and is
then accessed by the PAYE Expert System which recovers control. The PAYE may
then manipulate this data displaying the result and giving the user the option of
asserting any newly acquired facts onto the PROLOG data base.

Figure 5 shows top level predicate, in PROLOG, for the PAYE-INGRES interface. PAYE/COBOL interface predicate are somewhat different in detail but are handled in the same way as those of the INGRES interface.

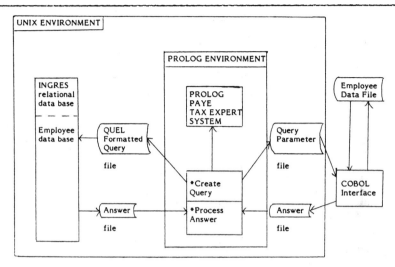

Figure 4
Query Interfaces and their Environment

* "Create Query" and "Process Answer" form the interactive interface to the rest of the computer environment.

ingres-query :-	create-query(Q), system-call, ! , accept-answer(ingres,T).
create-query(Q) :-	query-option, read(A), make-query(A,Q), translate(Q,QL,P,W), clear-query-list, add-query(QL,P,W), add-query(['/q',nL]), add-query(['/g',nL]), write-query-file.
system-call :-	system("csfile").
accept-answer(ingres,T) :-	see(dbanswer), copy-answer(T), print-answer(T), query-answer seen, assent-query.

Figure 5
Top-level PAYE-INGRES predicate interface

make-query is the predicate to construct the query in PROLOG
translate-quey is the predicate to translate query from PROLOG to INGRES
add-query is the predicate to build the query list

A sample interactive session using the PAYE/INGRES interface

do you wish to access:

the INGRES data base 1
the COBOL data base 2

ITEM? 1.

INGRES DATA BASE ACCESS AND MANIPULATION

do you wish to:

RETRIEVE RELATION 1
APPEND RELATION 2
DELETE RELATION 3
UPDATE RELATION 4

ITEM? 4.

UPDATE RELATION

SELECT   all
FROM   employee
WHERE   nino==ab245196f.

employee relation

1	2	3	4	5	6	7	8	9	10	11
nino	sname	pno	salary	payint	tax code	ni	sday	smon	syear	status
ab245196f	hall	110	120	w	250H	A	01	01	1986	new

which attributes do you wish to update?   4,11.
new value of attribute (4) salary?   140.
new value of attribute (11) status?   existing.
dbquery file written

START OF FILE

nino	salary	status
ab245196f	140	existing

END OF FILE
END OF QUERY

do you wish to assert these facts onto PROLOG data base ?   y.
INGRES updated facts are now asserted on PROLOG data base.

3.3 The Explanation Component

The explanation sub-system sits on top of the basic system and is used
to give the user the reasoning and justification of an action, advice or tax situation at
which the system arrived. The explanation sub-system has access to the proof tree

and generates a trace of the history of rules used to answer a query. The explanation given in terms of rules used, is however constrained by the limitation of a rule based model represented by PROLOG horn clauses.

The user may use any one of the following commands, available to him at any point during execution:

why: why a particular information is asked for or why a particular advice is given

how: how a goal, or advice is concluded and what conditions and rules are used in the process

whynot: why a particular decision cannot be made

explain: gives information, in English text, on specific items requested such as tax codes, what constitutes income, how to complete and prepare deduction working sheet etc.

The explanation has two other valuable purposes:

(i) as a check for the user; he may wish to query a set of actions and, given a display of all the information the system has discovered about employee X, the user may then decide if this information is incorrect in any way.

(ii) as a development aid for the designer/programmer when testing and debugging the knowledge base.

4. Discussions and Limitations

This section discusses lessons learned from the design, implementation and use of the PAYE Expert System.

(a) Analysis and formulation of tax rules from documentation

Logic is ideally suited for this kind of knowledge-based Expert System. It allowed high level specification of the rules and when expressed in PROLOG provided execution of the specification. The translation of the English description of rules into logic was easy and in particular the separation of knowledge, in the form of rules and facts, from control gave clear semantics to the system.

(b) The PROLOG language

. PROLOG is a powerful and flexible language, and was found useful as an implementation language for large and complex Expert Systems such as the PAYE. However, the expressive power of the horn clause is limited, typically one PAYE rule, in English form, mapped into 3 or 4 horn clauses, thus losing some of the semantics of the original rule. This limitation was particualrly noticeable when the explanation is given in terms of the horn clause.

. PROLOG is sensitive to clause and literal order. This resulted in a serious limitation to the complete flexibility of adding and deleting rules to the knowledge base, as it became necessary, without affecting system behaviour.

(c) The treatment of time

Time and events play important roles in tax rules. The proper treatment of time and events is the PAYE Expert System will greatly enhance its usefulness. To know the status of an employee during periods of employment, trade dispute or sickness are important factors in the reasoning of the system. Currently the PAYE does not treat time as a continuous parameter, but only as snapshots of time and therefore manual intervention by the user is essential. However, the next version of the system will include this facility as explained in section 2 above.

(d) Typing:

A critical feature found to be important, is the need for types in PROLOG or logic programming languages in general. Typing will increase system reliability, an essential requirment for a practical and large commercial Expert System.

5. Conclusion

A Tax Expert System (PAYE) was described in some detail. Using logic greatly eased the design and development of a complex and large Expert System. Rule specification and formalisation was made relatively simple in an otherwise complex situation. The PAYE system gives effective advice on a wide range of tax regulations and on particular employee tax status. The interface of the PAYE to existing employees' databases, INGRES and COBOL, was described and was argued to be necessary if the system is to be accepted by users in general. Finally, the construction of such an Expert System is an expensive and time consuming task. However, the end product is comparable in its performance to human experts in the field and it could form an important component in the complete automation of the entire tax system.

References

Allen, J. F. (1984). Towards a General Theory of Action and Time. A.I. **23**, 132-154.

Clocksin, W.F. & Mellish, C. (1984). Programming in PROLOG. Springer-Verlag, 2nd edition.

Kowalski, R.A. & Sergot, M. (1985). Logic-Based Calculus of Event. Internal paper, Imperial College, Dept of Computing, Feburary.

Stamper, A.K. (1973). The Legol project and language. Proc. Datafair Conference, British Computer Society, London.

Her Majesty's Stationary Office (HMSO) (1978). Income and Corporation Tax Act 1970.

HMSO (1982-1985). PAYE Guide to Employer P7.

HMSO (1982). National Insurance Contributions.

HMSO (1983). Statutory Sick Pay (SSP).

HMSO (1982-1985). PAYE Tax Tables.

OPERA: AN ASSISTANT FOR EDP OPERATORS

Ettore Decio [0] Sebastiano Di Pasquale [‡] Claudio Mordà [0]
Luca Spampinato [0]
(0) QUINARY - Milano - Italy
(‡) Banca San Paolo di Brescia - Brescia - Italy

Abstract

This paper describes OPERA, an expert system which helps an EDP centre
operator to diagnose and treat malfunctions in several securities and
bonds management procedures running on a Digital PDP11/70 computer.
OPERA is active during night, while operators are not supervised by
system manager. When a malfunction occurs, OPERA helps to identify its
cause, suggests a plan to make the system able to continue and finally
individuates a suitable point to restart the suspended procedure. The
representation of the knowledge necessary to the system's task shows the
typical problems of heterogeneous knowledge. OPERA is based on a frame
representation language and exploits the use of metarules in its control
strategy. The system consists of three different conceptual and
implementation levels and it was developed in Common Lisp.

1. Introduction

        An EDP centre has a crucial role in the regular operations of
a large company. In order to maintain a satisfactory level of
performance for both its hardware and software resources, expert
personnel must be devoted to the continuous planning and scheduling of
the centre's activities, while lower level technicians are concerned
with their actual execution and monitoring. The problem may arise that
they are unable to cope with unexpected hardware and/or software
failures, i.e. their experience with the computational resources
involved proves far too shallow in order to suggest a remedy.
        In situations like these, the system manager or a functional
equivalent of him must put forward an ad hoc solution to fix the
problem. Often the solution is simple, but to find it requires that
kind of thorough acquaintance with the system which only few people
possess. The net result is that these people become diverted from other
fundamental occupations, and this diversion can, in the worst cases,
interfere with scheduled activities. Failing to provide a solution
within a limited time lapse may cause, on the other hand, a serious
damage to the normal activities of a company.

2. Environmental considerations.

        OPERA (OPERator Advisor) is an expert system developed to
assist and advise an EDP operator at the data processing centre of the
Banca San Paolo di Brescia to diagnose and treat malfunctions in
several securities and bonds management procedures running on a Digital
PDP 11/70 computer. This hardware/software environment was chosen among
others for our advisor because of the relatively high rate of

malfunctions detected, partly due to the age of the hardware and partly to other software problems. OPERA is active during night, when operators are not supervised by the system manager.

Elementary considerations reveal that malfunctions can be divided into several layers according to their source, e.g. hardware device errors, system software errors, application software bugs, etc.

OPERA covers both hardware and system software errors, but when an application level software error gets spotted it gives up and notifies the operator. However, examining the log of past cases, we found that most problems arise from device mulfunctions, such as disk read/write errors, tape errors, etc., followed by a relatively large number of improper actions by the operator, such as skipping an argument to a command, misunderstanding system warnings, etc.

As a running procedure is halted and the PDP prints an error message on the console, the system manager (or the operator when the system manager is not there) has to:

1 identify the cause and the seriousness of the malfunction
2 operate to remove the cause and make the system able to continue
3 possibly restore a safe situation on files associated with the halted procedure, which might be in an inconsistent state
4 restart the halted procedure from a suitable point.

OPERA provides assistance to the operator while performing tasks 1-4 above, suggesting command and action sequences and requesting additional information from the user when needed.

To be effective, the system was designed to meet the following constraints:

• It had to run in a completely independent environment from the PDP and be invoked on request, i.e. when the operator recognizes an anomalous situation by means of an error message printed at the console

• It had to recognize and link those repeated faults having a common cause (e.g. a disk device malfunction can subsume two different error instances manifesting themselves as two read/write errors), as well as overlapping errors (i.e. errors occurring during the treatment of a former error).

• Finally it had to provide a report to explain what happened and its decisions so that the system manager could get a complete and updated view of the performance of the system.

The problem was well suited to the application of expert systems technology. In fact:

• The problem is constrained enough to be approachable with the current techniques

• A small group of experts exists who can carry out the task which the system is supposed to be implemented for

• Even a partial solution to the problem gives considerable advantages over the previous situation.

OPERA was developed in Golden Common Lisp™ by a team of three computer professionals and an EDP system manager (who provided the necessary knowledge and experience) over a period of six months. OPERA runs on an IBM AT personal computer. Currently it is a prototype system dealing with a significant subset (50%) of the procedures running on the PDP. It is now under extensive testing and refinement at Banca San

Paolo, and its operative release is scheduled by June 1986. A
relatively similar project, although dealt with in a larger setting and
with different aims, has been described in the International Workshop
on AI in Economics and Management, ETH Zurich, February 1985.

3. Knowledge analysis.

        The representation of the knowledge necessary to the
assisting task shows the typical problems of heterogeneous knowledge, in
that it does not lend itself to a unique paradigm. In other words it was
impossible to code the knowledge involved in the reasoning task by means
of a single formalism among the several normally used. Although
initially planned, a commercial, personal computer oriented, expert
system shell could not be used for the development due to this
requirement. In fact most of these shells extensively exploit (a
variation of) production rules as the main representation tool. As we
shall see in the sequel, not all of the types of knowledge needed in
OPERA fit into this well known pattern.
        A thorough analysis reveals that knowledge that is relevant
to the task at hand can be partitioned into the following usage classes:
Localizing Knowledge.
    It permits to discover where, in the halted procedure, the error
    occurred. As OPERA is not directly connected to the PDP, the
    localization takes place through an interactive dialog with the
    user. This dialog has the side effect of collecting a set of useful
    information for the system to be effective: among them we mention
    the devices involved and the operations needed to complete the
    procedure. All this implies a declarative description of the
    accounted procedures (we call them *external* procedures). A
    description specifies a procedure as a sequence of phases , where a
    single phase consists either of a restricted set of commands to the
    operating system or of particular actions to be performed by the
    operator. A procedure is partitioned in this way into a fine grain
    subdivision. Each phase has a set of logically related informations
    we referred to above.
Identifying Knowledge.
    Its role is to help in the diagnosis process, when OPERA has to find
    out which error type occurred (e.g. a disk error). It is not an
    actual diagnostic task in that every possible error message almost
    directly identifies a precise error context. The identification task
    may require additional information from the user, obtainable through
    a simple dialogue. This kind of knowledge can be easily put in
    tabular form. As a byproduct of the application of localizing and
    identifying knowledge we get a complete and accurate description of
    the error context: this makes possible to build its concrete
    internal representation.
Classifying Knowledge.
    It is fundamental when the expert has to relate the current
    malfunction to previous ones. For instance, multiple reported errors
    referring to the same physical device may in general require
    different corrective actions depending on the error frequency. The
    expert then, before taking any decision, examines the recent history
    of the system to properly cluster interdependent errors. This kind

of knowledge has an intrinsic local nature: the grouping of
different errors into a unique description depends on the context
they occurred in. It is best expressed as a set of production rules
that in the following are termed structural rules.
Decision Knowledge.
   It comes into play to select a satisfactory sequence of steps to
get rid of the malfunction and clearly lies at the heart of OPERA.
Based on the current error context created through the previously
described knowledge sources it selects a sequence of actions
corresponding to steps 2-4 above (where information about steps 3
and 4 is directly associated to the monitored procedure). It too is
straightforwardly coded in the form of production rules, that we
name intervention rules.
Operating Knowledge.
   It is a set of canned standard command procedure descriptions
(called *internal* procedures) that, when executed in some way,
implement phases 2 and 3 above, i.e. advise the user about how to
remedy to the malfunction. The overlapping constraint calls for a
uniform representation with external procedures, so that errors
while executing one of these procedures can be taken care of by the
same general mechanisms. The only difference between an internal and
an external procedure is the existence for the former of an
interpreter guiding the user through the actual execution of the
recovery task.

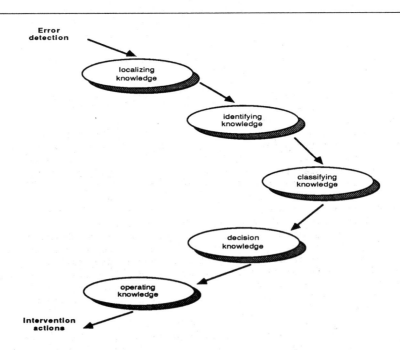

Figure 1. The knowledge structure of OPERA.

Most commercially available expert system shells for the PC AT were ruled out as unsuitable for the implementation because of their limited representation facilities (basically tied to production system formalisms). The need for a clean description of procedures was the major obstacle to the use of a commercial shell. We developed instead our own tools, briefly described in the following. The five knowledge classes are sequentially composed to define the overall behaviour of OPERA, as shown in Figure 1. The figure roughly corresponds to a block diagram of the system.

4. System structure.

OPERA consists of three different conceptual and implementative layers, each layer standing on top of the previous.

The ground layer is a fairly simple representation language, embedded in Lisp. It basically provides a common framework for knowledge description and access. QSL (Quinary Simple Language) features include most of the facilities found in frame based representation languages folklore, such as inheritance, if-added and if-needed methods, procedural attachment, etc. (Charniak, McDermott & Riesbeck 1980). QSL does permit cancellation between hereditarily linked frames, and so it does not avoid the conceptual problems that may arise due to this freedom (Brachman 1985). It also lacks a classification algorithm such as that of KLONE (Schmolze & Lipkis 1983).

Structured access to the data base takes place through a hierarchy of patterns, intermingled with the frame hierarchy, which permits economy of declarations, conceptual clarity and natural hooks for indexing. A pattern is a data structure, similar in a sense to a frame and subject to the same inheritance mechanisms, specifying a set of constraints which focus the access to data base.

The second layer comprises several tools of general use: a *production rules interpreter*, a *menu manager*, and an *interpreter of procedural descriptions*. All these tools come packed into a default hierarchical QSL taxonomy loaded at system initialization.

A domain level production rule is represented as a QSL frame, whose slots account for production's antecedent, consequent, specificity and implementation level data. This is nowadays quite a common practice in A.I. (Fikes & Kehler 1985). We chose not to hide the control strategy of the interpreter within its code, but instead to represent it explicitly by means of metarules. These share the same QSL format and antecedent evaluation method (which is actually distributed among different slots) with the domain level rules they control.

Currently two metarules are defined for the two domain level classes of structural rules and intervention rules. The control strategy for these two classes is completely different and is explicitely represented in several slots of the two metarules: structural rules have to be applied as far as possible to take care of distinct correlations between error contexts, whereas a single intervention rule needs to fire for each iteration.

Actually the particular criteria for selecting an instance of a production, be it at the meta or domain level, (e.g.· picking a domain rule out of several potentially relevant, or an error context out of the last few faults) are if-needed methods (i. e. Lisp code), which can be found scattered throughout the taxonomy. As a consequence, the production interpreter proved to be reasonably modular and easily tuned to different behaviours.

It seems to us that using the same frame format to represent both domain rules and metarules provides some additional advantages, in terms of modularity and conciseness, over the standard organization of domain rules into rulesets with an associated control strategy, e.g. the one adopted in STROBE, (Lafue & Smith 1985). In particular, using metarules it is possible to identify group of rules sharing properties and a control regime by means of pattern matching instead of explicit enumeration in the ruleset, as well as creating different levels of control (e.g. meta-metarules) simply exploiting the same general mechanism of pattern directed access to the data base.

Said in other terms, a STROBE ruleset is an object containing information about a set of rules which parameterize the behaviour of the interpreter over that set, while a QSL metarule itself is the part of the interpreter controlling the set of rules. In this way the user of the system is directly responsible of the internal structure and organization of the interpreter (we even more deeply stressed, respect to STROBE, the flexibility aspect in the flexibility/speed spectrum of production systems)

The procedure interpreter fills the gap between the declarative and the procedural import of procedural descriptions. It too consists of a portion of frame hierarchy with related slots implementing the interpreter. Recall that a procedure description is a sequence of phases, each phase being represented as a frame with slots containing information about the commands to be issued to the operator, the kind of action performed by these commands, the intervening devices, and so on. The methods contained in the slots which implement the interpreter specify how and when to ask the user to enter a PDP command, to prompt him for additional information, to select a branch based on the result of suggested commands or actions (a phase may be conditionally linked to different phases just as a programming language statement is executed subject to the positive result of certain test conditions).

It is important for the system to have a declarative and explicit representation of external and internal procedures:
• The characteristics (i.e. slot values) of the external procedures are crucial to analyze errors and to individuate a recovery treatment.
• The actual procedure which the operator is requested to follow are built out of concatenation of several internal procedures (for instance, the function call in the RHS of i-6 in Figure 2 links together three internal procedures). For this reason the representation of internal phases must be accessible for selection and modification.
• The OPERA's explanation mechanism produces a complete report for each error which occurred. This implies that the system have access to information about the procedures' behaviour in the procedures' representation itself.

As mentioned in the beginning, OPERA can deal with overlapping errors. As a consequence, during the execution of an internal procedure an error may occur which requires the very same procedure to be recovered. The solution to this problem is to create each time a new instance of an internal procedure from a prototype and reentrant version of it.

The domain knowledge belongs to the third layer. This includes actual representations of intervention and structural rules, external and internal procedures, error contexts, etc. according to the usage enforced by the level below. Some representations (error contexts) are dynamically created as the system runs and gathers new information from the user, while most of them are already known to OPERA at initialization time.

Figure 2 shows an example of a simple domain rule in English form along with its QSL translation. The description slot identifies, by means of a pattern, the error context which the rule refers to, while the predicate slot provides an additional constraint on it. Names whose first character is ~ stand for QSL variables. The interesting thing to notice is that the very same mechanism applies to metarules, where the description slot selects domain rules like i-6 which are represented themselves as QSL frames.

The operation of the system goes through the following main steps. Upon error notification by the PDP the fault is localized and identified by asking the user, and a QSL description of the context it occurred in is generated. OPERA is now able to invoke the production interpreter on structural rules to possibly relate the context to analogous situations previously noticed, and then on intervention rules to select the best way to take care of it. The selected procedure is finally executed by the procedure interpreter. This results in the user being asked to perform specific actions in a step by step fashion. Several data are recorded in frame format during the process thus allowing the system to eventually explain its behaviour.

---

if
a disk error on the same device has happened twice and the disk involved is not the system disk
then
it is necessary to change the device which the disk is mounted on, to restore a safe situation and to restart the halted procedure from a suitable point

```
(an intervention-rule WITH-NAME i-6 HAS
    description = {  (list (a-pattern-of error WITH-NAME ~fail HAS
                            type = DISK
                            object = ~obj
                            occurrences = 2)) }
    predicate = (not (eql ~obj 'SYSTIT))
    RHS = (let ((where (slot-value ~fail 'where)))
              (execute 'change-device
                       (slot-value where 'restore-procedure)
                       (slot-value where 'restart))) )
```

Figure 2. Example of an OPERA rule.

5. Conclusions.

We believe that an important result of the work we have described was to demonstrate that up-to-date A.I. programming techniques and methodology can be profitably introduced into productive settings at a reasonable cost, without giving up features normally found in more expensive applications.
Even if at the moment of writing OPERA is still in a developmental stage, it seems to us that the key factors to its success were the careful choice of the representation for the problem at hand coupled with a thorough but fully functional implementation of the appropriate tools. It is our opinion that commercial, low-cost, expert systems shells for personal computers cannot achieve at present a satisfactory level of flexibility to be able to cope with several different real world problems.

6. Acknowledgements.

Angelo Ongaretti's expertise was the *libretto* of OPERA. Gaetano Calì is the *impresario*. All the musicians gratefully thank them for their enthusiastic support.

7. References.

Charniak, E., Riesbeck, C.K., McDermott, D.V. (1980). Artificial Intelligence Programming. Hilsdale, NJ: Lawrence Erlbaum.

Schmolze, J. & Lipkis, T.A.(1983). Classification in the KLONE knowledge representation system. In Proc. Eigth International Joint Conference on Artificial Intelligence, pp.330-332. Karlsruhe,FRG.

Brachman, R.J. (1985). I lied about the trees. AI Magazine 6, No. 3, 80-93.

Fikes, R.& Kehler, T.(1985). The role of frame based representation in reasonin., Communications of the ACM 28, No. 9, 904-920.

Lafue, G.M.E & Smith, R.G.(1985). A modular toolkit for knowledge management. In Proc.Ninth International Joint Conference on Artificial Intelligence, pp. 46-52. Los Angeles, CA.

A KNOWLEDGE BASED SYSTEM TO ASSIST IN MEDICAL IMAGE
INTERPRETATION: DESIGN AND EVALUATION METHODOLOGY

Susan V. Ellam*, Michael N. Maisey**
* Department of Clinical Physics and Bioengineering, Guy's
Hospital, London SEl
** Department of Radiological Sciences, United Medical and
Dental Schools of Guy's and St. Thomas' Hospital, London SEl

Abstract

A specific area of medical imaging has been selected to test
whether a knowledge based system can provide a useful decision aid for
interpreting medical images. The system has been designed to use a
subjective description of the attributes of the image features as its
input and to provide the user with a differential diagnosis and
recommendations for further tests. The evaluation of various aspects of
the system, including the expert's variability, are described. The
conclusion is drawn that the problem is amenable to a knowledge based
approach , but that the variability in feature description between users
is sufficiently high to lead to significant degradation in performance
of the system. Thus, further work should be undertaken to derive more
quantitative feature descriptors directly from the images.

1. Introduction.

The interpretion of a medical image requires two tasks to be
performed – pertinent features in the image must be perceived and then a
diagnosis made based on these features. It has been demonstrated in a
number of studies , such as those by Garland (1959) and Yerushalmy (1969)
that the frequency of error in interpreting medical images is high. The
question should therefore be asked as to whether automation can assist in
reducing the error in either or both tasks.
We decided to concentrate our efforts on providing computer
assistance for the second task , making the assumption for the present
that human beings perform better at the perception task than machines as
they are able to apply prior knowledge about the image. A number of
workers have produced computer aided diagnostic systems in medical
imaging based on Baysian statistical techniques such as those of Lodwick
(1965) and Wilson (1965) and discriminant analysis such as that of
Templeton (1970), all of which have shown improved accuracy over human
observers. However both these methods require a very large library of
test cases which are difficult and expensive to acquire, may not maintain
their accuracy over time or in other populations, and have the inherent
deficiency of not being able to explain their conclusions other than in
mathematical terms.
As the knowledge based approach to computer aided decision
making promised to overcome these problems, we decided to build an expert
system in one specific area of medical imaging with a view to applying
the design and evaluation methodology to other areas. The area selected ,
the Tc^{99m} pertechnetate thyroid scan, was chosen for this initial work
because it is an uncomplicated image, diagnostic conclusions can be drawn
from the image alone without additional information such as patient

history and other test results, and it is an image about which inexperienced observers frequently make errors of interpretation.

2. Thyroid disease and the radioisotope thyroid scan.

The American Thyroid Association classification of thyroid disease details about 20 main classes of thyroid disease and about 60 subclasses. Many of these diseases give rise to under or over production of thyroid hormones. There are also a number of different types of thyroid cancer, the majority of which are treatable with excellant prognosis provided an early diagnosis is made. The radionuclide scan involves an injection of Tc^{99m} which is taken up by the thyroid. The 140Kev gamma ray emissions from the isotope are detected by a gamma camera and an image of the thyroid is produced. This image can have a large number of different presentations as illustrated by the examples in figure 1. The image is almost always acquired on computer as well as on X-ray film , and from the digital image the percentage of the injected isoptope which is taken up by the thyroid can be measured. The clinician who reports on a scan will include in the report a brief description of the features observed and an interpretation, with suggestions for further tests which may be considered suitable. If the thyroid function tests are available at the time the scan is seen, these will be taken into account, but often, particularly in small hospitals, this is not the case and the scan may have to be interpreted with no other information.

3. Design features of the system.

3.1. Input.

It was decided that for the initial prototype the user would describe the features he or she observed on the image, with the exception of the quantitative figure for percentage uptake. These features would be described in answer to a series of questions all of which would be asked on each occasion except where previous answers indicated that a particular question was not relevant. In this way it was hoped that the perception task would be easier for inexperienced observers as they would be forced to notice all features. As all the data would thus be available initially , the system would operate mainly in data driven mode.

3.2.Handling uncertain data.

Inevitably the user would be uncertain about some of the features observed but it was decided not to use numerical means for handling this. Instead the user would simply reply that he or she was uncertain and the system would explore the consequences of the alternative responses.

3.3. Accumulating evidence.

Due to problems inherent in using statistical data , as referred to earlier, it was decided not to use mathematical means for

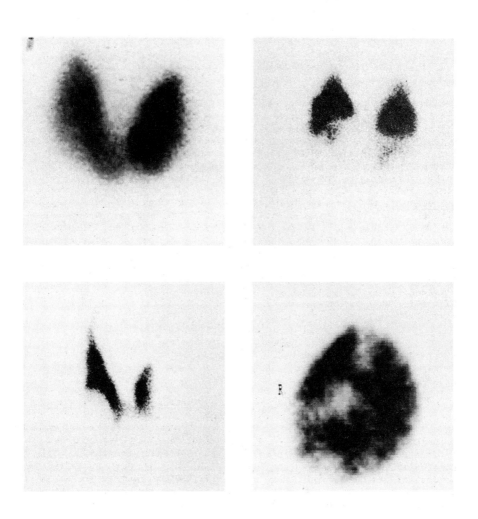

Figure 1

accumulating evidence but to use a version of the linguistic method
proposed by Fox (1985) by which linguistic concepts of uncertainty are
defined logically. The definitions chosen to be used in the system are as
follows : -
    X is possible if no necessary condition for X is violated
    X is impossible if an excluding condition is present
    X is suspected if X is possible and at least one piece of
evidence is favour of X is present
    X is likely if X is possible and the sum of evidence for X is
greater than the sum of evidence against X
    These definitions would be used in generalised inference rules
and in the final report, but the report would also indicate the exact
number of items of evidence for and against a particular diagnosis.

3.4. Output.

    The system should report suspected diagnoses and further test
recommendations, and should also mention any excluded diagnoses. The
reasons for each statement should be made explicit, and additional
information such as the potential consequences of a diagnosis, e.g.
possible malignancy, and the incidence of diseases provided.

3.5. User interaction.

    The user should be able to suggest possible diagnoses the
likelihood of which could be evaluated by the system and be able to ask
the system why a particular diagnosis or test recommendation was not
recommended.

4. Building the system.

4.1. Feature selection.

    It was necessary to derive a set of features with which any
thyroid scan could be completely described. This was done by asking 3
experts in the field to draw up a list of features and their possible
attributes, which they considered adequate. These 3 sets were combined to
give a final set of 30 features, each capable of taking from between 2
and 6 values.

4.2. Knowledge acquisition.

    The knowledge to be represented in the knowledge base was
acquired by asking the expert to work through 25 test cases selected to
represent a wide range of scan appearances and disease conditions. For
each case, the expert was asked to assign an attribute to each feature,
suggest as many diagnoses as were thought appropriate, and to give an
indication of the likelihood of each. The expert chose to express this
likelihood in probabilities. He was also asked to suggest further tests
which should be recommended and to give reasons for each diagnosis and
test recommendation.

4.3. Knowledge based tool.

The tool chosen with which to build the knowledge base was PROPS2, developed at the Imperial Cancer Research Fund by John Fox and colleagues. Among its features are the possibility to represent knowledge in pseudo English, to operate in data, goal or agenda driven mode, to use modular knowledge bases, and to store data in external datasets. PROPS2 is written in Prolog.

4.4. Knowledge representation.

The diagnostic categories are represented in hierarchical tree structures, there being seven main classes of disease with up to four levels of subclass. An example of a main class 'tree' is given in figure 2. This representation simplifies the inference task as the rules can be used recursively, as illustrated by the following rule, where words beginning with a capital letter represent variables :-

    if Class is suspected
    and Subclass is a type of Class
    and Feature,Value is evidence for Subclass
    and features include Feature, Value
    and Subclass is not impossible
    then Subclass is suspected

This rule also illustrates the logical definition of the term 'suspected' mentioned earlier.

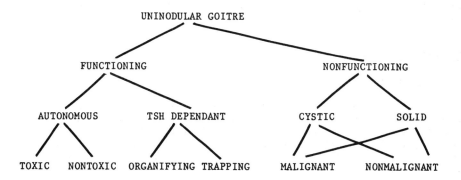

Figure 2. A main disease class and subclasses

It was evident from the test cases that the best way in which the scan features could be related to the diagnostic categories was to express values of features as excluding, necessary for , sufficient for, evidence for or evidence against particular diagnostic categories. In PROPS2 variables within a rule are instantiated to the complete set of matching values so generalised rules can be used for controlling the inference process and the specific domain knowledge represented as facts. A separate knowledge base was created for each of the 7 main diagnostic categories.

5. Evaluation.

This was considered to be a very important aspect of building the system as only by thorough evaluation of each part can assumptions be tested and quantitative value be placed on the system.

5.1. Expert variability.

The expert's variability was assessed by asking him to repeat the task described in the section on knowledge acquisition after an interval of a month. The variability in feature description, diagnoses, and probability statements was assessed. The results are shown in table 1.

25 scan training set

i)	Same most probable diagnosis in both sessions	19 (76%)
	Same most probable diagnosis in both sessions but > 30% difference in probability assigned	4
	:-Most probable diagnosis significantly different	10 (40%)
ii)	At least 1 diagnosis mentioned in only 1 session	17 (68%)
iii)	Total number of differences in feature description	40 (6%)
iv)	Total number of 'uncertain' responses to questions	11 (2%)

Table 1. Results of tests on expert variability

The first group of results indicate a significant inconsistency rate in the expert of between 25 and 40%. This is consistent with earlier studies in radiological imaging by Garland (1949) and suggests that an expert system should be of benefit even to an expert for difficult cases.

The second result suggests that an expert has difficulty in always remembering rare possibilities as most of the 17 cases were those assigned low probabilities.

The third result, although only representing an inconsistency in feature description of about 6%, does highlight the subjective nature of qualititative feature description. Results indicate that about 50% of these differences led to major differences in diagnostic conclusions with the other differences in diagnosis mainly being attributable to uncertainty in feature values. The number of uncertain responses is low but this result nevertheless emphasises the problems associated with subjective description of an image.

5.2. User / expert variability.

A radiologist who had completed his Nuclear Medicine training , and who represents a potential user of the system, was asked to perform the same task as the expert. The variability between him and the expert with respect to feature description, diagnosis , and probability statements was assessed. The results are shown in table 2.

25 scan training set

i) Same most probable diagnosis as expert   14 (56%)
    Most probable expert diagnosis not mentioned   9 (36%)
ii) Total number of differences in feature description 49 (8%)
    compared to expert
iii)Total number of uncertain responses to questions 35 (6%)

Table 2. Results of tests on user/expert variability

The first result confirms a high rate of variability between a trained but inexperienced observer and an experienced observer, and endorses the proposal that an expert system is needed.
The other results again illustrate the problems of subjective feature description.

5.3. Feature set and questions.

The adequacy of the feature set and the questions used to ascertain the values of each feature were assessed during the exercise mentioned in 5.2. As the user was answering questions he commented on ambiguities and inadequacies in the wording of the questions , and on features and values of features which he considered were redundant or should have been included. A number of improvements have been made to the questions as a result of this evaluation. Further work should be undertaken to evaluate the sensistivity of the system to changes in answers to questions in order to ascertain which features are most important.

5.4. Consistency of knowledge representation.

A knowledge base was written which performs a number of consistency checks on the other knowledge bases. An example of such a check is one which tests that all diagnostic categories mentioned in facts about particular features are mentioned in the tree structure of diseases. In this way any spelling and syntactic mistakes made when adding knowledge are detected. A number of errors have been detected in this way each time modifications have been made to the system.

5.5 Accuracy.

The accuracy of the system was tested using the 25 scan training set used for knowledge acquisition and a testing set of 50 scans. The latter represented the last 25 routine thyroid scans performed in the Nuclear Medicine department plus the last 25 routine scans marked as particularly interesting cases. The feature descriptions used as input to the system were provided by the expert. The expert diagnosis for each set was that produced by combining the diagnoses on two occasions. Two versions of the system were assessed with both sets of data - the initial prototype and a second version to which additions and modifications had been made as a result of the accuracy tests on the prototype.

The accuracy was expressed in terms of the number of diagnoses mentioned by the expert but omitted by the system, and the number mentioned by the system but not mentioned by the expert. A diagnosis was considered to be 'suggested' by the expert system if no necessary condition was violated , there was at least one piece of evidence for the diagnosis, and there was more evidence for the diagnosis than against. The results are shown in table 3.

	Training	Testing
Number of cases	25	50
Total number of diagnoses	52	116
Prototype version		
Expert diagnoses omitted by system	11 (21%)	37 (32%)
Extra diagnoses suggested by the system	25 (48%)	43 (37%)
Version 2		
Expert diagnoses omitted by the system	3 (6%)	34 (29%)
Extra diagnoses suggested by the system	22 (42%)	20 (17%)

Table 3. Results of accuracy tests of expert system

The diagnoses omitted by the system for both sets were mostly those with a very low probability. The rate at which extra diagnoses were suggested is high but these diagnoses include many subclasses. Further work should be undertaken to ascertain whether some of these additional diagnoses are in fact reasonable and have been forgotten by the expert. It is anticipated that with further work the percentage of extra and omitted diagnoses can be reduced to about 10% for any testing set. However it should be emphasised that these results were obtained using the feature descriptions provided by the expert and because of the variability in feature description between expert and the potential user, the performance would be degraded if the user feature descriptors were used.

5.6. Precision.

It is necessary not only to assess the accuracy of the system as stated above but also to assess the precision of the likelihood assigned to each diagnosis. As one of the design criteria was not to use numerical means for deriving conclusions, the degree of certainty attached to a diagnosis was initially expressed in terms of number of pieces of evidence for and against. Determination of the levels, in terms of aggregate of evidence , at which to mention a diagnosis was ascertained by assessing the accuracy at a number of different thresholds. The results are shown in table 4.

	Training	Testing
Prototype version		
Same most probable diagnosis as expert	22 (88%)	42 (84%)
Version 2		
Same most probable diagnosis as expert	24 (96%)	45 (90%)

Aggregate of evidence at which diagnosis mentioned	Training		Testing	
	Omitted	Extra	Omitted	Extra
sum for > sum against	3(6%)	22(42%)	34(29%)	20(17%)
sum for >= sum against	3(6%)	25(48%)	24(21%)	34(29%)
at least 1 item for	3(6%)	32(62%)	23(20%)	38(33%)

Table 4. Results of precision tests of expert system

The expert system is already yielding the same most probable diagnosis as the expert in over 30% more cases than the radiologist. The choice of threshold may need to be assigned separately for different diagnostic categories so as to be commensurate with the costs, human and monetary, incurred by misdiagnosis, as there will always be a compromise between extra and omitted diagnoses as the decision threshold is varied. Thus, for example, if there is any possibility of a disease being present which may be malignant it should be mentioned even if the aggregate of evidence is low. No attempt has so far been made to calibrate the aggregate of evidence with the probabilities assigned by the expert but this work should be undertaken in the future.

7. Conclusion.

The work described demonstates that a need for a computerised decision aid does exist in this field, as both intra- and inter-observer variability are high. It has also demonstrated the importance of a thorough evaluation of an expert system in the early stages of development as only by such an evaluation can assumptions be checked and the feasibility of the project assessed.

Our evaluations have shown that, given a reliable feature set, the expert system performs to a high level of accuracy, which will be further improved. However the system cannot be expected to perform well with unreliable input data and the evaluation has highlighted the high perceptual and/or descriptive variability of both expert and user. This would indicate that our initial assumption that human beings perform the perceptual task of image interpretation better than computers needs to be tested, and that work should be undertaken to derive as many features as possible quantitatively from the digital image. When this has been done it will be interesting to present the same and other subjects with the quantitative data and check the ensuing diagnostic variability and accuracy. In this way it should be possible to ascertain whether the main difficulty in arriving at a diagnosis from a medical image is in perception or in matching features with a diagnosis.

Acknowledgements

        We should like to thank John Fox of the Imperial Cancer
Research Fund for the opportunity to use PROPS2 for this work and for his
support and encouragement. We should also like to thank Tim Duncan and
David Frost of the ICRF for their help and suggestions, and Max Bramer of
the Thames Polytechnic for his valuable comments.

References

Fox J. (1965) Decision making and uncertainty in knowledge based systems.
Workshop on Artificial Intelligence and Statistics, Bell Laboratories

Garland L.H. (1949) On the scientific evaluation of diagnostic
procedures. Radiology 52, no. 3, 309-327

Garland L.H. (1959) Studies on the accuracy of diagnostic procedures.
American Journal Roentgenology 97, no. 4, 901-905

Lodwick G.S. (1965) A systematic approach to the roentgen diagnosis of
bone tumours. Tumors of bone and soft tissue , Year Book Publishers,
Chicago, pp.49

Templeton A.W.,Bryan K.,Waid R.,Townes J.,Huque M.,Dwyer S.J. (1970)
Computer diagnosis and discriminate analysis decision schemes. Radiology
95 ,47-55

Wilson W.J.,Templeton A.W., Turner Jr. A.H.,Lodwick G.S. (1965) The
computer evaluation of roentgenographic signs in benign and malignant
gastric ulcers. Radiology 85, 1064-1073

Yerushalmy J. (1969) The statistical assessment of the variability in
observer perception and description of roentgenographic pulmonary
shadows. Radiologic Clinics of North America 7, no. 3

OBSERVATIONS ON THE DEVELOPMENT OF A HIGH PERFORMANCE SYSTEM
FOR LEUKAEMIA DIAGNOSIS

P L Alvey* and M F Greaves§
* Imperial Cancer Research Fund, London WC2A 3PX
§ Leukaemia Research Fund Centre,
   at The Institute of Cancer Research, London SW3 6JB

Abstract

         A tree structured logic program diagnoses leukaemia from the
results of monoclonal antibody tests. It gives an acceptable conclusion
in 400 test cases, with concise explanations and suggestions for further
tests to improve the conclusion. The expert was asked how he performs the
task, repeated clarifications were sought to ensure good comprehension of
the subject, and the system was built in a flexible way, being modified
continuously around the knowledge engineer's increasing understanding of
the domain. The most difficult component of the development was the
formulation of an overall specification for the problem.

1.0 Introduction

         Standard haematological tests allow leukaemia to be classified
into four major categories, but a more precise subclassification is now
possible with monoclonal antibodies and related tests that detect specific
cell markers (Figure 1). The extra information assists with the prognosis
and treatment of patients and the antibodies are commercially available.
But interpretation of the results is not easy since most markers may also
be found on normal cells. Particular combinations are only significant
when they are present on cells that are otherwise known to be leukaemic.
This assessment may require the experience of a specialist immunologist
and these experts are available in only a small number of centres.
         Our program performs this interpretation and is based on the
expertise of one immunologist (MFG). It is not a finished system but the
performance problems have been overcome and future development will
involve extending its scope, improving its format, and evaluation against
other experts in the field. Our primary objective has been to produce a
usable system that can give a sound opinion in virtually any case. At all
stages dogma has been subordinate to the practicalities of the application
and we have not attempted to solve problems we did not need to solve.

2.0 Pilot System

         Chris Myers had built an EMYCIN pilot system (Fox et al 1985)
but its limited conclusions were correct in only 70% of a subsequent test
set (using a benevolent scoring system). Analysis of its internal logic
(Alvey et al 1984) exposed three major hazards for further development:
the use of non-logical features obscured the interrelationship between the
rules; positive conclusions based on the inability to prove some
condition are not fail-safe (they conceal errors by allowing correct
conclusions to be made "for the wrong reasons"); most test cases are
simple enough for a naive system but a significant minority of complex
cases would require fundamental revisions to the whole system.

ACUTE LYMPHOBLASTIC LEUKAEMIA	ACUTE MYELOBLASTIC LEUKAEMIA
eg T-ALL, Null ALL Common ALL	eg Myeloid, Megakaryoblastic Monocytic, Erythroid
Typically TDT +ve MYELOID -ve	Typically TDT -ve MYELOID +ve

CHRONIC LYMPHOCYTIC LEUKAEMIA	CHRONIC MYELOID LEUKAEMIA
eg Monoclonal B cell CLL T cell Leukaemia TDT -ve MYELOID -ve	

Figure 1   The Major Classification of Leukaemia
Clinical and haematological data may enable a case to be assigned to one of the 4 major types, but marker information is required for the majority of subtypes (shown in lower case). The major markers of acute disease are TDT and the MYELOID markers, which are positive in acute lymphoblastic leukaemia (ALL) and acute myeloblastic leukaemia (AML) respectively. However each of these markers may be falsely negative in approximately 5% of cases and TDT may be spuriously positive in 5% of cases of acute myeloblastic leukaemia.
There are no simple markers for the curious condition of chronic myeloid leukaemia, which may undergo transformation into either ALL or AML (or a mixture of both) by a process called blast crisis.

3.0   Development of the New System

New knowledge was obtained at 15 discussion sessions of approximately 3hr duration, held at intervals of 4 to 6 weeks. Initially the basic biology of leukaemia and its classification were discussed; subsequently the interpretation of sample data was covered. The knowledge was represented as a logic program and the new system soon gave a suitable conclusion in more than 70% of the test cases of the pilot system (using strict scoring criteria). But it proved difficult to push the performance beyond 83% - as though there were some barrier at that level. Repeatedly it was found that amendment of the rules to suit some difficult case would degrade performance on cases previously diagnosed "correctly". Review of these cases in turn would reveal facets that had been oversimplified and which required a more thorough explanation of the underlying biology before the existing rules could be modified appropriately.
Eventually the system passed the 83% barrier and it soon gave a suitable conclusion for every case. Similar problems occured with the next set of 100 cases: initially 17 were diagnosed incorrectly and 3 of these were difficult cases, of a type that had not been represented in the previous set (Figure 5). Extensive modifications were required to handle these cases without adversely affecting others, and 10 months elapsed before all 100 cases were diagnosed correctly.

With two further test sets there have been few problems in
updating the system and the minor modifications have not affected the
performance on previous test sets, as indicated in the following table.

Test Set	Initial Performance	Date of 100% Accuracy	Effect on Previous Test Sets		
			1st	2nd	3rd
1st	47%	19-Nov-84			
2nd	83%	27-Sep-85	99%		
3rd	96%	29-Oct-85	100%	100%	
4th	96%	14-Mar-86	100%	100%	100%

4.0 Format of the System

The current system is written in Edinburgh University PROLOG
running on a DEC-20 mainframe computer (a micro-PROLOG version is being
prepared). There are three major components: a set of domain rules
(approx 700) arranged as a tree-structured logic program; a set of tools
for obtaining, storing and performing specific logical operations on the
patient data; and a user-interface, written by Nicola Preston. After
obtaining the clinical details and test results the system gives its
conclusion, a concise summary of its reasons, and suggestions for further
tests that may be of benefit.

4.1 Structure of the Rules

All groups of rules are designed to succeed under all
circumstances and to return only one conclusion. The top level checks the
final conclusion and declares that there is a bug in the program if the
rules fail, or give more than one conclusion. Genuine ambiguity is
expressed within the structure of the single conclusion, eg
'UNCLASSIFIABLE-MYELOID'('Monocytic' or 'Erythroid').
This mechanism has proved extremely useful as a safety net,
not only for detecting trivial coding errors but also for unsuspected
errors in the logical completeness of sets of rules. Whenever a new set
of rules is added, its constituents must be mutually exclusive and
mutually exhaustive, and this can be checked without having to test the
system on all known cases at frequent intervals. It is also advisable for
the rules and the steps in the logic to be kept as simple as possible.
The system's negative conclusion - 'UNCERTAIN PHENOTYPE' - is
always made in a positive manner. If a case defies diagnosis then a truly
expert system should be able to recognize the relevant features and
describe them in its explanation. Systems offering trite explanations
based on a closed world assumption are unlikely to impress professional
users and our experience suggests they will be breeding grounds for bugs.
The undiagnosable cases can be the most testing ones for our
system, because it has to suggest which extra tests, if any, might make a
diagnosis possible. This must be done skilfully: in some case the real
problem is that few tests were done initially because of the limited
quantity of the original sample (usually blood or bone marrow). Our
system gives a conclusion in every case, regardless of the number of tests

```
'evidence of leukaemic cells is'( Present_or_Absent, Y, S, Pt_Sa ):-
        positivity( 'BLAST COUNT', 30, Pt_Sa, BLASTS ),
        leuk_ev_when_blasts( BLASTS, Present_or_Absent, Y, S, Pt_Sa ).

leuk_ev_when_blasts(        positive(Y),            present, [Y], [], _ ).
leuk_ev_when_blasts( not_positive(negative,Y), absent, [Y], [], _ ).
leuk_ev_when_blasts( not_positive(unknown,Yb),    Ans,    Y,   S, Pt_Sa ):-
        positivity( 'PLATELET' or 'ERYTHROID', 50, Pt_Sa, PorE ),
        leuk_when_P_or_E( PorE, Yb, Ans, Y, S ).

leuk_when_P_or_E(        positive(Ype),     Yb, present, [Ype],    [] ).
leuk_when_P_or_E( not_positive(_,Ype), Yb, absent, [Yb,Ype],
        [suggest('BLAST COUNT',[to,allow,'AML',to,be,considered])] ).
```

Figure 2   Example of IF-THEN-BECAUSE-SUGGEST Rules
These are used in determining whether acute myeloblastic leukaemia
(AML) should be considered. The most reliable factor is whether the
blast count (percentage of immature cells) exceeds 30%, but if this
is unknown the presence of many cells bearing markers of specific
myeloid subtypes would be an acceptable substitute.
    The positivity tool determines whether the value of any member of
the specified test groups exceeds the specified threshold. In its
last argument it returns (or confirms) one of the values:
positive(Y), not_positive(negative,Y) or not_positive(unknown,Y).
The variables with the initial letter Y are components for the
explanation, S is the list of appropriate test suggestions and Pt_Sa
contains the identity of the patient and sample.
    The format of the rules makes it easy to check that all possible
combinations of results are covered and that appropriate reasons and
suggestions are given. No side-effects are used yet nothing is
computed twice and first argument indexing aids efficiency.

---

performed. If none has been done the user will be given a somewhat
predictable conclusion and a list of test suggestions that almost
corresponds to the basic set performed on all samples in our laboratory.
In fact the system can be used in a stepwise manner - a few tests at a
time - using the suggestions to guide the choice of subsequent tests.

4.2 Explanations

        A complex explanation system is not required in this
application: haematologists will only want the relevant components in the
reasoning and they will appreciate the absence of unnecessary verbosity.
But the factors that constitute the "relevant components" will vary from
conclusion to conclusion in a way that defies generalization. The
justification for diagnosing a condition with pathognomonic features may
be very brief, whereas a diagnosis by exclusion would be more complex, and
a case of 'UNCERTAIN PHENOTYPE' would require so many "why not" components
that each should be kept mercifully concise.
        The explanations in our system are hand-crafted within the
individual rules: when a rule succeeds it returns one value for its
conclusion and another for the reason - usually a list, often an empty
list (see Figure 2). The final nested list is printed out in an indented
format that reflects the tiers of the logic.

4.3 Suggestions

The suggestion mechanism was added at a relatively late stage, when it was noticed that rules making negative conclusions on the basis of unknown test results could easily be adapted to suggest the tests in question. Throughout the development period the format of the rules has evolved from the IF-THEN format of the pilot system to IF-THEN-BECAUSE rules and finally to IF-THEN-BECAUSE-SUGGEST rules.

4.4 Tools

The logical operations performed on the data consist mainly of testing whether individual values or the sums or ratios of paired values exceed specified thresholds. This is complicated by the fact that each marker may be identified by more than one antibody and the results of these do not always correspond. A set of tools has been developed for gathering and storing the test data and for testing their significance. These are purpose-built in efficient PROLOG and they would be of little value in any other application. Their format has evolved with the rest of the system and, in addition to values, they also return building blocks for the explanations, and in one case for the suggestions also. If they were written as production rules the system would be impossibly slow.

4.5 Uncertainty

Uncertainty is not a major feature of the system and the qualitative method of the expert is used. Conclusions may be qualified by one of: "definitely", "probably", "compatible with", "possibly" or (occasionally) "minor population of". The qualification for certain goals are the fuzzy minimum of those of its subgoals, although most conclusions use only "definitely" or "compatible with". When there is positive evidence for more than one condition, the expert usually concludes that the case is compatible with either one alone, or in some circumstances with a mixture of the two, and he may go on to suggest further tests to discriminate between the possibilities. He does not use numerical methods to get rid of competing hypotheses and the system has been designed to follow his methods as closely as possible.

5.0 Observations on the Knowledge Elicitation

5.1 The Expert's Knowledge is Coordinated by Common Sense

The expert's knowledge is not in the form of a comprehensively coordinated overall scheme: it consists of a multitude of simple items with no pre-planned method of integration. Only at the time of making a decision are they interrelated and then by a process of common sense, intuition and judgement acquired from years of experience.

This coordination process does not have a fixed format. In analyzing some case aloud he might follow one line of reasoning initially but then discover a confounding feature causing him to abandon that reasoning and start again. On another occasion he may spot the confounding feature first and arrive at the same final conclusion by a different route, although using the same fundamental "items" of knowledge.

Computer Diagnosis for pt_27 test_1 :-

definitely T-LYMPHOMA/LEUKAEMIA (Helper Cells)

   because mature T cells are present
         because CD3 > 20
           and CD1 =< 5
           and TDT MARKERS are negative
              because TDT =< 5
      and the T Cell subtype is: Helper cells
         because CD4 : CD8 ratio >= 5 : 1

Data for pt_27 test_1

AGE 75			SAMPLE TYPE . MARROW	
SEX . . . . FEMALE			BLAST COUNT . 75	
CLINICAL DIAGNOSIS . ACUTE LEUKAEMIA			WBC . . . . . >131071	

CD1 (NA134) .	4	CD7 (WT1) .	67	MOUSE-ROSETTES .	2
CD10 (A12) . .	0	CD8 (C3) .	0	MY906	6
CD2 (OKT11A) .	98	DA2	5	SHEEP-ROSETTES .	11
CD3 (T28) . .	84	J0	0	SMIG	5
CD4 (OKT4) . .	86	KAPPA . . .	9	TDT	0
CD5 (S33) . .	86	LAMBDA . .	9		

Figure 3   Conclusions for a Simple Case.
  Data in the upper block are clinical details and results of tests
performed in the referring hospital (blast count is a percentage).
The marker results are in the lower block and the values are the
percentage of cells positively stained by the immunofluorescent
antibodies.

5.2 A Decision Tree Assists Knowledge Elicitation

        An expert system needs both the fundamental items of knowledge
and a coordinating mechanism, but clearly the major problem is the
coordinating mechanism. We have made no attempt to simulate common sense
in our system but in its place we use a decision tree to unite the basic
knowledge. In the early stages the expert would explain the basic issues
using small decision trees of his own and it was quite natural to base the
whole system on a method with which he is familiar.
        The elicited knowledge was represented as logical PROLOG which
was used at the subsequent discussions for establishing whether the topics
had been fully understood. With a little instruction in syntax the expert
could easily follow the code, and seeing his knowledge laid out in this
way provided a powerful stimulus that enabled him to criticize and
elaborate on the relevant features with much greater ease than when
describing a new topic from scratch.
        In considering a new topic, attention is naturally
concentrated on the major features, but it is also important to ensure
that all possible combinations of values are provided for, including
unknowns. With the draft rules in the form of a logic program it is easy
to spot the missing components and the expert was soon volunteering the
information needed to fill the gaps without being prompted.

On occasions the elicited knowledge for a new topic seemed bewilderingly complex but some form of decision tree was always made, however daunting the task appeared. At the next discussion session it was always possible to resolve the major problems, and the act of drawing up an incorrect set of draft rules seemed to have a powerful effect in exposing the misunderstandings.

6.0 Observations on the Implementation of the System

6.1 The Interrelationships between Rules are Crucial

High performance depends on whether the rules cover the intended scope of the system without any gaps or contradictions. The expert has the ability to view each particular topic in a number of ways and the difficulty in designing a comprehensive system lies in ensuring that related topics are viewed in a similar way. If he were asked: "how do you identify the various types of mature T cell disease?" he might give one scheme on one occasion, but a completely different version on another. Both would be equally correct: they would simply represent different ways of looking at the same problem. But it is vital that the rules for immature T cell disease should have a complementary format. It would be disastrous if the system had to diagnose a case of T cell leukaemia with equivocal evidence of maturity and neither rule set covered the case or both sets did so with inconsistent conclusions.

6.2 The System Evolves

The maintenance of an effective system through many generations is facilitated by the decision tree, but the best format for the rules and the best layout for the tree are only determined by trial and error. This seems to proceed through three phases. Initially, understanding is limited and a naive generalization may be used; subsequently the specific details of special cases require individual treatment and general mechanisms are used less and less. Finally, understanding of the topic improves and the mass of detail can be integrated into a new overall plan. At this stage much superfluous detail can be removed but there are usually so many exceptions and special cases that little semblance of generality remains.

6.3 Generalizations Can Be Harmful

In the early stages naive generalizations served their purpose but they could be harmful if kept for too long, and it was not always easy to detect this situation. For example, all intermediate and final conclusions were represented as a list of two elements (qualification and value), but one difficulty was traced to the rigidity of this conclusion format. In a few cases of acute lymphoblastic leukaemia (ALL) the expert's opinion would oscillate between "definitely COMMON ALL" and "compatible with COMMON ALL" and the rules were modified back and forth in pursuit. This was considered to be a performance problem, but eventually it was recognized that the case is best described as: "COMMON CELLS definitely present; DISEASE compatible with COMMON ALL". The real error lay in forcing the expert's opinion into a restrictive format.

Computer Diagnosis for pt_83 test_1 :-

UNCERTAIN PHENOTYPE

```
    because monoclonal B cells are not suggested
            because KAPPA & LAMBDA are unknown
        and a mature T cell diagnosis cannot be made
            because CD3 +ve mature cells are ruled out
                    because CD3 =< 20
                and miscellaneous mature T cells are not suggested
                    because fewer than 2 T cell markers exceed 50
                            because CD1 & CD2 & CD3 & CD4 & CD5 & CD8 =< 50
        and an ACUTE DIAGNOSIS is NOT SUGGESTED
            because TDT MARKERS are negative
                    because TDT is in the range 6 to 20
                    and SAMPLE TYPE is MARROW
                and MYELOID MARKERS are unknown
                    because CDw13 & MY9 are unknown
                and ALL cannot be considered (without +ve TDT)
                    because BLAST COUNT is unknown
                and early myeloid cell type is unknown(unclassifiable)
                    because evidence of leukaemic cells is absent
                            because BLAST COUNT is unknown
                            and J15 & J15/AN51 & R10 are unknown
```

Further test suggestions for pt_83 test_1 :-
```
    KAPPA & LAMBDA . for consideration of monoclonal B cell disease
    BLAST COUNT  . . to allow ALL to be considered
    BLAST COUNT  . . to allow AML to be considered
```

Data for pt_83 test_1

AGE . 2	CLINICAL DIAGNOSIS . unknown	BLAST COUNT . unknown
SEX . MALE	SAMPLE TYPE . . . . MARROW	

CD1 (NA134) .	0	CD5 (S33) .	9	SHEEP-ROSETTES .	0
CD10 (J5) . .	47	CD7 (WT1) .	6	SMIG	40
CD2 (OKT11A) .	8	CD8 (C3) .	0	TDT	10
CD3 (T28) . .	3	DA2	16		
CD4 (OKT4) . .	2	J0	0		

Figure 4   Output for an Undiagnosable Case
    The rules shown in Figure 2 contributed to the explanation and the
suggestions. From these data it is not certain that the patient has
leukaemia so the suggestions are just those that could confirm this.

With hindsight there was no particular merit in the single
conclusion format but it seemed to work with simple cases and in the early
stages there were many more serious problems to be solved. A three-part
conclusion format is now being installed (Figure 6) and the need for this
is embarrassingly obvious now. It will require modifications to the whole
system but that is a commonplace event: the best specifications only
emerge from many cycles of trial and error, and the change will enable
many of the rule sets to be simplified considerably.

6.4 Efficiency Matters

Initially the system was written in a declarative style that facilitated amendments, but as it grew it slowed down considerably and efficiency had to be improved. Values required by different rules are now pre-computed, and the tools have undergone a series of revisions to the point that they are very procedural (though free of side-effects).

7.0 Overview

This project demonstrates the feasibility of high performance in a program written directly from human expertise. However, the result is extremely specific and this is primarily a consequence of the domain itself. There are few opportunities for useful generalizations: hardly any situation is free of special cases and the methods for dealing with them are usually unique. There is no extractable shell and the tools would be of little use in other applications. The value of our work for others lies not in the code that can be copied or the knowledge bases that can be shared but in the lessons that we have learned.

7.1 The Most Difficult Task is Knowledge Formulation

The building of our system involved three major components: elicitation of the basic items of knowledge, formulation of a coordinated overall scheme and representation in a computer language. All three were inter-dependent and were only be accomplished through many cycles of trial and error. By far the most difficult component was the formulation of a comprehensive specification of the expert's knowledge - since this is not something that already exists. The basic knowledge was easily elicited but it could only be organised with a good understanding of the domain.
The decision tree contributed greatly to the knowledge formulation. It is artificial in the sense that the expert does not use one; but he can easily relate his knowledge to it, and it provided an important basis for discussion. Furthermore, its structure aids debugging; many bugs have been removed from the system - not just simple coding errors but also errors in the logic. Because each part of the tree should have a predictable behaviour it has been relatively easy to detect and correct many of these logical aberrations. Without the structure of the system this would not have been so easy and it is disturbing to consider what would happen in a system of independent production rules.

7.2 The System is Built from Partial Ignorance

The most salutary lesson - obvious in retrospect - is that at every stage the knowledge engineer designs the system from his incomplete understanding of the domain. This will improve with experience but in the nature of things it will always be imperfect. A high price may be paid for over-zealous attempts to use deep knowledge or general mechanisms.
In the early stages almost any method can be chosen to represent the various concepts of the domain, but as the complexities unfold the oversimplifications have to be corrected. It is time consuming to change all the rules in the system to accommodate an improved representation of some feature but in the pursuit of performance there is

Computer Diagnosis for pt_5004 test_1 :-

compatible with T-ALL

    because ACUTE MARKER CATEGORY is compatible with "LYMPHOID or MIXED"
        because TDT MARKERS are definitely positive
            because TDT > 50
        and MYELOID MARKERS are unknown
            because CDw13 & MY9 are unknown
    and early lymphoid cell type is probably leukaemic Pre-T
        because pre-T markers are positive(leukaemic)
            because CD7 —< 20
                and the PRE-T marker may be a false negative
                    because at least 2 T cell markers overlap TDT
                        because CD2 & CD3 & CD4 & CD5 + TDT >
                                    120%
        and HLA-DR markers are unknown
            because DA2 & CA2 & anti-HLA-DR are unknown
        and CD2 > 20

Further test suggestions for pt_5004 test_1 :-
CDw13 or MY9 . . . . to rule out mixed disease
DA2 or CA2 or anti-HLA-DR . to improve the certainty of T-ALL

Data for pt_5004 test_1

      AGE 63   SAMPLE TYPE . BLOOD
      SEX . . . . FEMALE   BLAST COUNT . unknown
      CLINICAL DIAGNOSIS . T-CELL-LYMPHOMA   WBC 77000

        CD1 (NA134) .   0   CD4 (OKT4) . 72   CD8 (C3) .   0
        CD2 (OKT11A) . 76   CD5 (S33) . 91   JO   0
        CD3 (T28) . . 89   CD7 (WT1) .   1   TDT . . . 80

Figure 5   One of the 3 Problem Cases from the Second Test Set.
    There is enough evidence to suggest that this case is acute
lymphoblastic leukaemia of precursor T cells, in which the principal
pre-T marker (WT1) is spuriously negative. If the MY9 and DA2 tests
are done and prove to be negative then the remaining doubts would be
removed, whereas if the DA2 result were strongly positive the case
would be quite unclassifiable.

---

no alternative. When the knowledge engineer writes his first prototype
system he cannot possibly know the best format for the knowledge, but if
he does not write the prototype he will never find out. Similarly if he
does not modify it in the light of experience it will never get out of the
demonstrator class. A crude system may get about 70% of cases correct
with only a handful of rules but getting them all right is another matter.
        Doubtless the perfect representation will not be found but
successive versions should get closer to it. Likewise a really expert
system will never be complete - because the knowledge engineer can always
improve his understanding of the domain and the expert is continually
augmenting his knowledge of it.

Computer Diagnosis for pt_5123 test_1 :-

    CELL TYPE: definitely B CELLS
    CLONALITY: definitely MONOCLONAL
    DISEASE: compatible with CLL or PLL

Cell Type is: definitely B CELLS
    because KAPPA : LAMBDA ratio >= 10 : 1

Clonality is: definitely MONOCLONAL
    because KAPPA : LAMBDA ratio >= 10 : 1

Disease is: compatible with CLL or PLL
      because CLL is possible
            because MOUSE-ROSETTES > 25
    and PLL is possible
            because FMC7 > 20
            and CLINICAL DIAGNOSIS suggests PLL

Further test suggestions for pt_5123 test_1 :-
BLAST COUNT . to help determine the subtype of B cell disease

Data for pt_5123 test_1

AGE . 63   CLINICAL DIAGNOSIS . ?PLL   BLAST COUNT . unknown
SEX . FEMALE   SAMPLE TYPE . . . . BLOOD

   DA2 . 80   KAPPA 87   SHEEP-ROSETTES . 0
   FMC7 . 83   LAMBDA 0   SMIG 68
   J0 . . 0   MOUSE-ROSETTES . 50   TDT 0

Figure 6   An Example of the New Three-Part Conclusion Format.
It is certain that this is a case of monoclonal B cell leukaemia but there is mildly conflicting evidence for the subtype. The main possibilities are prolymphocytic leukaemia (PLL) and simple chronic lymphocytic leukaemia (CLL), although disseminated monoclonal B cell lymphoma (B-ALL) cannot be ruled out without a low blast count.
It is certain that this is a case of monoclonal B cell leukaemia If the conclusion were simply "compatible with CLL or PLL" the certainty of leukaemia would not be communicated and the clinician would not know whether to treat the patient or send another sample.

7.3 Flexibility is Important

The major difficulty in developing the system has been the search for an executable specification for the problem. The use of PROLOG as a logic programming language has allowed the knowledge representation to be modified around a continuously changing understanding of the domain. Every component of the system has been revised many times and massive changes can be made without the need for frequent testing at intermediate stages. Others may prefer different programming environments but the test of their suitability lies not in an ability to hold the final product but in their flexibility to support the exacting developmental stages.

7.4   The Dream and Reality of Expert Systems

       The expert system dream is of computer programs developed from
human expertise, solving and explaining problems as a human expert would,
and built in a modular way that allows easy expansion.   This may be
achieved in a trivial way in a demonstrator system but, at the level of
performance required for a useful leukaemia system, the amount of unique
detail severely restricts the scope for converting the dream to reality.
       Unfortunately the expert's knowledge is not in the form of a
complete and integrated set of rules to which we can simply help
ourselves, and we have avoided the problems of meta-knowledge by using a
decision tree.   Good coordination between the rules is essential since an
occasional stupid answer cannot be tolerated, in contrast to demonstrator
systems.   Similarly, explanations cannot be produced by general methods
because the resulting verbiage would defeat its purpose.
       Amendments can only made to the system by those who understand
the domain and also the coordination of the rules.   We consider this to be
a characteristic of any high performance solution in a complex domain
since functionally important interrelationships would exist between the
rules regardless of whether the system contained any organising structure.
       On the subject of generality we have an open mind.   There are
no easy generalizations in our field, but these are early days.   When we
have more experience and have revised the system a few more times a "grand
plan" may emerge - but we are not optimistic.   However, we are certain
that unwarranted generalizations and poor knowledge representation hinder
progress and are not a substitute for a good understanding of the domain.
       What we have produced is a substantial system with reasonable
performance and a robust capacity for further development.   New
immunological findings can easily be incorporated and major revisions can
be made without adversely affecting overall performance or inactivating
the system.   At present the views of one immunologist are represented but
if an international consensus were to emerge it would be easy to modify
the system accordingly;   it would entail modifications and rearrangements
of the tree of rules but we are experienced at that.
       The gulf between the expert system dream and the realities of
our practical application is very wide and we see no prospect of bridging
it.   Perhaps the dreamers should go back and modify their specification,
as we have modified ours - many times.

REFERENCES

Fox, J., Myers, C.D., Greaves, M.F. & Pegram, S.   (1985).   Knowledge
Acquisition for Expert Systems: Experience in Leukaemia Diagnosis.
Meth. Infor. Med. 24, 65-72.

Alvey, P.L., Myers, C.D. & Greaves, M.F.   (1984).   An Analysis of the
Problems of Augmenting a Small Expert System.   In Research and Development
in Expert Systems: Proceedings of The Fourth Technical Conference of The
British Computer Society Specialist Group on Expert Systems,
ed. M. Bramer, pp. 61-72.   Cambridge: Cambridge University Press.

ADVANCES IN INTERACTIVE KNOWLEDGE ENGINEERING

Mildred L G Shaw & Brian R Gaines
Dept. Computer Science, University of Calgary, Alberta, Canada T2N 1N4

Abstract

This paper gives a state-of-the-art report on the use of techniques based on personal construct psychology to automate knowledge engineering for expert systems. It presents the concept of *knowledge support systems* as interactive knowledge engineering tools, states the design criteria for such systems, and outlines the structure and key components of KSS1 and its KITTEN implementation. KSS1 includes tools for interactive repertory grid elicitation and entailment analysis that have been widely used for rapid prototyping of industrial expert systems. It also includes tools for text analysis, behavioral analysis and schema analysis, that offer complementary and alternative approaches to knowledge acquisition. The KITTEN implementation integrates these tools around a common database with utilities designed to give multiple perspectives on the knowledge base.

1. Knowledge Support Systems for Automating Knowledge Engineering

Problems of knowledge engineering have been recognized since the early days of expert systems. It was possible that knowledge engineering might develop as a profession on a par with systems analysis and programming, and that an initial shortage of skilled knowledge engineers would cause problems to be overcome eventually be as the profession developed. However, this scenario now appears less and less likely. There is certainly a shortage of knowledge engineers and problems in developing applications, but doubts have been cast on the notion that human labor is the appropriate solution to the knowledge engineering problem:

• The decline in costs of both hardware and software support for expert systems has brought the technology into a mass-market situation far more rapidly than originally envisioned;

• This has lead to a growth in demand for expert systems that is proceeding far more rapidly than the growth in supply of trained and experienced knowledge engineers;

• The declining costs of expert system technology are also making the expense of human labour in tailoring the technology for particular applications appear to be the dominating constraint and an excessive cost;

• A move towards a labor-intensive activity such as knowledge engineering is contrary to all trends in industry;

• In particular it is contrary to the trend towards automatic programming techniques in the computing industry;

• The role of the knowledge engineer as an intermediary between the expert and the technology is being questioned not only on cost grounds but also in relation to its effectiveness—knowledge may be lost through the intermediary and the expert's lack of knowledge of the technology may be less of a detriment than the knowledge engineer's lack of domain knowledge.

The considerations of the previous section have heightened interest in the possibility of providing *knowledge support systems* (KSSs) to automate knowledge engineering as a process of direct interaction between domain experts and the computer. In 1980 we proposed that *personal construct psychology* (Kelly 1955, Shaw 1980) could provide foundations for expert systems, particularly in systems that combined interactivity with database access and expert advice to provide decision support, and gave examples of algorithms and programs that extracted entailment rules from repertory grid data (Gaines & Shaw 1980). In 1983 we reported at the first BCS Expert Systems Conference on further enhancements of these techniques and a preliminary experiment to validate them empirically as a knowledge engineering technique for priming expert systems (Shaw & Gaines 1983). This work led to industrial studies of the methodology applied to the development of expert systems: Boeing Computer Services (Boose 1984, 1985, 1986) and Lockheed Software Technology Center (Wahl 1986) have reported success in applications; and validation has been reported in a statistics domain (Gammack & Young 1985).

This paper gives a state-of-the-art report on the use of techniques based on personal construct psychology to automate knowledge engineering for expert systems. It is based on four areas of advance since the previous paper:

• Improved techniques for the derivation of rules from repertory grid data which give: a natural knowledge representation for uncertain data combining fuzzy and probabilistic logics; and an information-theoretic measure of the significance of a derived rule (Gaines & Shaw 1986a);
• Widespread applications experience in prototyping expert systems using the methodology (Boose 1985, Gaines & Shaw 1986b);
• Improved interactive techniques for on-line knowledge engineering from groups of experts interacting through a computer network (Shaw 1986, Shaw & Chang 1986);
• KSS1, and its KITTEN implementation, a knowledge engineering workbench that provides next generation KSS facilities including textual analysis, induction of models from behavior, multi-level and multi-expert repertory grid elicitation, and hierarchical construct laddering, to automate knowledge engineering for a wide range of problem domains.

2. Knowledge Support System Design Considerations

We see knowledge engineering in very broad terms as: *the acquisition, elicitation, structuring and encoding of knowledge for application in inferential, goal-directed, explanatory, decision and action support systems.* We see knowledge support systems as having even broader scope, encompassing both aids to knowledge engineering and support of human knowledge processes—in the long term the division between knowledge engineering tools and expert system shells will break down, and integrated systems will be necessary. The general requirements for a KSS are:
1. The KSS tools should be domain independent;
2. The KSS tools should be directly applicable by experts without intermediaries;
3. The KSS tools should be able to access a diversity of knowledge sources including text, interviews with experts, and observations of expert behavior;
4. The KSS system should be able to encompass a diversity of perspectives including partial or contradictory input from different experts;
5. The KSS system should be able to encompass a diversity of forms of knowledge and relationships between knowledge;
6. The KSS system should be able to present knowledge from a diversity of sources with clarity as to its derivation, consequences and structural relations;
7. Users of the KSS should be able to apply the knowledge in a variety of familiar domains and freely experiment with its implications;
8. The KSS should make provision for validation studies;
9. As much of the operation of the KSS as possible should be founded on well-developed and explicit theories of knowledge acquisition, elicitation and representation;
10. As the overall KSS develops it should converge to an integrated system.

All of these requirements are subject to caveats—some domain dependence may be appropriate for efficiency in specific KSSs—some human intervention may be helpful or necessary when an expert is using a KSS—and so on. However, the broad design goals stated capture the key issues in KSS design currently.

The PLANET system for repertory grid elicitation and analysis (Shaw 1980, 1982, Shaw & Gaines 1986b,c) is a primitive KSS satisfying requirements 1 and 2 for domain independence and direct use. Its foundations in personal construct psychology, which itself has strong systemic and cognitive science foundations (Gaines & Shaw 1981, Shaw & Gaines 1986a), are attractive in terms of requirement 9. Boose (1985) in evaluating ETS has noted the limitations of basic repertory grid techniques in terms of requirement 5—that the methodology is better suited for analysis than for synthesis problems, for example, debugging, diagnosis, interpretation and classification rather than design and planning, and that it is difficult to apply to *deep* causal knowledge or strategic knowledge—and is attempting to overcome these use grid hierarchies in NeoETS (Bradshaw & Boose 1986). The TEIRESIAS extension to MYCIN is an early form of KSS providing debugging support for an expert system using basic analogical reasoning (Davis & Lenat 1982). The development of KSSs has become a major area of activity recently, for example, MORE (Kahn, Nowlan & McDermott 1985), SALT (Marcus, McDermott & Wang 1985), SEAR (van de Brug, Bachant & McDermott 1985), and MOLE (Eshelman & McDermott 1986).

The following section describes our work on KSS1, a knowledge support system that draws on many concepts and techniques for knowledge engineering to begin to encompass requirements 3 through 8, while attempting to satisfy 9 by relating them all through personal construct psychology, and 10 by building a workbench of tools around a common database.

3. KSS1: A Knowledge Support System

Figure 1 shows the structure of KSS1 (in its workstation implementation termed KITTEN: Knowledge Initiation & Transfer Tools for Experts and Novices). KSS1 consists of a: knowledge base; various analytical tools for building and transforming the knowledge base; and a number of conversational tools for interacting with the knowledge base. The KITTEN implementation is written in Pascal and currently runs on a coupled IBM AT and Apple Macintosh to combine processing power and interactivity.

The KSS1 structure is best understood by following sequences of activity that lead to the generation of a *rule base* and its loading into an *ES shell*:
• A typical sequence is *text input* followed by *text analysis* through *TEXAN* which clusters associated words leading to a *schema* from which the expert can select related elements and initial constructs with which to commence *grid elicitation*. The resultant grids are analyzed by *ENTAIL* which induces the underlying knowledge structure as production rules that can be loaded directly into an ES shell (Gaines & Shaw 1986a).
• An alternative route is to monitor the expert's behavior through a verbal protocol giving information used and decisions resulting and analyze this through ATOM which induces structure from behavior and again generates production rules (Gaines 1977).

These two routes can be combined. KSS1 attempts to make each stage explicit, and, in particular, to make the rule base accessible as natural textual statements rather than technical production rules. The ES shell being used in KITTEN currently is Nexpert (Roy 1986) which gives a variety of textual and graphical presentations of the rule base enabling the expert to see the impact of different fragments of knowledge.

The group problem-solving component of KSS1 is particularly important because it goes beyond the stereotype of an "expert" and "users", and allows the system to be used to support an interactive community in their acquisition and transfer of knowledge and mutual understanding. The *SOCIO* analysis allows members of a community to explore their agreement and understanding with other members, and to make overt the knowledge network involved (Shaw 1980, 1981).

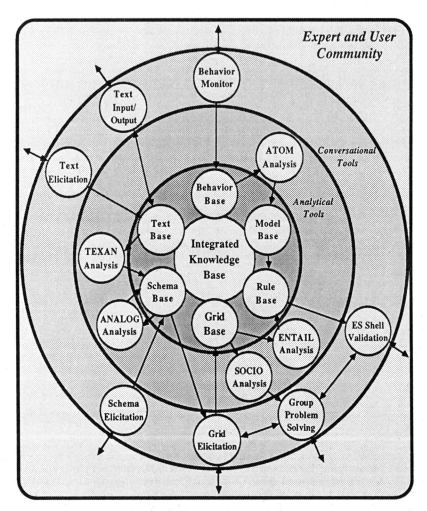

Figure 1 KSS1—KITTEN—
Knowledge Initiation and Transfer Tools for Experts and Novices

The KITTEN implementation is an initial KSS1 prototype offering a workbench with minimal integration of the knowledge base, but each of tools has already proven effective, and their combination is proving very powerful in stimulating experts to think of the knowledge externalization process from a number of different perspectives. The following sections describe and illustrate some of the tools.

3.1 ENTAIL: Entailment Analysis

PLANET and ETS access the expert's personal construct system by interactively eliciting a repertory grid of constructs classifying elements characterizing to part of the domain of expertise. A repertory grid, such as that of Figure 2, may be viewed as a component of a database in entity-antribute form with elements as *entities*, constructs as *attributes* and ratings of elements on poles of constructs as *values*.

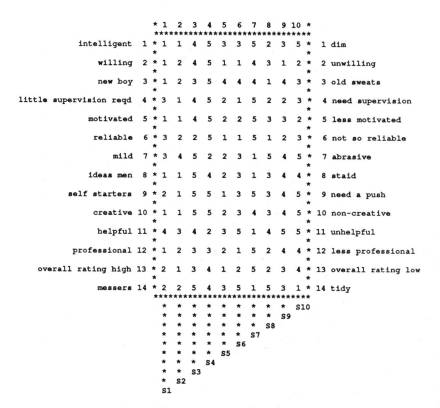

```
                            *  1   2   3   4   5   6   7   8   9  10  *
                            **********************************
        intelligent    1  *  1   1   4   5   3   3   5   2   3   5  *  1 dim
                            *                                      *
            willing    2  *  1   2   4   5   1   1   4   3   1   2  *  2 unwilling
                            *                                      *
            new boy    3  *  1   2   3   5   4   4   4   1   4   3  *  3 old sweats
                            *                                      *
little supervision reqd 4 * 3   1   4   5   2   1   5   2   2   3  *  4 need supervision
                            *                                      *
          motivated    5  *  1   1   4   5   2   2   5   3   3   2  *  5 less motivated
                            *                                      *
           reliable    6  *  3   2   2   5   1   1   5   1   2   3  *  6 not so reliable
                            *                                      *
               mild    7  *  3   4   5   2   2   3   1   5   4   5  *  7 abrasive
                            *                                      *
          ideas men    8  *  1   1   5   4   2   3   1   3   4   4  *  8 staid
                            *                                      *
       self starters   9  *  2   1   5   5   1   3   5   3   4   5  *  9 need a push
                            *                                      *
          creative   10  *  1   1   5   5   2   3   4   3   4   5  * 10 non-creative
                            *                                      *
           helpful   11  *  4   3   4   2   3   5   1   4   5   5  * 11 unhelpful
                            *                                      *
      professional   12  *  1   2   3   3   2   1   5   2   4   4  * 12 less professional
                            *                                      *
  overall rating high 13 *  2   1   3   4   1   2   5   2   3   4  * 13 overall rating low
                            *                                      *
           messers   14  *  2   5   4   3   5   1   5   3   1  * 14 tidy
                            **********************************
                            *   *   *   *   *   *   *   *   *   * S10
                            *   *   *   *   *   *   *   *   * S9
                            *   *   *   *   *   *   *   * S8
                            *   *   *   *   *   *   * S7
                            *   *   *   *   *   * S6
                            *   *   *   *   * S5
                            *   *   *   * S4
                            *   *   * S3
                            *   * S2
                            * S1
```

Figure 2 Repertory grid elicited on staff appraisal

The entailment analysis of a repertory grid treats each pole of a construct as a fuzzy predicate to which the elements have degrees of membership given by their ratings, and induces the logical implications between these predicates. The original ENTAIL program produced all entailments consistent with the grid and allowed the expert to prune any that seemed spurious before using them as inference rules in an expert system. ENTAIL II rank orders entailments in terms of the uncertainty reduction they induce in the distribution of the data, and hence tends to reject spurious entailments (Gaines & Shaw 1986a).

Figure 3 is an ENTAIL II analysis of the grid of Figure 2. The entailments are shown with three values in the range from 0 to 1: first, the truth value of the hypothesis; second, the probability of the hypothesis being true; and third, the information content (uncertainty reduction generated) of asserting the hypothesis. For example, L1→L9 has a truth value of 0.80, a probability of 1.00, and an information content of 0.29. The information content measures the significance of the hypothesis and is used to ensure that trivial entailments consistent with the data are pruned.

The data of Figure 2 are those of an expert on staff appraisal concerned with deriving his *overall rating* (construct 13) from behavioral assessments such as *intelligent* and *creative*. The ENTAIL analysis of Figure 3 shows that L1, L4, L6, L9, L10 and L12 imply L13, that *intelligent, creative, reliable and professional self-starters requiring little supervision receive a high overall rating*, whereas R2, R4, R5, R6, R9 and R12 imply R13, that *being unwilling, less motivated, not so reliable, less professional, needing supervision and needing a push leads to a low overall rating*.

Entail	Truth	Prob.	Inf.	(Cutoff 0.17) Implication Usually
L 1 → L 9	0.80	1.00	0.29	intelligent→self starters
L 9 → L13	1.00	1.00	0.29	self starters→overall rating high
R 9 → R 1	0.80	1.00	0.28	need a push→dim
L10 → L 8	1.00	1.00	0.28	creative→ ideas men
L 1 → L10	0.80	1.00	0.26	intelligent→creative
R 8 → R10	1.00	1.00	0.26	staid→non-creative
L10 → L 9	0.80	1.00	0.26	creative→self starters
R13 → R 6	0.80	1.00	0.26	overall rating low→not so reliable
L 9 → L10	0.80	1.00	0.24	self starters→creative
R10 → R 1	0.80	1.00	0.24	non-creative→dim
L10 → L 1	0.80	1.00	0.23	creative→intelligent
R13 → R 9	1.00	1.00	0.23	overall rating low→need a push
R 4 → R13	0.80	1.00	0.22	need supervision→overall rating low
R 5 → R 4	0.80	1.00	0.22	less motivated→need supervision
R 5 → R13	0.80	1.00	0.22	less motivated→overall rating low
R 9 → R10	0.80	1.00	0.22	need a push→non-creative
L 1 → L 3	0.80	1.00	0.21	intelligent→new boy
L 6 → L13	0.80	1.00	0.21	reliable→overall rating high
R10 → R 9	0.80	1.00	0.20	non-creative→need a push
R 1 → R 6	0.60	1.00	0.19	dim→not so reliable
R 1 → R10	0.80	1.00	0.19	dim→non-creative
R 9 → R 4	0.60	1.00	0.19	need a push→need supervision
R 9 → R12	0.60	1.00	0.19	need a push→less professional
R 9 → R13	0.60	1.00	0.19	need a push→overall rating low
R12 → R13	0.80	1.00	0.19	less professional→overall rating low
R13 → R 4	0.80	1.00	0.19	overall rating low→need supervision
R13 → R12	0.80	1.00	0.19	overall rating low→less professional
L 4 → L 5	0.80	1.00	0.18	little supervision reqd→motivated
L 4 → L 9	0.60	1.00	0.18	little supervision reqd→self starters
R 6 → R 4	0.80	1.00	0.18	not so reliable→need supervision
R 6 → R13	0.80	1.00	0.18	not so reliable→overall rating low
L12 → L 9	0.60	1.00	0.18	professional→self starters
L13 → L 4	0.80	1.00	0.18	overall rating high→little supervision reqd
L13 → L 5	0.80	1.00	0.18	overall rating high→motivated
L13 → L 9	0.60	1.00	0.18	overall rating high→self starters
L 1 → L 8	0.80	1.00	0.17	intelligent→ideas men

Figure 3 ENTAIL analysis of repertory grid on staff appraisal

Figure 4 shows Nexpert in operation loaded with the entailments of Figure 3. Interaction with Nexpert enables the expert to see the derived rules in action. He can determine their consequences with test data, analyze new hypothetical cases, and see the inter-relations between rules presented graphically. The logging and explanation facilities of Nexpert enable him to track down spurious inferences that may arise with the rules derived by ENTAIL, or proper inferences that are missing. He can then edit the rules and test the revised system using Nexpert's facilities.

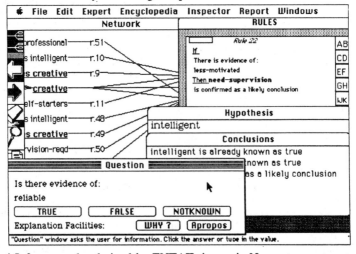

Figure 4 Inference rules derived by ENTAIL in use in Nexpert expert system shell

3.2 TEXAN: Text Analysis

Repertory grid techniques depend on eliciting elements and constructs from experts that are representative of a domain and comprehensive in their classification. The interative elicitation program PEGASUS in PLANET uses online analysis of the grid to feed back comments to the expert which stimulate the addition of elements and constructs to achieve comprehensiveness (Shaw 1980). However, this structural feedback is only applicable when a grid has been partially completed and the initial selection of elements has had no computer-based support.

TEXAN is a text analysis program designed to pump-prime the grid elicitation process when a manual or text book is available that the expert regards as having reasonable coverage of the domain. It uses techniques that were originally designed to map subject matter concepts against student concepts in computer-managed instruction systems (Smith 1976). The text is fully indexed by all non-noise words grouped by their stems, and a coupling matrix of word associations is calculated using a simple distance-in-text measure. The high-frequency associations in the text are clustered and presented to the expert as a prototypical schema for the subject area which he can edit for spurious words and associations, and then use to suggest knowledge islands and associated elements and constructs.

Figure 5 shows a TEXAN clustering of an evaluation study of data logging, analysis and presentation methodologies for human performance evaluation in complex systems (Gaines & Moray 1985). Figure 6 shows an independent mapping of the main knowledge islands for an expert system design based on the analyzed report (Gaines 1986). The TEXAN analysis was done some time after the production of Figure 6, and the shading of Figure 5 shows the relationship of some of the groupings in the schema with the knowledge islands. There is not a one-to-one correspondence but this, and similar analyses, show that basic text analysis can focus attention on salient features of the domain and pump-prime the knowledge elicitation process.

In the long term more sophisticated text analysis techniques may be used to derive knowledge from text without human intervention. However, for many domains the knowledge is not yet that explicit and pump-priming of elicitation from experts will remain a significant requirement.

3.3 ANALOG: Schema Analysis

The groupings of Figures 5 and 6 when combined with the construct classifications of repertory grids as in Figure 2 may be viewed as schema structuring a knowledge domain. ANALOG is a program that maps schema to schema based on their structure without regard to content. It is based on a theory of analogy that explicates analogies as pullbacks of faithful functors between categories (Gaines & Shaw 1982) and generates maximal sub-graph isomorphisms between two classificatory data structures. It may be regarded as a generalization of the copy-edit process being used in the encoding of commonsense knowledge in CYC (Lenat, Prakash & Shepherd 1986). ANALOG produces meaningful results on artificial examples and grids in related domains. It will also find meaningless analogies between unrelated domains which cannot be rejected by information-theoretic statistical procedures such as those used in ENTAIL and ATOM. It seems likely that effective application of ANALOG depends on the expert pump-priming the matching with known or hypothesized relations and the program extending these rather than attempting to generate them completely.

3.4 ATOM: Behavior Analysis

Michalski and Chilausky (1980) have demonstrated that inductive modeling of an expert's behavior may produce effective rules when those elicited by interview techniques are clearly inadequate. ATOM is an algorithm for inducing the structure of a system from its behavior using a search over a model space ordered by complexity and goodness of fit. As in ENTAIL, models are evaluated in terms of the uncertainty reduction induced by the model in the distribution of the modeled behavior

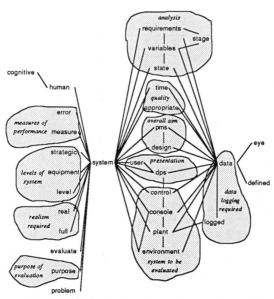

Figure 5 TEXAN clustering of word associations from text
with annotation showing knowledge islands

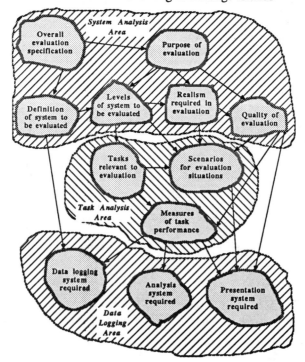

Figure 6 Knowledge islands specified by expert for performance measuring system

(Gaines 1976, 1977, 1979). We have incorporated a version of ATOM in KITTEN that takes a set of sequences of arbitrary symbolic data and generates a set of production rules that will reconstruct it. These can be loaded into the ES shell to give a simulator of the behavioral system. This has proved effective with inter-personal interaction data such as that analyzed by Mulhall (1977) and interactively elicited by Stevens (1985).

3.5 SOCIO: Mutual Agreement and Understanding Analysis

We have already emphasized the need for knowledge elicitation methodologies to cope with a group of experts as well as the individual. Much expertise only resides within the social context of cooperating individuals and requires elicitation across the group. The SOCIO analysis program supports group elicitation techniques in which the construct systems of a number of users are compared. Grids are elicited separately but then exchanged in two ways: a user can place elements on a colleague's constructs from his own point of view, and the analysis system then allows him to explore their *agreement*; or he can attempt to place them from his colleague's point of view and hence explore his *understanding*.

The SOCIO program has been used to develop a *Participant Construct System,* PCS, which supports multiple interacting users in group problem solving activities through terminals on a network of Macintoshes (Shaw 1986). It follows the paradigm suggested by Chang (1986) of a *participant system* in which computer-based communication between multiple users is *essential* to the performance of their tasks, rather than merely incidental to their use of a timeshared computer or computer network. PCS supports its users in:
• seeing the relationship of their points of view to those of others;
• exploring differing terminology for the same constructs;
• becoming aware of differing constructs having the same terminology;
• extending their own construct systems with those of others;
• providing others with constructs they have found valuable;
• exploring a problem-solving domain using the full group resources.

Figure 7 shows a construct being elicited using the natural click-and-drag techniques of the window/mouse interaction rather than numeric rating scale of Figure 2. Figure 8 shows the natural representation of the construct match screen supporting element elicitation. Figure 9 shows the presentation of agreement when one participant has made his own assignment of elements to constructs elicited from another participant.

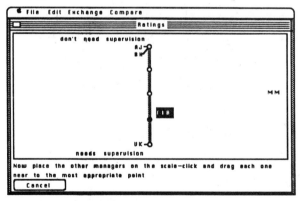

Figure 7 Rating elements on a construct spatially using click and drag

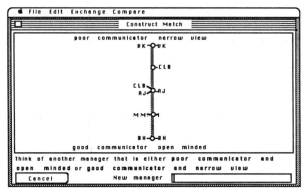

Figure 8 Eliciting an element by breaking a construct match

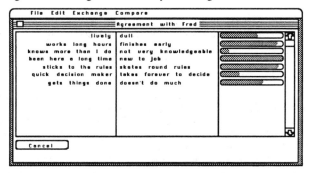

Figure 9 Presentation of degrees of agreement when one participant has
rated elements using another's constructs

4. Conclusions: Steps Toward an Integrated Knowledge Support System

This paper has presented the concept of knowledge support systems as interactive knowledge engineering tools, stated the design criteria for such systems, and outlined the structure and key components of KSS1 and its KITTEN implementation. KSS1 consists of a set of knowledge engineering tools, some of which already have track records of successful use in knowledge acquisition studies. In developing KITTEN we have preserved the integrity of each of these tools, enabling each to be utilized effectively in a stand-alone mode. However, we have also made the first steps towards an integrated knowledge support system by building the tools around a common database, providing access to the same data in each of its intermediate forms, and providing conversion utilities between different data forms.

The objective of integrating the tools has raised a number of new and significant questions. ENTAIL transforms a repertory grid to a set of production rules—is it possible, and useful, to convert production rules to a repertory grid? Technically the result is a possible world of grids that might have generated the rules, and the capability does prove useful, particularly given the other grid analysis tools available in KITTEN. Similar considerations apply to the transformations between other forms of knowledge representation. We see the next generation of knowledge support tools as increasingly flexible in handling all aspects of knowledge acquisition, representation, processing and presentation. They will not be optimized with a particular knowledge representation, uncertainty calculation, inference mechanism, and so on, that are in some sense right. Rather they will provide a wide range of perspectives on the knowledge base, preserving source data and chains of derivative processes, so that users can freely explore the knowledge or follow a very specific path according to their choices and needs.

Acknowledgements

Financial assistance for this work has been made available by the National Sciences and Engineering Research Council of Canada. The PCS implementation is being carried out by Alberta Research Council. We are grateful to John Boose and Jeff Bradshaw of Boeing AI Center, and Ernie Chang of Alberta Research Council for stimulating discussions relating to knowledge support systems.

References

Boose, J.H. (1984). Personal construct theory and the transfer of human expertise. Proceedings AAAI-84, 27-33. California: American Association for Artificial Intelligence.

Boose, J.H. (1985). A knowledge acquisition program for expert systems based on personal construct psychology. International Journal of Man-Machine Studies 20(1), 21-43 (January).

Boose, J.H. (1986). Rapid acquisition and combination of knowledge from multiple experts in the same domain. Future Computing Systems, In press.

Bradshaw, J.M. & Boose, J.H. (1986). NeoETS. Proceedings of North American Personal Construct Network Second Biennial Conference. pp. 27-41. University of Calgary: Department of Computer Science (June).

Chang, E. (1986). Participant systems. Future Computing Systems, in press.

Davis, R. & Lenat, D.B. (1982). Knowledge-Based Systems in Artificial Intelligence. New York: McGraw-Hill.

Eshelman, L. & McDermott, J. (1986). MOLE: a knowledge acquisition tool that uses its head. Technical Report. Carnegie-Mellon University: Department of Computer Science.

Gaines, B.R. (1976). Behaviour/structure transformations under uncertainty. International Journal of Man-Machine Studies, 8(3), 337-365 (May).

Gaines, B.R. (1977). System identification, approximation and complexity. International Journal of General Systems, 3, 145-174.

Gaines, B.R. (1979). Sequential fuzzy system identification. International Journal of Fuzzy Sets and Systems, 2(1), 15-24 (January).

Gaines, B.R. (1986). Development of performance measures for computer-based man-machine interfaces: Application to previous SHINMACS evaluation. Technical Report DCIEM-PER-SUP:MAR86.

Gaines, B.R. & Moray, N. (1985). Development of performance measures for computer-based man-machine interfaces. Technical Report DCIEM-PER-FIN:JUL85.

Gaines, B.R. & Shaw, M.L.G. (1980). New directions in the analysis and interactive elicitation of personal construct systems. International Journal of Man-Machine Studies 13(1) 81-116 (July).

Gaines, B.R. & Shaw, M.L.G. (1981). A programme for the development of a systems methodology of knowledge and action. Reckmeyer, W.J., Ed. General Systems Research and Design: Precursors and Futures. pp. 255-264. Society for General Systems Research (January).

Gaines, B.R. & Shaw, M.L.G. (1982). Analysing analogy. Trappl, R., Ricciardi, L. & Pask, G., Eds. Progress in Cybernetics and Systems Research. Vol. IX, pp. 379-386. Washington: Hemisphere.

Gaines, B.R. & Shaw, M.L.G. (1986a). Induction of inference rules for expert systems. Fuzzy Sets and Systems, 8(3), 315-328 (April).

Gaines, B.R. & Shaw, M.L.G. (1986b). Knowledge Engineering for an FMS Advisory System, Proceedings of AMS 86, to appear (June).

Gammack, J.G. & Young, R.M. (1985). Psychological techniques for eliciting expert knowledge. Bramer, M., Ed. Research and Development in Expert Systems, pp. 105-116. Cambridge University Press.

Kahn, G., Nowlan, S. & McDermott, J. (1985). MORE: an intelligent knowledge acquisition tool. Proceedings of the Ninth International Joint Conference on Artificial Intelligence. pp. 581-584. California: Morgan Kaufmann.

Kelly, G.A. (1955). The Psychology of Personal Constructs. New York: Norton.

Lenat, D., Prakash, M. & Shepherd, M. (1986). CYC: Using common sense knowledge to overcome brittleness and knowledge acquisition bottlenecks. AI Magazine 6(4), 65-85.

Marcus, S., McDermott, J. & Wang, T. (1985). Knowledge acquisition for constructive systems. Proceedings of the Ninth International Joint Conference on Artificial Intelligence. pp. 637-639. California: Morgan Kaufmann.

Michalski, R.S. & Chilausky, R.L. (1980). Knowledge acquisition by encoding expert rules versus computer induction from examples—A case study involving soyabean pathology. International Journal of Man-Machine Studies, 12, 63-87.

Mulhall, D.J. (1977). The representation of personal relationships: an automated system. International Journal of Man-Machine Studies, 9(3), 315-335 (May).

Roy, J. (1986). Expert systems in Nexpert. MacTutor, 2(2), 48-51 (February).

Shaw, M.L.G. (1980). On Becoming a Personal Scientist. London: Academic Press.

Shaw, M.L.G. (1981). Conversational heuristics for eliciting shared understanding. Shaw, M.L.G., Ed. Recent Advances in Personal Construct Technology. pp. 31-44. London: Academic Press.

Shaw, M.L.G. (1982). PLANET: some experience in creating an integrated system for repertory grid applications on a microcomputer. International Journal of Man-Machine Studies, 17(3), 345-360.

Shaw, M.L.G. (1986). PCS: a knowledge-based interactive system for group problem solving. Proceedings of 1986 International Conference on Systems, Man and Cybernetics, to appear (October).

Shaw, M.L.G. & Chang, E. (1986). A participant construct system. Proceedings of North American Personal Construct Network Second Biennial Conference. pp. 131-140. University of Calgary: Department of Computer Science (June).

Shaw, M.L.G. & Gaines, B.R. (1983). A computer aid to knowledge engineering. Proceedings of British Computer Society Conference on Expert Systems, 263-271 (December). Cambridge.

Shaw, M.L.G. & Gaines, B.R. (1986a). A framework for knowledge-based systems unifying expert systems and simulation. Luker, P.A. & Adelsberger, H.H., Eds. Intelligent Simulation Environments, 38-43 (January). La Jolla, California: Society for Computer Simulation.

Shaw, M.L.G. & Gaines, B.R. (1986b). Interactive elicitation of knowledge from experts. Future Computing Systems, 1(2), to appear.

Shaw, M.L.G. & Gaines, B.R. (1986c). An interactive knowledge elicitation technique using personal construct technology. Kidd, A., Ed. Knowledge Elicitation for Expert Systems: A Practical Handbook. To appear. Plenum Press.

Smith, R.A. (1976). Computer-based structural analysis in the development and administration of educational materials. International Journal of Man-Machine Studies, 8(4), 439-463 (July).

Stevens, R.F. (1985). An on-line version of the personal relations index psychological test. International Journal of Man-Machine Studies, 23(5), 563-585 (November).

van de Brug, A, Bachant, J. & McDermott, J. (1985). Doing R1 with style. Proceedings of the Second Conference on Artificial Intelligence Applications. IEEE 85CH2215-2, pp. 244-249. Washington: IEEE Computer Society Press.

Wahl, D. (1986). An application of declarative modeling to aircraft fault isolation and diagnosis. Luker, P.A. & Adelsberger, H.H., Eds. Intelligent Simulation Environments, pp. 25-28 (January). La Jolla, California: Society for Computer Simulation.

QUESTION CLASSIFICATION IN RULE-BASED SYSTEMS

Sheila Hughes
Department of Computer Science
University of Liverpool
Chadwick Building
PO Box 147
Liverpool
L69 3BX

Abstract

The HOW and WHY questions in rule-based systems are often
hailed as rudimentary "explanation" facilities based on the
identification of rules. Although obtaining answers to HOW and WHY is
straightforward and domain-independent, the semantics involved is
ill-defined. What is the meaning and nature of these questions? Are
they really what the user wants to ask? What can the system not answer?
This paper shows how a development of W G Lehnert's question
classification system can be used to shed light on the nature of HOW and
WHY.

1. Introduction

The two modes of explanation of a rule-based system are
described as HOW and WHY questions. The object of both types of enquiry
is a term present in either a premise or a conclusion of a rule in the
system. The application of WHY to a term generates a description of the
inferences which can be made using the truth value of that term. The
application of HOW to a term asks about the factors which influence the
truth value of that term. Both questions can in theory be asked in the
general sense or with reference to a particular situation. So, if no
problem-solving has taken place one may ask "WHY would the system need to
know X?". Explanation can then be provided by finding all the rules
which have X as a premise term, and quoting them as possible reasons for
trying to establish X. During or after problem solving, one can ask "WHY
did the system need to know X?". This time, only those rules having X as
a premise term and which were actually fired or which are currently under
active consideration to be fired, will be quoted. The mirror image of
these two questions can be constructed to answer the corresponding
questions "HOW would you prove Y?" and "HOW did you prove Y?" For HOW
questions, Y is matched against rule conclusion terms and rules showing
such a match are quoted.

This paper reviews Lehnert's classification of questions in
text understanding systems and analyses HOW and WHY questions in the
light of a modification of that classification. It highlights the
restrictions imposed by the rule-based formalism, and illustrates how
questions put to experts in real situations commonly belong to categories
unreachable by HOW and WHY.

2. Lehnert's Question Classification

Lehnert recognised that understanding of text is convincingly demonstrated by the ability to answer an assortment of questions about that text. Lehnert's module QUALM [Lehnert 1978] could translate natural language queries into a Conceptual Dependency (CD) representation, and then access the associated instantiated causal chain to obtain an answer [for details of CD Theory and causal chaining, see Schank 1975].

This was achieved by dividing a question into two conceptual parts: the question category and the question concept. Lehnert's question concept is the CD assertion which is present in the question. This contains no interrogative force, but clearly may also have one or more unknown values.

For example, using a story about John going to London by train in order to go to the theatre, we may consider the following questions:

How did John go to London?
When did John go to London?
Why did John go to London?

Although all three example questions are clearly different and require different answers, if the interrogative force of each query is removed, we are left with a common central concept:

John went to London.

This simple sentence is readily representable in CD terms, and is the question concept for our three example questions.

Answers to the three questions are obtained in different ways by reference to the question category for each question. Lehnert identifies thirteen categories of questions. For example a concept completion question whose question concept must be an act rather than a state, eg. 'When did John go to London?'. At least one slot or descriptive feature in the question concept is unknown and the question is answered by providing the appropriate feature.

A similar category based on slot filling for CD states is called Feature Specification: for example, 'What colour is your car?' Questions in another category, goal orientation, ask about the goals which prompted an action, eg 'Why did John go to London?'. Lehnert says "this presupposes that the actor of the question concept is a human who acts of his own volition". Goal orientation questions are meaningless outside of the context of a sentient actor. Answering such questions necessitates looking ahead in the causal chain to see what major events are subsequently enabled by the question concept. Thus, for this question category, the question-answering mechanism must shift its attention to conceptualisations in the causal chain other than that which matches the question concept.

Lehnert's other categories are Procedural/Instrumental, Causal Antecedent, Enablement, Causal Consequent, Verification, Disjunction, Expectational, Judgemental, Quantification and Requests. Thirteen classes are named and described, but interrelationships and dependencies between them are not examined: they are organised only into a single-level hierarchy.

3. A Reappraisal of Lehnert's Classification

While Lehnert's classification of question types works well enough for
the domain of simple news stories, it is not entirely appropriate to the
discussion of problem-solving behaviour nor to industrial and technical
processes. Lehnart's classification is based on common utterances:
questions used in daily conversation about well-understood (from a human
viewpoint) events. This style of communication does not give rise to the
same set of question categories produced by examination of questions
asked in consultation with a technical expert.

Only one existing question category becomes completely
irrelevant in the changed domain: requests. There does not appear to be
any reason to phrase a request to a computer system as a question; it
would naturally be phrased as a command. Another class, disjunction, can
be usefully metamorphosed into a class of "comparison"
questions, which have the form

Which has more of attribute X, entity A or entity B?
This class is more than a disjunction of two confirmatory questions.
Since entities A and B have an attribute in common, yet each has an
individual value for that attribute, the question class cannot be simple
slot-filling. It is proposed, then, that these Comparison questions
replace the Disjunctive class.

One extra class of questions should be added to the scheme.
This is the Definition class. This encompasses all requests for
definitions of entities, and in English is often recognisable as a "What
is a ..." question. This class is, in fact, appropriate to Lehnert's
original domain as well as to an industrial problem-solving domain, and
would have been worthy of consideration in her work.

There is considerable structure in the classification itself.
Lehnert simply postulates her categories leaving them organised only into
a single level. Relationships exist between the categories, but these
relationships are not made explicit. This work clarifies and organises
the relationships between categories, using ideas that underlie the
description of primitive script-manipulation tasks; since in answering
questions about the domain one must indeed undertake various movements
around a causal chain. This yields a more richly descriptive and deeper
hierarchy into which the categories can be ensconced. Instead of a
shallow, flat tree of dependencies, the structure shown in Figure 1 is
obtained.

Classifying questions in this way stems directly from the view
of question-answering as the process of moving in characteristic ways
around a causal chain. A primary distinction is made between questions
which require movement along causal links (causal) and those which do not
(acausal). The causal category is then divided into cause-seeking and
result-seeking classes. The result-seeking class is characterised by a
movement of attention from the question concept in the causal chain
toward a resultant state or enabled act. It is this forward traversal of
the causal links which is common to each of the three categories in this
class. The identification of causal consequent and goal orientation as
result-seeking categories is straightforward.

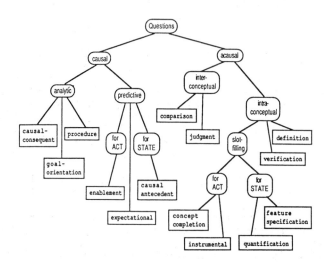

Figure 1

The procedure category has been distinguished from instrument questions. Procedure queries require the traversal of a detailed causal chain, for which the act in the question concept is a 'title' or summary. This detailed causal chain is traversed forwards (hence result-seeking) to mimic the time sequence of the description. For example:

Q How did you find the book in the library?

A I went to the index, looked up the author, found the index card, noted the classification number ...

Categories in the cause-seeking class are similarly related by the need to traverse causal links in finding an answer to the query. In this class, however, the causal links are traversed backward up the causal chain; moving from the question concept toward enabling state or causative act. The distinction between causal antecedent and enablement has been more sharply defined. A enablement question has an act as a question concept, and enquires about the state which enabled it. Symmetrically a causal antecedent query asks about an act which caused the state in the question concept. The expectational category may have either an act or a state as its question concept.

The atemporal class is also divided in two. The intraconceptual subclass requires that only a single conceptualisation in the knowledge base, matching the question concept, be examined. Its relationships, causal or otherwise, with other conceptualisations are not relevant to the answering of the query. Several categories constitute a sub-class of the intraconceptual class. These are the slot-filling categories. They can be further divided into slot-filling for acts and slot-filling for states. The instrument category is a slot-filler for an act. It is interesting that a shift in the level of detail required can transform the relatively simple instrument query into the more complex causal procedure question. For example:

> Q How do you get to London? (instrumental)
> A By train.
> Q How do you get to London? (procedural)
> A You take a taxi to the railway station, buy a ticket, get on the train ....

Methods for disambiguating the natural language question depend on the context in which the question is asked and on the repondent's view of the enquirer. This is outside of the scope of the work reported here.

The interconceptual subclass requires consideration of two conceptualisations, which are related not by causal links, but by relationships within some hierarchy. These relationships are often 'sibling' links, in that both conceptualisations are instances of the same domain class. For example, the two entities may be a drying-oil coating and a chlorinated rubber coating: both are instances of the 'coating' superclass.

The two categories in the interconceptual subclass, the judgement and comparison categories, are related to each other. Examples of the comparison question category are:

> Which is easier to implement, causal consequent or goal orientation?
> Is drying–oil-paint more viscous than a chlorinated rubber coating?

An example of the judgement question category is:

> What do you think of bitumen coatings?

The judgement class of query is seeking information about a comparison of the object of the question concept with some ideal in the same hierarchy; in the example, this is the coating hierarchy. This notion of comparison can be seen most clearly if a Comparison question is contrasted with a Judgment query having a closely related question concept.

> Q Which is more resistant to mechanical damage, a chlorinated-rubber coating or a bitumen coating? (Comparison)
> A A bitumen coating.
> Q What do you think of bitumen coatings? (Judgment)
> A ... bitumen coatings have poor resistance to mechanical damage ...

So the bitumen coating wins over the chlorinated-rubber coating, yet is judged 'poor' in relation to some other unspecified standard. This standard or ideal can be thought of as an aggregation of the strongest attribute values available in the relevant hierarchy. So if the best possible available mechanical damage resistance is obtained from sprayed–metal coatings, then this is the criterion against which all other coatings will be judged in general sense; that is, as intended in a Judgment question.

4. Analysis of HOW and WHY using the revised classification

The aim of this analysis is to distinguish
    i   the nature of the question concepts
    ii   the correct question category
for HOW and WHY questions in rule-based systems.

4.1. The WHY question

Consider this example dialogue fragment from a rule-based system for selection of anti-corrosive paints.
    What is the standard of surface preparation?
    ** WHY
    I am trying to establish a value for COATING ADHESION
        Rule: If surface preparation > 2
            Then coating adhesion is good
Consider the meaning of what is being asked. The question can be expanded in English in several ways.
    Why did you ask me that question?
    Why is that concept important?
    Why do you need to know?
    In what way will that information be used?
The question concept deals with the availability of information:
    You asked me a question.
    That concept is important.
    You need to know.
    That information will be used.
The contents of "that question", "that concept" or "that information" are only of secondary importance. The central acts or states in the question concepts are concerned with the manipulation of information; "ask", "... is important", "need to know ..." and "information ... used". All the expansions, in more or less circuitous ways, are enquiring about the system's current 'goal', that is toward what desirable state it can logically move when the sought-after information is provided. These are 'system-level' acts and states, often taking whole domain-level assertions (ie "that concept") as objects of the verbs.

The most appropriate category for WHY questions is goal orientation. Here, the system is functioning as the sentient agent which has definable goals. Its actions in pursuing those goals form the question concepts of WHY questions.

4.2. The HOW question

We can elaborate the HOW question in a manner similar to that used for WHY.
    What made you reach that conclusion? (Causal antecedent)
    What enabled the system to prove that? (Enablement)
Also similarly, the question concepts are at the system level.

You reached a conclusion.
The system proved something.
The questions are asking about the states of knowledge which have led to
a certain conclusion being drawn.

It is tempting to think of HOW questions as procedural or
instrumental. If this were so, the following would be obtained:
Q How did the system prove that?
A By modus ponens
The answer is a shorthand way of describing the detailed mechanism for
carrying out the verb in the question concept.

This is certainly not the kind of response provided by
rulebased systems; neither is a step-by-step account of how modus ponens
can be implemented. The true intent of a HOW question is to establish
the attributes of a situation which enable a conclusion to be drawn. The
HOW question is causal; further, it is cause-seeking. The absence of a
well-defined meaning for the HOW question makes further differentiation
difficult. HOW questions can be couched as Causal Antecedent or as
Enablement without losing the essence of the question.

5. Other Question Categories and the Rule-Based Formalism

We can use this classification and the idea of a "question
concept" to delineate the extent to which single-level rule-based systems
are capable of answering questions.

Kidd [Kidd 85] gives general examples of questions commonly asked of
human experts by callers in radio phone-in programmes. She points out
that the user plays a major role in the problem-solving dialogue. The
user has views on the essential components of the problem definition, and
ofter on the nature of an acceptable solution. This leads to a
negotiation between the expert and the user. Many of the questions put
to the expert belong to categories other than goal orientation or causal
antecedent. For example:
Is X a good remedy? (Judgment)
Which is the best remedy: X, Y or Z? (Comparison)
How does remedy X work? (Procedure)
Why doesn't remedy X work? (Expectation)
What happens if remedy X is used? (Causal consequent)
If all the categories in Figure 1 other than goal orientation
and causal antecedent are beyond the capabilities of conventional
rule-based systems, then clearly such systems cannot hope to support a
genuine co-operative dialogue with the user. Other paradigms must be
employed. A script-based approach to causal modelling, and to the
modelling of problem-solving behaviour, is clearly indicated by the basis
of the question analysis. A script-based system supporting both expert
problem solving and flexible querying is currently being reimplemented
following the construction of a prototype.

It is also interesting to note that the question concepts
concern domain-level ideas. Examination of the conventional HOW and WHY
questions has demonstrated that this domain level is beyond their reach,

and yet it is precisely this level which has been shown to interest enquirers in an unconstrained situation. In reality, then, it seems that the user asks questions in categories not accessible to HOW and WHY.

6. Conclusion

Understanding the nature of explanation is gravely hampered by the collection of ad hoc 'types of explanation' with no attempt to identify the relationships between the proposed classes, and it is this problem which has been addressed. The classification proposed in this work may not be relevant in its entirety to other domains or problem-solving tasks. For example, causal question types may be irrelevant in straightforward classification problems. However, such a classification does offer a good initial 'handle' on questions in many applied science and engineering domains. Using the classification, it will be possible not only to build real systems having far greater expressive power, but also to begin to quantify the communicative shortcomings of existing systems.

The application of the modified question classification to HOW and WHY in expert systems highlights their severely restricted nature. The acts which take part in the question concepts refer only to the system's actions and goals, and the system has only limited information about this already small set. The user cannot interact freely with such a system, and such cramped windows into the system's reasoning prevent the most flexible and natural use of the knowledge present.

7. Acknowledgements

I would like to thank Brian Walsh, Brian Ward and Stuart Moralee for their constructive comments on drafts of this paper.

Bibliography

Clancey, W. J. (1983). 'The Epistemology of a Rule-Based Expert System - A Framework for Explanation'. Artificial Intelligence 20, pp 215-251.

Clancey, W. J. (1981). 'NEOMYCIN: Reconfiguring a Rule-based Expert System for Application to Teaching'. Proc Int Joint Conference on Artificial Intelligence - 7.

Cullingford, R. E. Krueger, M. W. Selfridge, M. & Bienkowski, M. A. (1981). 'Towards Automating Explanations'. Proc Int Joint Conference on Artificial Intelligence - 7.

Davis, R. & King, J. (1981). 'An Overview of Production Systems' Machine Intelligence 8, eds E. W. Elcock and D. Michie, Ellis Horwood.

Jackson, P. & Lefevre, P. (1984). 'On the Application of Rule-Based Techniques to the Design of Advice Giving Systems'. Int Journal of Man-Machine Studies 20, pp 63 - 86.

Johnson-Laird, P. N. (1983). 'Mental Models'. Cambridge University Press.

Kidd, A. L. (1985). 'What do Users Ask - Some Thoughts on Diagnostic Advice'. Expert Systems '85, ed M. Merry, Cambridge University Press.

Lehnert, W. G. (1977). The Process of Question Answering'. Lawrence Earlbaum Associates.

Schank, R. C. (1975). 'Conceptual Information Processing'. North-Holland.

Schank, R. C. (1981). 'Representing Meaning: An AI Perspective'. Yale University Cognitive Science Technical Report 11.

Schank, R. C. & Abelson, R. P. (1977). 'Scripts, Plans, Goals and Understanding'. Lawrence Earlbaum Associates.

Sinnhuber, R. (1984). 'Explaining and Justifying the Reasoning of Expert Systems: a Review of recent Work'. University of Sussex AI in Medicine Group Report AIMG-4.

EXPERT SYSTEMS FOR THEORETICALLY ILL-FORMULATED DOMAINS

Sharon Wood
Cognitive Studies Programme
University of Sussex
Brighton BN1 9QN

Abstract

This paper describes the work of a project to develop an expert system for a theoretically ill-formulated domain: the domain of the school-based teacher-tutor who is adviser on classroom practice to the trainee teacher. This work has involved the development of a technique of knowledge elicitation involving the use of video tapes, and the representation of a model of knowledge about classroom process in the format of an augmented transition network. The research described has enabled the specification of an expert system which forms the basis for work on system implementation currently underway.

As an example of work on the development of an expert system for a theoretically ill-formulated domain, this project may serve as an exemplar for the potential development of expert systems in similar 'soft science' domains such as general management, personnel management, etc.

1. Introduction

Success in the development of Expert Systems has been quite marked for systems in many 'skill-based' areas, as has been remarked upon (D'Agapeyeff, 1984). For other areas, progress has not been so impressive. Among the collection of reasons put forward is that problem solving in some domains may require redress to 'first principles', rather than reliance on derived knowledge which may be used heuristically in reasoning about that domain. For this reason, the solution of qualitatively modelling the expert's 'deep' knowledge, has been proposed.(1)
Problems exist in attempting to do this: obtaining a suitable representation in order to model the acquired knowledge adequately being not the least of them; but such endeavours are usually able to assume the verification of such models to begin with. Should the domain be so ill-formulated that such models exist only in the minds of its expert practitioners, the problem becomes that much harder.
The Expert Systems in Teacher Education (ESTE) project is a collaborative venture between the Cognitive Studies Programme and the Education Area at Sussex, undertaking the development of an expert system - the Trainee Teacher Support System (TTSS). This project focusses on just such an ill-formulated domain: the domain of the school-based teacher-tutor who is adviser to the trainee teacher. The teacher-tutor's expertise reflects knowledge of both the classroom and teaching, and on how to advise in such a way as to facilitate the development of the trainee's own teaching expertise, through encouraging an understanding of classroom process and the effect of teaching practice.
A problem typical in the development of theories of social domains, is that there is no existing theory to account for classroom practice - educational theories in general being rather more abstract from the pragmatic concerns of the practising teacher. Yet the nature of the advice that is given demands interpretation of the trainee's teaching problems according to that very knowledge which exists in the practical expertise of experienced teachers.(2)

As a result, progress on the development of a TTSS which embodies a model of classroom processes accountable for this expertise, has involved the design of our own techniques in the fraught areas of knowledge elicitation and representation. In addressing the former, we developed a technique involving the use of videos of trainee teachers taking lessons, to prompt experienced teachers to discuss classroom processes. In addressing the problem of representation, we have adopted a transition network model, to capture the transition of classroom processes into qualitatively distinct states. Such a model may potentially be used diagnostically or opportunistically in advising users.

2. Preliminary Work

An observation study of sessions between trainee teachers and teacher-tutors initially revealed to us the nature of their interaction in giving and receiving advice about classroom practice (Wood, 1984). The findings of this study were used to outline the model on which the TTSS might be based with regard to both input and output, and mechanisms underlying the production of that output given the input. These mechanisms include the representation of classroom processes and the use of this representation in interpreting the input and formulating the output of the system.

The interaction underlying the seeking and giving of advice which took place during these observed sessions between trainee teachers and teacher tutors appeared to be aimed at diagnosing specific difficulties raised by the trainees themselves. The tutor would follow this up with questions about the context surrounding the situation the trainee described: previous activities, previous classwork, aims of the trainee for the lesson etc. The tutors then appear able to re-construct the scenario the student described, making an interpretation of the situation and responding accordingly with an explanation and advice; although the explanation the tutor provides is not always acceptable to the trainee, and sometimes the interpretation to be put on the situation is 'negotiated', until both parties are happy with it. In all these cases, the teacher tutors were being consulted regarding lessons they had not observed.

Some of the discriminations teachers make in responding to a trainee's problem are made possible by appeal to knowledge about classroom processes. By recourse to their appreciation of these processes, tutor's are able to infer the possible antecedents to the events trainees describe. Without this, their sole response would be to the superficial characteristics of a situation as it presents itself, without being able to direct attention towards those factors which contributed to the problem arising in the first place. The following example indicates what is meant by a process:

trainee: "As I was talking, the group started to split off into small groups which were talking amongst themselves."

tutor: "The attention span of the fourth year CSE group is not long enough for a whole lesson based around a talk; if the standard is low, you must go quicker to keep attention and relate the content to the pupils more."

A more formal description of a process might be: a phenomenon which may be affected by events taking place in a particular setting (the classroom, for instance), to the outcomes of which they contribute, especially in whether they engender a situation conducive to learning.

Experienced teachers possess knowledge that enables them to
ascertain which processes are of paramount influence in a given
situation.   This combines abilities to assess which events in the
classroom carry implications for the outcome of the lesson, i.e. are
critical in teachers' decision making; to make valid inferences about
the processes underlying the current situation; to reason about how that
situation may have come about; and to evaluate those factors which have
most likely brought about the current situation.   Reasoning about how a
situation came about requires an understanding of the causality of
events on processes and interactions between processes.

3. Knowledge Elicitation Using Videos of Trainee Teachers

It was especially knowledge about classroom process that we
wished to articulate in developing the knowledge base of the TTSS.
However, tutors' knowledge is implicit in responses made to trainees.
To gain access to this beyond the evidence provided through observation
requires in-depth investigation involving follow-up interviews, etc., to
arrive at an understanding about what led a tutor to ask particular
questions or to give specific advice.   This is a difficult task:
techniques available are generally problematic (Gammack and Young, 1984)
and not helped by the tendency when reflecting upon events to
rationalise decisions which were made (Calderhead, 1984, pg4.
Successful 'knowledge elicitation', therefore, often involves the
development of one's own techniques suited to the domain under
investigation.   For our particular domain, we developed a technique
involving the use of videos of trainee teachers taking lessons, to
prompt discussion of classroom processes, in order to discover what
teachers' knowledge of classroom processes might be (Wood, 1985).

Experienced teachers were shown videos of trainee teachers
taking classes and were invited to comment. It was hoped that witnessing
these would encourage the teachers to make explicit those aspects of the
classroom situation they felt relevant to teaching appropriately, of
which perhaps the trainees had failed to take account or were unaware.
Thus we might identify critical aspects of the classroom situation,
important to the teaching process and classroom management, which would
provide a contextual framework through which to interpret trainee
teachers' descriptions of classroom events.   We also aimed to indentify
processes underlying transitions from one classroom state to another.

The videos were not custom made for our purposes.   They were
made during the course of PGCE students' training year, specifically for
the purpose of giving individual students feedback on their classroom
manner, presentation etc. These videos are not made as a matter of
course, but are made especially for those students who are suffering
persistent problems in the classroom; they tend therefore to be examples
of ineffective teaching rather than exemplary, tending, therefore, to
highlight critical situations.

This was a preliminary study: it was not clear to what
extent this methodology would elicit the desired information or
knowledge.   Some variations in the strategy of obtaining information
were made between sessions, therefore, in the hope of improving
technique.   These might be variations in how the video was presented:
all at once, or in stages; in whether a discussion took place and/or a
questionnaire was used; and in the questions included in the
questionnaire.   The questionnaires, where these were used, were compiled
without any validation (whether they elicited the desired information).

A comparison of sessions with regard to their usefulness in
obtaining the desired information, favoured showing a video in its
entirety, following this with a discussion and providing participants
with a questionnaire.   The discussion is very useful in ascertaining

what teachers mainly focus on in making their interpretation and enables follow-up enquiries to be made there and then. It may also provide participants with some bare bones to flesh out in questionnaire responses and even predispose them to think analytically about what they saw, in doing this.

4. Modelling Classroom Processes

An analysis of the information integrated from all the video sessions revealed experienced teachers apparently referring to a range of processes. We have currently identified seven of these (the list will probably grow rather than shrink), which have been labelled according to their identifying characteristics:

control: the extent to which a class is engaged in task appropriate behaviour;

motivation: the class's predisposition to participate in the lesson and to pay attention, listen, understand and make the effort to learn;

comprehension: the process by which pupils come to understand the material presented to them through its structure and relationship to previous knowledge, and pacing according to the pupils' rate of comprehension;

communication: the extent to which pupils are aware of what they should be doing and why (contrasting with content of learning materials);

learning: the result of all the aforegoing processes which goes beyond mere rote memory of the material presented, involving its apprehension and retention as the basis for subsequent learning and application to new situations;

forgetting: the ommission of learning between lessons (or even during them!) and over longer periods of time such as the duration of a course;

relationship: describes the development of a relationship between class and teacher

These processes were modelled formally according to the following criteria. Processes may move into various phases or states; one state can be distinguished from another on the grounds that there is a qualitative (rather than a quantitative) distinction between the two. The criteria for making this distinction might be where one can characterise two (or more) situations to which the effects of one's response vary (rather than that the response carries a greater or lesser weight or effect). For instance, interactions between processes depend on the state a process has been allowed to get into – so comprehension may be motivating, and inability to understand subject matter may reduce motivation; but in a state of very low motivation (perhaps brought about by inability to understand) improving understanding will not alter motivation. Something purely motivational has to be done to regain attention (alter the state of the process) before one can get back to a situation where the influence of comprehension again applies. This differential response of motivation to the affects of comprehension characterises at least two distinct states of motivation.

Similarly when low motivation leads to loss of control: one doesn't get around a rowdy class through motivation (bribery or pleading, say) once control has been lost, but purely through control measures. These would be legitimate grounds for distinguishing between two states of a process. Other grounds might be internal restrictions on a transition: one might want to characterise a state of motivation (of a highly participant class, say) where it was inconceivable, except under some extreme conditions, that a class could make a direct transition into the state of motivation where it would only respond to purely motivational measures. Thus the state a process is in may lead it to suffer the effects of causes and other processes in characteristically different ways (underlying the variable effects of one's response), depending on the internal state of the process.

5. Representing Classroom Processes

The findings of the video study and the subsequent development of a formal model of classroom process, enabled the completion of the specification for a TTSS which included a formal description of the mechanics of internal reasoning, which would enable advice to be provided based on some deep understanding of classroom process.

The process model itself is represented as an augmented transition network: a network of states connected by pathways corresponding to the transitions from one state to another. Transitions between states are recursive and mark the passing of processes into either the same or different states over a period of time. Three different sets of conditions have been identified in marking transitions between one state and another: the internal state of the process, primary context of events and secondary context of other processes.

Internal state conditions: these specify which states a process may lapse into given the existing state of that process. For instance, if a process is in one of three states, it may be valid for state A to pass into state B, and for state B to pass into state C, but not for state A to pass directly into state C - representing that it is not possible to make transitions over a certain magnitude.

Primary context: certain conditions appear causal in the way they affect a particular process; their existence, alone or in combination with other events, may also mark the transition of a process. However, they may be choosy in which transitions they mark. For instance, a condition may be significant in marking a transition from state A to state B, but perhaps not vice versa; or say from state A to state B but not state B to state C, as in the variable appropriateness of control measures, discussed above.

Secondary context: the state of other processes sometimes has a bearing on the kinds of state transitions that can be made. The causes acting on other processes may not have a bearing themselves on the state of the process; but should they engender a transition in another process - that resultant state can. Thus the causal influences on one process may have an indirect bearing on another, as when participation in work during an activity requiring the active involvement of pupils (e.g. class discussion) enhances control through motivation. These conditions implicitly embody constraints on legal combinations of process states.

6. Mechanism of Interpretation

Diagnosis may be achieved through reference to the process model by identifying (according to their observed characteristics) the problem state of the class and state(s) prior to that. Read as a grammar, transition rules can describe possible pathways from one (perhaps desirable) state to another (perhaps less desirable) state, under alternative contextual conditions. This representation may then be used to identify possible pathways from an earlier state to the problem state; including the potential causal agents operating on such a transition. Once the transitions which may have taken place have been pointed out in this way, investigation of the conditions known to contribute to a transition is made possible. Interpreting the underlying route of a problem might involve evaluating these causal properties in order to identify protagonists: these protagonists might operate directly through events; via other process states (indirectly through events); or through the state the process has been allowed to get into itself, making it less responsive to measures for preventing problems and therefore requiring quite different remedies.

By focussing on the context in which a problem state has arisen, this representation presents the means for addressing novel problems. Hence this model is capable of supporting the kind of reasoning usually associated with recourse to 'first principles'. One cannot possibly anticipate all the things which might possibly go wrong for a teacher in any classroom i.e. using a 'checklist' approach. Nevertheless, part of the task of uncovering the root of a problem lies in being able to pose the right questions.

For instance, some initial diagnosing might suggest a problem communicating with a class; the task is then to pinpoint how this has come about. Knowing the contexts in which lack of communication arises enables sensible questioning strategies to be formulated. Say the problem were the old chestnut: the shiny blackboard. If one can discount the class having not actually been told what to do, then one might focus on the _means_ of communication. Verbal instructions are known for their failings: you need the _complete_ attention of _all_ the class - failings of memory apart. So in a situation where instructions must be referred to over a period of time, or where their importance to some operation is paramount, e.g. a biology practical, they are best written down somewhere: in a book, on a worksheet or on the board, for instance. This situation, however, is satisfied in this example, as the instructions are constantly accessible in this way. Therefore, one might begin to suspect a _problem_ with the medium of communication: poor photocopying or printing which is too faint to read; or with a blackboard the problem might be one of many: dark chalk on dark board; shortsightedness of class members; distance seated from the board; size of handwriting; legibility of handwriting; _shininess_ _of_ _the_ _board_!

One does not need a checklist of such failings, however - what pinpoints the problem is knowing that questioning the medium of communication is sensible and appropriate. It works just as well if the medium involved is a book, for one may discover, for instance, that a child has reading difficulties. We as intelligent users can be quite creative in pinpointing a problem, once we know the type of problem and where we should be looking.

The potential also exists for this model to be used opportunistically: i.e. given an current state and a desired state, one may advise upon how to achieve the desired learning state by reference to the conditions associated with a transition; or comment upon the potential of achieving a desired state from a given situation or intended plan of action. However, we do not seek to impose prescriptions for trainees' teaching practice: there are many ways to teach a lesson successfully, and one may also wish to encourage the development of individual style, especially where this capitalises on the strengths of the individual concerned and avoids their weaknesses. We would prefer to view the potential user of a TTSS as an intelligent collaborator in identifying appropriate solutions to problems. The TTSS, therefore, would not be the manufacturer of solutions to problems; but the interpreter of problems in a non-superficial way, in order to provide information or explanation of a kind that will assist and guide the user in making his/her own decisions. It could therefore be called a 'decision support system' (Freyenfeld, 1984). It becomes clearer as time goes on that the position we have chosen to adopt on this may be the only acceptable one to users of expert systems (cf discussion of the ATTENDING system (Miller, 1981) which gives informed feedback to anesthetists on their proposed plans for anesthetic management of patients undergoing operations)(3).

7. Summary

     The findings of the ESTE project have resulted in a specification of system's requirements and how these may be met, and forms the basis for current work on a first approximation to the TTSS. This work may serve as an exemplar for the potential development of experts systems in theoretically ill-formulated domains, typically social domains; it may thus have implications for the development of expert systems in similar domains such as the 'soft science' business domains of management, personnel, etc.

Footnotes

(1)   For a good description of what is implied by the term 'deep' knowledge, see Basden 1985.

(2)   Some argue that the expert knowledge of teachers is very close to commonsense knowledge: 'craft' or 'folk' knowledge. We do not subscribe to this view, but believe the knowledge of teachers is, in fact, professional knowledge (in use) and that it is the inadequacy of educational theory to account for what happens in practice in the classroom which has led to teachers' professional knowledge being labelled as craft or folk knowledge. We suspect the difficulty is presented by a lack of theoretical knowledge about social domains such as the classroom. Consequently, we are lacking in concepts and a vocabulary through which to articulate the domain specific professional knowledge of teachers. It is certainly the case that it has not been until recent years that educational theorists have been prepared to acknowledge the pragmatic issues of teaching (see Halkes and Olson, 1984). Until educational theory can account for the why of classroom practice, such practice will continue to be perceived as dependent on a kind of knowledge, craft or folk knowledge, itself somehow regarded as deficient.

(3)   This contrasts with systems such as MYCIN (Shortliffe, 1976) which attempt to simulate a medical expert's decision making process. Instead, it is assumed the physician has evaluated a patient and has certain thoughts as to management; rather than duplicating this process, ATTENDING critiques it. In this way, interaction with the ATTENDING system mimics how a physician usually asks another for advice. Miller cites as an important outcome of this approach that it forces the physician to grapple with problem himself and to think through any difficulties, consequently keeping the physician centrally involved in the decision making process.

Acknowledgements

The ESTE Project is funded by the Renaissance Trust which serves to support projects specifically in innovatory areas. The project has a steering group whose members include Ben du Boulay, Trevor Pateman, Mike Scaife and Aaron Sloman, to whom much is owed for the successful progress of this research.

References

Basden, A. (1985). 'What is Deep Knowledge?'. Report on Alvey Workshop on Deep Knowledge, University of Sussex, 11-12 July 1985.

Calderhead, J., (1984). *Teachers' Classroom Decision Making*. London: Holt, Rhinehart and Winston.

D'Agapeyeff, A. (1984). 'Report to the Alvey Directorate on a short survey of expert systems in UK business'. *Alvey News*, Supplement to issue No. 4, April 1984.

Freyenfeld, W.A., (1984). *Decision Support Systems*. Oxford: NCC Publications.

Gammack, J.G. and Young, R.M. (1984). 'Psychological Techniques for Eliciting Expert Knowledge'. In M. Bramer, (Ed.), *Research and Development in Expert Systems*. Cambridge: Cambridge University Press.

Halkes, R. and Olson, J. (1984). *Teacher Thinking*, Lisse, Netherlands: Swets and Zeitlinger.

Miller, P.L. (1984). *A Critiquing Approach to Expert Computer Advice: ATTENDING*. London: Pitman Publishing Ltd.

Shortliffe, E.H. (1976). *Computer-Based Medical Consultations: MYCIN*. Oxford: Elsevier.

Wood, S. (1984). 'Observation of School Tutoring Groups'. Progress Report, Cognitive Studies Programme, University of Sussex.

Wood, S. (1985). 'Eliciting Teaching Expertise using Videos of Trainee Teachers'. Progress Report, Cogntive Studies Programme, University of Sussex

GENERAL ROTATIONAL MACHINERY EXPERT SYSTEM

Dr R H Bannister and M P Moore
School of Mechanical Engineering, Cranfield Institute
of Technology, Bedford, MK43 0AL, England.

Abstract

The proposed rotational machinery expert system aims to perform the functions of fault:

(i)   detection,
(ii)   identification, and
(iii) alleviation.

Each of these problems represent separate but logically sequenced aspects of machinery management. Hence within the expert system, these problem areas are individually described as a Chapter. All three Chapters are capable of functioning as separate entities within the expert system. The system, however, is designed to be used as a complete package, hence some facilities are utilised for the transfer of global information when more than one Chapter is used within the same consultation session. The methodology of construction within each Chapter is highly modular. This is partly to accommodate the large number of machines which fall under the broad 'rotational' classification. But it is also advantageous, in allowing the system to provide, when the possibility exists, several measurement options, instead of dictating just one. This prevents the alienation of potential users who may otherwise have lacked the necessary vital instrumentation to carry out the stated measurement. Modules within each of the three Chapters are capable of functioning separately. Throughout the system facilities are provided to guide the novice user from one module to another or from one Chapter to the next. However experienced users, may utilise commands provided for immediate access to modules.

1. Introduction

Companies without highly developed condition monitoring systems currently rely on the vigilance of operating personnel, observing an abnormality in the behaviour of a rotating machine, and communicating it to an expert for advice. An inevitable time delay occurs between this petition to a higher authority and the conveyance of a response. Meanwhile the machine continues to function, leading to a possible further degradation in its mechanical condition. Alternatively the whimsical tripping of a machine can prove extremely costly in terms of lost production. Although machinery monitoring equipment for vibration, sound and temperature is highly developed, the task of accurate interpretation and correlation of the readings with machine operating conditions requires highly proficient personnel. The skill and experience to carry out this work is in short supply and further threatened by naturally occurring events such as staff departures. In an attempt to overcome these present

short-comings in rotational machinery management, work has started on
the construction of an off-line computerised system, incorporating the
competence of a human expert. With the adoption of expert system
technology it is hoped that all levels of workers will have instant
access to an expert 24 hours a day. But how is the methodology,
knowledge and experience of such a proficient person captured and
coded? Currently, the best guide to expert system production is to
emulate the problem specific thoughts and reactions of a human expert.
How then does a rotational machinery expert respond when confronted
with an entreaty for the health of a machine? The code of practice
employed by such an expert may be broken down into a fundamental trio
of questions. The primary question deals with QUALIFICATION:

> Are the current running conditions of the
> machine likely to result in damage?

Note, a negative response to this question disqualifies the use of the
remaining questions, as the machine may be regarded as normal. Hence
no further analysis is required. The second question concerns
DIAGNOSIS:

> What fault is the machine suffering from?

And lastly ACTION:

> What can be done to improve the situation?

Work on the present computerised system has been broken down into
three areas to provide answers to these questions.

2.   Chapters of the Expert System

The proposed rotational machinery expert system aims to
perform the functions of fault:

  (i)   detection,
 (ii)   identification, and
(iii)   alleviation.

Each of these problems represent separate but logically sequenced
aspects of machinery management. Hence within the expert system,
these problem areas are individually described as a Chapter. All
three Chapters are capable of functioning as separate entities within
the expert system. The system, however, is designed to be used as a
complete package, hence some facilities are utilised for the transfer
of global information when more than one Chapter is used within the
same consultation session. The methodology of construction within
each Chapter is highly modular. This is partly to accommodate the
large number of machines which fall under the broad 'rotational'
classification. But it is also advantageous, in allowing the system
to provide, when the possibility exists, several measurement options,
instead of dictating just one. This prevents the alienation of
potential users who may otherwise have lacked the necessary vital
instrumentation to carry out the stated measurement. Modules within
each of the three Chapters are capable of functioning separately.

Throughout the system facilities are provided to guide the novice user from one module to another or from one Chapter to the next. However, experienced users, may utilise commands provided for immediate access to modules.

2.1 Qualification Chapter

The Qualification Section or Chapter currently functions with only one module. However, the contents of this Chapter will not remain static, since (Sell 1985).

'Expert systems, like works of art, are never finished, merely abandoned'.

The present module deals with vibration tolerance levels. Its development has taken precedence, because of its potential higher reliability for assessing machine health compared to other methods. For example, the quality of the signal obtained by means of sound readings often suffers in its transmission from the machine surface to the pickup microphone. However, to utilise as many diverse forms of information as possible, later prototypes hope to include modules for sound and temperature evaluation. Interpretation of vibration is not without its problems, as vibration is a naturally occurring event in operating machinery. This means that levels of vibration need to be set, distinguishing between acceptable and unacceptable machine behaviour. The problem is compounded by the dependence of the acceptable vibration level on the type, size and speed of the machine. Fortunately a multitude of vibration tolerance assessment charts have been developed to determine machine condition (Anon. 1964; Blake 1964; Baxter & Bernhard 1967). These and other vibration tolerance charts form the heart of the Qualification Section. The Chapter functions by prompting the user to input his vibration readings along with supplementary information, such as the location of the measurement points, type of bearings, and the machine speed, since these factors will all influence the vibration tolerance region that the significant data may fall in. A deliberate policy of not asking the user for a specific form of measurement has been adopted in an attempt to make the program as convenient and flexible as possible. At most prompted questions from the system, further information can be displayed by making use of simple Help and Why facilities. Here, entering Help provides the user with assistance on answering the question, often with example entries. Entering Why forces the program to justify its question. To further satisfy the curiosity of the user, bright green boxes occasionally appear on the screen, containing reference numbers to publications, from which the current information displayed has been extracted. The user by noting the appropriate number can later call up the full reference to the article. Further facilities will ultimately also be available for viewing within the system, all the information contained in the knowledge base.

Once the initial input stage has been completed, a bar chart and accompanying table, as shown in Figure 1, is displayed. From this, the user can perform a visual check on the inputed vibration information. Perhaps also utilising previous experience, to quickly identify and generally assess the vibration tolerance levels in the bearings. The next step in the program allows the user to select an

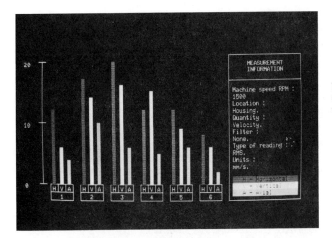

Figure 1
Confirmation of Input
Vibration Measurements

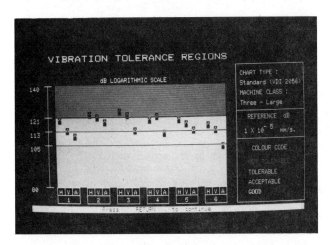

Figure 2
Assessment Option for
a Set of Overall
Vibration Readings

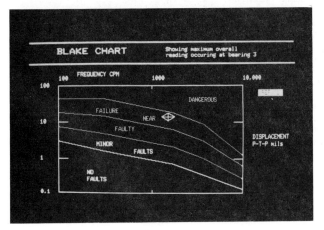

Figure 3
Assessment Option for
a Filtered Vibration
Reading

appropriate tolerance chart from a displayed menu. The options appearing on the menu, hinging on whether the measured signal has been filtered. Figure 2 shows one of the vibration tolerance charts applicable to a set of unfiltered vibration readings. With this type of chart immediate recognition of the offending bearing or group of bearings is possible. Figures 3 and 4 present two of the possible chart options for filtered readings. Here the user is allowed to display only one reading at a time. In practice this is usually the maximum value measured in a radial direction. Thus, in brief, the principle function of the Qualification Chapter is to provide the necessary tolerance charts that a human expert would call upon, with the extra encoded know-how to allow the user to access the most appropriate chart for the type of measurement and conditions under which it is taken. Final results concerning the condition of the machine are presented in graphical form by displaying the appropriate chart with the users inputed readings indicated. If the Qualification Chapter reveals that the vibration level is unacceptable then the user has the option of entering into the Diagnosis Chapter.

2.2 Diagnosis Chapter

A vast majority of machines, such as turbo-generators, electric motors and centrifugal pumps, contain a rotating shaft as the central operating component. Because of this shared link, it may be expected that rotating mechanical devices will suffer from a common range of operating problems, or systemic malfunctions. This has been found to be the case. In fact a notable diagnosis chart (Broekmate 1979) covering a wide range of machines has been devised. However, fault diagnosis probably remains the most complex of the three Chapters in which a catholic level of use can be obtained. This is partly due to the contrasting environments under which machines operate. Two extreme examples being the conditions experienced by centrifugal pumps and turbo-alternators. But it is also due to the uniqueness of each individual machine monitored. As no two machines of the same type will display exactly the same dynamic behaviour. Thus, for effective diagnosis the Section will probably be forced to contain three specific classes of knowledge:

(i)   unique to a particular machine,
(ii)   specific to a type of machine, and
(iii)   systemic information, relating to
        general rotational machinery.

To assist in the analysis process for complex machinery, construction of a finite element or difference model for each individual machine could prove necessary.

Development of the fault Diagnosis Chapter has been hampered by the reluctance of companies to openly admit problems with their machines. Further, information that is published is not in the required form to be of much assistance in expert system construction. Fortunately, the invaluable work of a particular turbomachinery consultant (Sohre 1980) has been recognised by a number of co-workers in this field (Stuart & Vinson 1985; Stewart 1985). His charts relating cause and effect have to a certain extent, enabled the speedy development of a prototype fault Diagnosis Section for

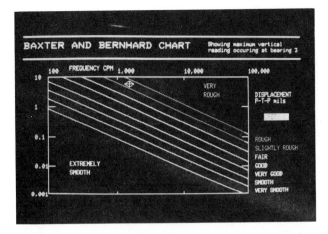

Figure 4
Alternative Assessment
Option for a Filtered
Vibration Reading

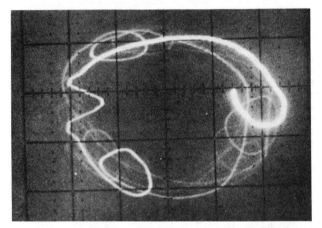

Figure 5
Lissajous Figure
Obtained from a
Submersible Pump,
Experiencing Severe
Vibration Problems

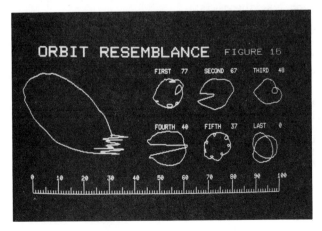

Figure 6
Ranking Digitised
Lissajous Figures
According to their
Resemblance to Figure
5

turbo-machinery.

The design of the Section is highly modular. This method of construction has been adopted not only for ease of production, maintenance, and with an eye on future expansion to incorporate changing measurement/analysis technology, but to allow the user to select only those modules for which he has the available equipment to take the necessary readings. Two prototype modules contained in this Section concern frequency analysis and orbit recognition.

Frequency analysis is a powerful diagnostic method in which the vibration signal is decomposed into its individual frequency components and associated relative amplitudes. The result of this process is utilised in the frequency analysis module. Here the knowledge base contains terms consisting of lists of malfunction likelihood values, whose predicates are specific orders of shaft speed or rotor frequency (R_F).

> e.g. one_X_R_F ([90, 25, 40, 10 .....]).
>   two_X_R_F ([30, 50, 20, 10 .....]).

Orders are preferred to Hertz for expressing vibratory information, when machines of variable shaft speed need to be accommodated. Also considerable correlation between faults and orders seem to exist. The position of each likelihood value in the list relates it to a specific malfunction. Each value represents the certainty of the malfunction affecting the amplitude of the specified frequency category or order. For example, in the above two lists, 90 and 30 indicate the likelihood of unbalance, 25 and 50 the likelihood of misalignment, 40 and 20 the likelihood of bearing damage, and so on, affecting the associated labelled frequency category. The program functions by asking the user to input the frequency category which has undergone the greatest change since the last frequency analysis, then the next greatest change and so on, until all the noticeable changes have been input. The user is also requested to input the corresponding amplitude ratio change (present/past value), for that particular order. This change in amplitude is then used to weight the associated list of malfunction likelihoods for that particular category. Heuristic rules may also form part of the final ranking process.

> IF the fundamental AND harmonic amplitudes both change,
> THEN double the effect of the ratio weighting on the
> harmonic malfunction likelihood list.

The user can eventually view, specific frequency category rankings of malfunctions, or a single ranked list of faults for the frequency signature as whole. This is obtained by an ad hoc combination of each of the frequency category rankings.

An important tool for diagnostics is the oscilloscope, because it allows the actual motion of the monitored part to be observed. The oscilloscope can be operated in two modes to present time base or orbital information. Orbital shapes or Lissajous figures are obtained by displaying in the XY mode the output from two separate orthogonally positioned proximity probes, located in the vicinity of the shaft bearings. An actual picture obtained from an oscilloscope screen monitoring the behaviour of a submersible pump during commissioning is shown in Figure 5. The pump subsequently failed due to the generation of large vibrations as a result of hydrodynamic instability, causing damage to a number of bearings. The figure on the screen is effectively the trace of the shaft centreline as the shaft rotates in the bearing. From this motion it is possible to extract information concerning the conditions under which the machine operates, and hence speculate at the likely fault which has arisen as a result of these conditions. An initial step in the module involves matching the figure's pattern with typical digitised orbit shapes stored in the program. The present prototype module works by the program displaying consecutively, different orbit shapes, and the user keying in a resemblance factor, by means of a scale, for each figure. As an aid to this initial resemblance ranking process, the system is capable of displaying on the computer screen simultaneously, the top five members of the list in order, along with the current lowest ranked figure. Figure 6 illustrates the general scheme. Here, a user is in the process of matching the real orbit in Figure 5 with the stored shapes in the module. Because different users operate at variable levels of ranking, it is not the individual values of the resemblance factors which are of importance, but their relative values. That is, different users of the system, pattern matching the same oscillosocope image with the stored shapes, should end up with identical or very similar orderings, although the attached resemblance factors may vary widely from one rank to another. Most of the displayed figures are unfortunately not mutually exclusive, in that an orbit shape is not representative of a single fault, but several. For example in Figure 6, the orbit labelled FIRST could typically indicate mechanical looseness or a hit and bounce rub. The THIRD orbit could be a light hit and bounce rub or hydrodynamic instability. The FIFTH orbit may be a medium rub, while internal spikes in the SECOND and FOURTH orbits suggest that the rotor is hitting and bouncing off the labyrinth. The LAST orbit could suggest transverse cracking. To the left of the picture the large orbit shows an electrostatic shaft voltage discharge effect, which could lead to bearing damage. Because a one to one relationship between orbit shape and fault does not exist, a further series of related questions such as the number of phase markers, and reactions to changes in operating conditions need to be answered before a local list of ranked faults is obtained.

It is anticipated that the fault Diagnosis Section will eventually contain time base analysis, orbit recognition, frequency analysis, run-up, run-down behaviour and airborne sound modules. Each of these measurement/observation modules is capable of forming a local ranked list of faults. This approach perhaps simulates best the behaviour of a human expert, who usually seeks local answers before arriving at his global conclusion. The procedure of carrying out local rankings for each module, is a practical way of avoiding the unrealistic assumption that only one fault is present. In reality a major fault is usually accompanied by several minor faults, each exerting a different influence on the ranking process for each measurement/observation module accessed. In the fault Diagnosis Chapter, the conclusive ranked list of malfunctions is achieved with a syndrome assessment module, which is capable of combining the global information generated from each accessed module. Ideally, the more modules accessed, the greater the accuracy of the final overall ranking.

2.3 Action Chapter

Unbalance is perhaps the commonest cause of rotating machinery problems. Hence the third Action section of the system is devoted solely to the correction of unbalance. Unfortunately, there is a tendency in industry to rebalance rogue machinery without fully understanding what has caused the increase in vibration levels. This is due to the widely held false assumption that 90% of all rotating machinery problems can be cured by balancing. Balancing will usually have apparent short-term success, since it reduces the vibration level, masking the presence of the actual fault. The rogue machine though is too unstable to remain in this state for long, and inevitably the initial fault will surface again, with perhaps greater destructive effect than before. It is thus highly advisable to use the Diagnosis Section prior to the consultation of any of the balance modules. By adopting this approach you can be sure that the machine will only be balanced when there is a legitimate need to do so.

In the Action Section, individually functioning modules perform either a procedural or calculation role for a variety of single-plane, two-plane, three-plane and mixed modal balancing methods. Facilities for the advanced user allow direct access to modules. Otherwise the user can be taken gradually through the different levels of the program. This Section again makes extensive use of graphics. One step in the approach to aiding the user in selecting a method of balancing, has been to display simple colour coded sketch diagrams of machine arrangements. Green indicating that a specific method of balance is suitable, red not suitable and blue possible. Sketches in magenta are a sign that only the indicated part of the represented machine can be balanced by the relevant method. This kind of formula for single-plane balancing is depicted in Figure 7. One of the intermediate vector diagrams presented to the user in the single-plane calculation module is shown in Figure 8. In this module the user is taken step-by-step through the calculation process. The final display indicating the mass and position of the correction weight needed to balance the machine. Again for complex machinery, a finite element or difference model of the rotor would prove invaluable for qualitative assessment of the reaction of the rotor to the balancing process.

It has been recognised that procedural files, explaining how to carry out a particular method of balancing would greatly benefit from the use of interactive video (Roberts 1985; Sargent 1985). Allowing the user to easily digest, by means of still and moving video images, coupled with sound and supplemented by computer generated text and graphics, the basic practical skills required for a selected balance method. At present, interactive video remains prohibitive because of the high costs involved in cutting a disc. However, utilisation of a computer controlled video tape recorder, may provide a satisfactory economical alternative. On the practical side though, tape systems suffer from slowness in operation, preventing the construction of a fully interactive system. Such a system also lacks the massive storage capacity of disc or the ability to produce high definition images.

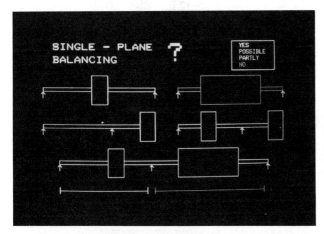

Figure 7
Decision Aid for the
Suitability of
Employing Single-Plane
Balancing

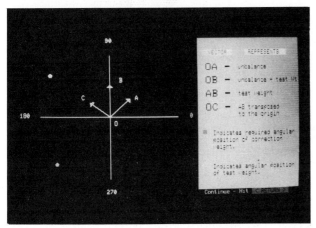

Figure 8
Vector Diagram
Utilised in the
Single-Plane Balancing
Calculation Module

3. Implementation

Prolog contained as a sub–system in Sussex POPLOG, has been chosen as the main language for implementing the system. Its syntax corresponds closely to Edinburgh or DEC-10 prolog. Heavy mathematical operations for performing the balancing calculations are written in fortran, and accessed from prolog by means of an external linking routine written in POP-11, POPLOG's core language. This allows the passage of data from prolog to fortran and vice versa, via POP-11. The system also makes use of DEC's ReGIS (Remote Graphics Instruction Set) (Anon. 1981) via a prolog interface, to provide graphical displays. Adopting the method of using escape sequences to generate local graphics, greatly speeds up the process of drawing images on the screen, since no complex interfacing to an external graphics package such as GINO–F is involved. Graphics has been the deliberate preferred means of out–putting results, throughout the system. Allowing the user to easily and rapidly pick up the required information, and therefore avoid the slow tedious task of reading text. The expert system currently runs on a VAX 8650 or 780, under the VMS operating system.

4. Conclusion

A major design criterion for the system is to make it of use to as many a number of companies as possible. This we feel is best achieved by utilising a modular method of construction. All three Chapters contained in the expert system are designed to function independently. Within a Chapter, a user has free access to any of the contained modules, enabling the conveyance of beneficial local results or information to the user. With this type of approach, the present system can tackle immediately some of the problems associated with rotating machinery. The systems level of contribution growing as more modules are completed.

The intended function of the expert system is to act in an interactive manner with the user. Its operation is quite separate from any monitoring system employed on the machine. However, the transfer of this technology to an on–line system, removing the worker from the loop, or to one incorporating useful features of both systems would be relatively simple, because of the inherent flexibility of A.I. systems.

The authors have found that A.I. programming differs from the conventional carefully defined, well specified systems analyst approach, in that the final programs are the result of much prototyping, and contain many heuristic relationships.

Acknowledgements

The authors would like to thank J. P. Stead in the School of Industrial Science at Cranfield, who initially suggested the use of ReGIS, and subsequently allowed the extraction of many useful ideas from his own prolog interface PROREGIS.

References

Anon. (1981). GIGI/ReGIS Handbook. Order number AA-K336A-TK. Software Distribution Centre, Digital Equipment Corporation, Maynard, Massachusetts 01754.

Anon. (1964). Assessment Criteria for Mechanical Vibrations in Machines. VDI Code of Practice 2056.

Baxter, R.L., Bernhard, D.L. (1967). Vibration Tolerances for Industry. ASME Paper No. 67-PEM-14.

Blake, M.P. (1964). New Vibration Standards for Maintenance. Hydrocarbon Processing, Vol. 43, No. 1, 111-4.

Broekmate, A. (1979). The Diagnosis of Machinery Vibration. DSM Nieubouw/Engineering, WE-Dept., P.O. Box 10, 6160 Mc Geleen, The Netherlands.

Roberts, P.S. (1985). Intelligent Computer Based Training. In: People and Computers: Designing the Interface, eds. P. Johnson, S. Cook. British Computer Society Workshop Series, pp 264-72.

Sargent, M. (1985). Living in the Real World. Personal Computer World, February 196-8.

Sell, P.S. (1985). Expert Systems - A Practical Introduction. Macmillan.

Sohre, J.S. (1980). Turbomachinery Problems and their Correction. Chapter 7 of Sawyer's Turbomachinery Maintenance Handbook, Vol.II (Steam Turbines, Power Recovery Turbines), pp 7-1 to 7-56, Turbomachinery International Publications, 27 South Smith St., Norwalk, Conn. 06855, USA.

Stewart, R.M. (1985). The Way Ahead for Machinery Health Monitoring as a Subset for Plant Control. Part II. Noise and Vibration Control Worldwide, March, 81-6.

Stuart, J.D., Vinson, J.W. (1985). TURBOMAC: An Expert System to aid in the Diagnosis of Cause of Vibration-Producing Problems in Large Turbomachinery. Radian Technical Report No. ST-RS-00968. Presented at the 1985 ASME International Computers in Engineering Conference and Exhibition, Boston, Massachusetts, August 4-8th.

A LOOPED INFERENCE ENGINE FOR CONTINUOUS EVOLUTIONARY PROCESS EXPERT SYSTEM CONTROLLING

Morizet-Mahoudeaux P., Fontaine D., Le Beux P.
Université de Technologie de Compiègne
Département de Génie Informatique, UA CNRS 817,
B.P. 233
60206 Compiegne-Cedex, France.

Abstract

This paper presents improvements of the expert system shell SUPER, to monitor evolutionary processes. The first step has been to develop functions to manage an evolutionary fact base. The procedures to enter or deduce new facts have been modified to take into account their successive values, to ensure consistency of the fact base and to manage the system change of states. Since facts can be added or deleted to the base, special care has been taken to allow non-monotonic revision of judgement. A looped inference engine is then defined. It is mainly based on selection, inhibition and reactivation functions for goals and rules. Sets of justifications are built, it allows to know for each fact if it confirms, denies or reactivate any goal or sub goal. Goals are ordered according to the known facts which are in favor, not in favor and not in relation with each of them. Rules are organised in networks, it is then possible to compile these networks and to built efficient path. A rule can be flagged as used or not used and be used many times with the evolution of the data base. First results and enhancement of the system are presented.

1. Introduction

Most of the expert systems that have been developed are dedicated to diagnostic aid, decision aid, theorem proving or hypothesis confirmation (Hayes-Roth & al. 1983). In most cases they use production rules, which may be structured in an AND/OR tree (Khan & al.

1985; Fontaine & al. 1986), a grammar oriented model, a frame structure
or an algorithmic tree (Shortliffe 1976; Weiss & al. 1978; Duda & al.
1981; Khan 1984). The inference engine chooses the most appropriate
goals or sub-goals, according to the facts that are known at the
moment, and a forward or backward inference strategy. With the
completion of the unknown facts, it can then find all the possible
solutions and stop with a success or a failure. These systems are very
efficient in constituting consistent knowledge bases and in diagnosis
consultation.

On the other hand, these systems are unable to reason
about evolutionary fact bases (Charniak & McDermott 1985; Fink & al.
1985), which are characteristic of evolutionary processes. Furthermore,
they usually do not allow endless loop in order to monitor a
continuous process.

We present here improvements of the SUPER expert system
shell (Fontaine & al. 1986) to manage evolutionary processes, with a
cycled inference engine working on an evolutionary fact base.

2. The expert system SUPER

SUPER is an *application oriented expert development
system*, its essential characteristic is to use a *backward chaining*
expert rules *network, controlled* with a *forward chaining* adjunct
rules *network*. The expert network corresponds to what is usually
referred to as the knowledge base and the adjunct network contains
rules of logical, semantic, algebraic relations, as well as rules of
thumb for the search efficiency and the search performance.

A production rule contains several premises and one
action. Each premise or action is called a proposition, it contains
mainly a number, a statement and a positive or a negative sense. The
positive sense means that the statement with its affirmative meaning is
true, the negative sense means that the statement with its negative
meaning is true.

A rule editor allows to enter, modify or delete any rule
interactively. It ensures the logical consistency and the optimality of
the expert rules network.

The diagnostic session begins with the introduction of initial facts (if they exist). The goals are then ordered according to these known facts and the justifications' sets that contains the antecedants as defined bellow:

Definition 1 : A proposition p is a *mandatory antecedant* of a proposition q if and only if the realization of q implies the realization of p.

Definition 2 : A propostion p is a *possible antecedant* of a proposition q if and only if the realization of p contributes to the realization of q.

In other words, the mandatory antecedants of a proposition figure on any path of the expert network that leads to that propostion, whereas the possible antecedants figure on at least one path. We note, $A_p(p)$, the *set of the possible antecedants* of a proposition, and $A_m(p)$, the *set of the mandatory antecedants* of a proposition .

The goals ordering function, that we will define more precisely in the fourth section, computes for each goal G the ratio of:

1) the number of the initial facts that belong to $A_p(G)$

2) less the number of the initial facts that are in opposite sense to $A_p(G)$

3) less the number of the initial facts that do not belong to $A_p(G)$

4) divided by the size of $A_p(G)$.

Goals are then ordered in a decreasing order. The systems tries then to complete the diagnosis with the addition of the missing facts via a query directed by a backward chaining on the first goal. Rules are selected in the same way thanks to the network structure. The goal order is computed again each time a goal has been reached or rejected according to the previous query.

Explanations about the reasoning and the conclusions are available at any moment during the interrogation session.

SUPER has been successfully used in medical (Fontaine & LeBeux 1983; Fontaine & al. 1985) and in signal processing (Li & al. 1985; Prugneau & al. 1986) applications.

3. Evolutionary fact base maintenance

The first step has been to give to SUPER the possibility of updating the fact base in any case of insertion of new facts including modification of the sense of a proposition, new value, deletion, etc ... Details are presented in (Morizet-Mahoudeaux & al. 1986).

The chosen solution has been to update the fact base according to two principles :

Principle 1 : for each recursive trial of the inference engine with a selected rule, it is possible for the user (or any input/output system) to enter any number of propositions. In this case the recursive inference engine is stopped.

Principle 2 : any entered or deduced fact may exist in the fact base with only one value. If there is a contradiction, only one value is retained, it is chosen either by the user or a predefined algorithm.

A *recursive insertion function* adds $A_m(p)$ to the fact base when the proposition p has been entered and removes any proposition of the opposite sense that would exist in the fact base.

A *recursive testing function* will then analyse each proposition and the sets of its mandatory antecedants. If some direct or deduced contradiction appears deletion or completion of facts can then happen.

A special sequence of rules, called *change of state rules* has been added to the adjunct network to reflect the evolution of parameters characteristic of a change of state of the system analysed. In this paper we consider that the system's state has changed for a proposition P if and only if there is a sequence of n rules R_i in which p is the premise of the rule R_1 and $(\neg p)$ is the action of the rule R_n.

If inserted in the expert network, such a sequence leads to a conflict during the interrogation session since it is not possible to find a goal, the later being defined as a proposition that does not appear as premise in any rule. The sequence is then inserted in the adjunct network. This is justified since this network has been developed to optimize the choice strategie of the most pertinent rules and to lower the query by avoiding questions about facts that can be deduced in forward chaining with it. In the present case the aim of these rules is to update the fact base consequently to a change of state of the system carcacterised by the given sequence. The main difference with the initial use of the adjunct rules network is that, with the use of the functions defined in the previous section, it may lead to deletion of facts.

We can then conclude that addition of information may induce revision of judgement, that is, if some previous fact held before the introduction of this new information, it may not hold afterwards. Formally speaking, the deduction system that we use corresponds to the so called first order logic theory of the *sentential calculus* and may be written as:

Let S be a set of formulas (the set of initial facts for example), A the set of the axioms of the sentential calculus, and the rules of inference defined by:

Modus Ponens : from p and p $\supset$ q, infer q (noted p $\rightarrow$ q) The theory defined by $\text{Th}\{S\} = \{p: S \rightarrow_A p\}$ has generaly the property of *monotonicity* that is:

$$\text{If } S_1 \subset S_2 \text{ then } \text{Th}(S_1) \subset \text{Th}(S_2),$$

which means that if a sentence follows from a collection of sentences S_1 it necessary follows from any collections of sentences that contains S_1. In other words addition of information cannot deny any previous proof. This does not correspond to the human way of reasonning and to what we have called the revision of judgement.

The maintenance of the fact base as described above has now the property of *non-monotonicity* as defined in (McDermott & Doyle 1980). The main difference with the Truth Maintenance System described in (Doyle 1979) is that the justifications sets are built during the interrogation session very efficiently with the help of the antecedants sets that have been built during the learning session. Passing information between the data base maintenance system and the inference engine has been, by the way, considerably reduced.

4. Looped inference engine

Evolutionary processes modeling leads to the idea of a looped inference engine. Clearly, one or any goals or sub-goals, which have been selected at a consultation step may not be of interest after any number of the fact base state modifications. We have then to reconsider the SUPER functions that compute the goals order and the candidate rules order.

For any new added fact, due to a query of the expert system or an user initiative, the recursive backward inference engine is stopped. The fact base is updated according to the principles and functions given above. Any facts that may be deduced from the adjunct rules are added to the base in the same way. The goal order and the candidate rules order are then computed.

The goal ordering function has been modified so that no goal will now be rejected. If a goal is not accessible, its coefficient is set to zero. For any other goal G its coefficient is computed as a function of the size of $A_m(G)$ and $A_p(G)$, and of the facts that are present in the fact base, which contributes in the direct sense and in the opposite sense to the realization of the selected goal or sub-goal. Let us define a goal G with $A_p(G) = \{ \ldots, p, \ldots \}$ and a fact base FB. We define ¬FB the symetrical set of FB, as the set of the propositions p so that (¬ p) belongs to FB. The computation of the goal order coefficient C(B) is :

If $\exists\ P \in A_m(B)\ |\ (\neg p) \in$ FB then C(B) = 0.

Else let us define the following sets :

Set of the referees to B:

$$\text{REF}(B) = A_p(B) - \{p|\ p \text{ and } (\neg p) \in A_p(B), \text{ and } (\neg p) \in \text{FB}\}$$

In other words, if P and (¬ p) are both possible antecedents of B then we only consider the antecedent that belongs to FB. The number of elements of REF(B) corresponds to the number of propositions that may contribute to the realization of B.

Set of the elements in favor of B:

$$\text{PRO}(B) = A_p\{\text{REF}(B) \cap \text{FB}\},$$ where A_p computed on a set represents the union of the possible antecedants of the propositions of this set. The set PRO(B) is reduced as above with

$$\text{PROB} = \text{PRO}(B) - \{p|\ p \text{ and } (\neg p) \in \text{PRO}(B), \text{ and } (\neg p) \in \text{FB}\}.$$

PRO(B) represents the set of the antecedants of B with their possible antecedants existing in the fact base. To estimate the weight of the elements in favor of B we have to consider the set of the propositions that are attached to them.

Set of the elements not in favor of B:

ANTI(B) = A_p{REF(B) $\cap$ $\neg$FB} .

ANTI(B) is reduced with

ANTI(B) = ANTI(B) - {p| p and ($\neg$ p) $\in$ ANTI(B), and ($\neg$ p) $\in$ $\neg$FB}

ANTI(B) represents the set of the antecedants to B with their possible antecedants existing in the opposite sense in the fact base. The appearance of the set of the possible antecedants is due to the same arguments as above.

Set of the elements that are not related to B:

EXT(B) = A_p{FB} - A_p{B}.

EXT(B) consits of all the facts that are not related to the selected goal B. We delete from the fact base all the facts and their possible antecedants that may contribute to the proof of B.

We compute then the ratios :

C_1 = Card(PRO(B)) / Card(REF(B)), in favor of B,

C_2 = Card(ANTI(B)) / Card(REF(B)), not in favor of B,

C_3 = Card(EXT(B)) / Card(A_p{FB}), not related to B.

The goal order coefficient is then :

$C(B) = (C_1(B) - C_2(B) - f(C_3(B)) + 2)/3$, where f is a function which measures the attenuation due to the facts not related to B and which expression is dependant of the application.

The inference engine is then initialized and started up with the new state, the goals being ordered in the decreasing order of the coefficients.

Rules selection is built on the same way. Let us consider that the fact base has been updated and the goals have been ordered. All the rules of the adjunct network that can be inferred have been triggered. For each goal or sub-goal G, that has been selected with the goal order function, we determine the rules whose G is action. The premises of these rules are either known or considered as sub goal.

If one of the premises of a rule R is p and if ($\neg$ p) belongs to the FB then the rule is rejected.

If one of the mandatory antecedants of p of the rule R is
Q and if (¬ Q) belongs to FB then the rule is rejected.

In any other cases the coefficient of the rule is
computed owing to the possible antecedants of its premises and their
contraries refered to the facts existing in the base and the
coefficients computed as above for its action (considered as a
sub–goal) that is :

REF(R) = $A_p\{p \mid$ p is a premise of R$\}$,

PRO(R) = REF(R) ∩ PRO(SG), where SG is the sub goal
corresponding to the rule R (its action),

ANTI(R) = REF(R) ∩ ANTI(R).

We can then compute :

$C_1(R)$ = Card(PRO(R)) / Card(REF(R)), in favor of R,

$C_2(R)$ = Card(ANTI(R)) / Card(REF(R)), not in favor of R.

The weight of the rule is then : $C(R) = C_1(R) - C_2(R)$. The
rule with the highest coefficient is selected and the recursive
analysis is pursued.

The problem is now to create restrictive conditions for
any goal that has been reached. The difficulties are

i) to forbid the inference engine to conclude to this
goal with the next loop, since all the rules and propositions of the
corresponding sub–tree are present and valid in the fact base,

ii) to allow the engine to reach the same goal by any
other path in the tree as soon as the facts and rules on this path are
validated,

iii) to release the restriction at any moment if
justified (the user wants to reach the same goal again with the same
path, some facts of $A_m(G)$ have changed or been deleted, ...).

The first problem has been easily resolved with the use
of the goal ordering function, that gives a negative value to any
reached goal.

The second one has been resolved by testing if any new
fact does belong to a path, that has not yet been used, going to any
restricted goal. This implies the building of the corresponding
sub–trees dynamically during the interrogation session. The use of
$A_m(G)$ and $A_p(G)$ has been very helpful for this dynamic instantiation.

The third has been resolved by testing if any new facts does not yet exist in the fact base. If it exists with the same value or sense and if it is on a path going to an already reached goal, we have to test if the user wants to reach this goal again. If it exists with a different value or sense and if it is on the only actived path that leads to the reached goal, we have to release the restriction (the fact base state has changed, and the goal is not more accessible .This implies that the goal order function will now run normally). This lead to consider rules previously ignored and to take care of not rerunning rules as in (de Kleer 1986).

5. Conclusion

The system is now on hand in three application domains, in medicine (for the neonatal resuscitation protocol follow up), in signal processing (digital filtering and spectral analysis) and in production control (water production, non-destructive control). The next step will be to interface the system with instruments to enter information (facts) on line.

The first results have shown that the system, when the user is not satisfied with the deduction results or changes the fact base state, can find the right node in the expert rules network where to start reasoning again. Let us consider an example of the spectral application given in the figure 1. Suppose that the fact base contains $\{1,2,6\}$, then the system concludes to $\{5,10,9\}$ and executes the FFT (Fast Fourier Transform) algorithm with the Hamming windowing.

If on one hand the user is not satisfied with the attenuation, but asks the system to diminish the sidelobes $\{2\}$ anyway, the system knows that the previous windowing path has been used $(R_6-R_4-R_1)$. Then it finds the path that leads to a greater attenuation with the Blackmann windowing and starts deduction again at this node, which will draw inference to FFT with the Blackmann windowing. Consequently it will use the rule R_6 again, but with the rules R_5 and R_2 instead of the previous rules.

If on the other hand the user changes the fact base state from $\{1,2,6,(5,10,9 \text{ deduced})\}$ to $\{1,2,4,6,(5,10,9)\}$, then the system

References

Charniak, E.& McDermott, D.(1985). Introduction to artificial intelligence, Reading Mass.: Addison Wesley.

de Kleer, J. (1986). An assumption-based TMS. Artificial Intelligence, 28, n☐ 2, 127–162.

Duda, R., Gaschnig, J. & Hart, P.(1981). Model design in the PROSPECTOR consultant system for mineral exploration, in Readings in Artificial Intelligence, B. Weber and N. Nilson (eds.), pp. 334–348, Palo Alto, CA: Tioga.

Doyle, J. (1979). A truth maintenance system, Artificial Intelligence, 12, 231–272.

Fink, P.K., Lusth, J.C. & Duran, J.W.(1985). A general expert system design for diagnostic problem solving, IEEE Trans. on Patt. Anal. and Mach. Intell., 7, n☐5, 553–560.

Fontaine D.& Le Beux P.(1983) An expert system for rubella consultation, in MEDINFO, van Bemmel/Ball /Wigertz (eds.) IFIP-IMIA (North-Holland).

Fontaine, D., Le Beux, P.,, Trigano, P., Henry, C.& Morizet-Mahoudeaux, P.(1985). SUPER: An expert system: application to neonatal infection, Intern. Working Conf. on Comput. Aided Med. Decis. Making, Prague.

Fontaine, D. & Lebeux P.(1986). A knowledge acquisition system for expert systems. Technique et Science Informatique, 11, n☐5, 7–20.

Hayes-Roth, F., Waterman, D.A.& Lenat, D.B. (1963). Building expert systems. Reading, Mass.: Addison-Wesley.

Khan, G.(1984). On when diagnostic systems want to do without causal knowledge, in Proc. Adv. Artif. Intell., Pisa, Italy understands that he wants to calculate the FFT via an other algorithm, that is using the new path R_7–R_3 that leads to the goal 9 via 8.

Lastly if he changes 2 to ¬2 then 5, 7 and 9 are not consistent and are suppressed from the base. If 2 is valid again the base will be in the same state as at the beginning.

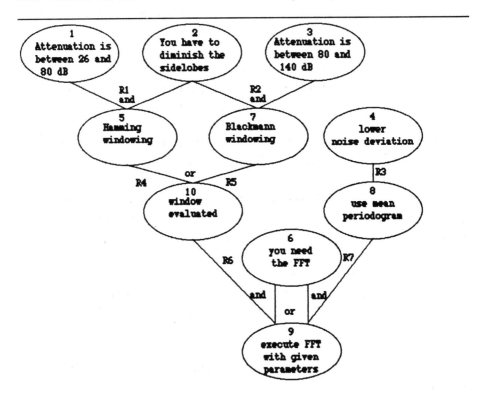

Figure 1: example of the signal processing application network

An improvement direction would be to study the case of controlling a production system during its starting or stopping phases. The expert system would be responsible of the starting check list control, and should correctly react when the system evolves normally or when some failures are detected. The problem will not be only to perform failure diagnosis but also to recognize normal states evolution.

Khan, G., Nowland, S. & McDermott, J.(1985). Strategies for knowledge acquisition, IEEE Trans. on Patt. Anal. and Mach. Intell., 11, n□5, 511-522.

Li, X., Morizet-Mahoudeaux, P., Fontaine, D. & Gaillard, P.(1985). Expert system for spectral analysis, 10 ème colloque sur le traitement du signal et ses applications, GRETSI, Nice,France.

Li, X., Morizet-Mahoudeaux, P., Trigano, P., Gaillard, P.(1985). A spectral analysis expert system, Applied signal processing and digital filtering, IASTED Intern. Symp., Paris, France.

McDermott, D. & Doyle, J.(1980). Non-monotonic logic I, Artificial Intelligence, 13, n□1 and 2, 41-72.

Morizet-Mahoudeaux, P., Fontaine, D & LeBeux, P.(1986). An expert system for evolutionary process control: application to the neonatal resuscitation protocol following, MEDINFO, Washington.

Prugneau, P., Morizet-Mahoudeaux, P., Trigano, P., Gaillard, P.& LeBeux P. (1986). Resources sharing between an expert system and a sofware package; 6th International conference on expert systems and their applications, Avignon , France.

Shortliffe, E.(1976). Computer-based medical consultations : MYCIN, New York: Elsevier.

Weiss, S., Kulikowski, C., Aramel S. & Safir A.(1978). A model-based method for computer-aided medical decision making, Artif. Intell., 11, 145-172.

Rule-based Surface Classification Using
Specular Sonar Reflections

J C T Hallam, J B H Kwa, J A M Howe
Dept of Artificial Intelligence,
University of Edinburgh,
Forrest Hill, Edinburgh EH1 2QL.

Abstract

This paper describes an approach to real-time surface
classification using specular sonar reflections. Initially, when the
surface is insufficiently sensed, multiple uncertain hypotheses pertaining to the surface type can be posted. These are revised incrementally as more evidence is received, leading eventually to a correct
dominating hypothesis. The evidence combination method is based on the
Dempster-Shafer theory and makes extensive use of a set of rules.
These rules are established by case analysis of the combinations of
observer motion and primitive surfaces. Results based on simulated
noisy data indicate that this is a feasible technique for classifying
primitive surfaces.

1. Introduction

Classification of stationary primitive surface patches can
be achieved by analysing the specular sonar echoes sensed from the
same platform which carries the sonar system. This is possible by
virtue of the physical imaging constraints due to the curvature of the
surface.

In this paper, we present an approach to surface classification using sonar data. The classification process is data-driven and
involves three main phases -- feature extraction; hypothesis formation
and evidential reasoning.

The immediate objective of the analysis is to extract
relevant topological and geometric information (feature extraction)
from a set of specular echoes. Relevant features include measures of
parallelism, cylindricality, point of convergence and the dimension of
the observer motion. Using some of these measures, an intermediate
conclusion can be made on the class of echoes. This intermediate
result and the information about the observer motion is then matched
against a rule set to obtain the possible surface classification
hypotheses.

The rule set to support hypothesis formation is constructed by case analysis of how various observer trajectories with
respect to various primitive surfaces can give rise to the classes of
echoes. Multiple hypotheses are possible when the echoes are insufficiently constrained. Furthermore, some of these trajectories may seem
more contrived than others and hence the associated class of echoes
will be less likely. By subjective analysis of the relative likelihood of the cases, we can impute rough estimates to the certainty of
the surface classification hypotheses.

Since subjective estimates of the certainty of hypotheses are inevitably imprecise, the chosen specification takes the form of a numeric range instead of a point probability estimate. As more sets of echoes are gathered and analysed, the certainty estimates of candidate hypotheses are updated incrementally using the Dempster-Shafer theory of evidence combination.

Experiments using simulated noisy data (0.3m s.d. with ranges up to about 40m) have shown that this approach to surface classification is able to correctly identify ellipsoidal, spherical, cylindrical and planar primitive surface patches when given sufficient data.

2. Background

In previous work, Hallam (1985a) has shown that it is possible under certain conditions to resolve the observer's motion as well as the motion (if any) of detected objects. Position data from different objects intermingled in a stream of sensed data can be segmented using conventional techniques. This provides object-specific position data streams, each with a corresponding stream of observer positions from which object positions were measured. Each pair of corresponding observer-object position data constitutes a view-vector. All the view-vectors which can be obtained from the object form its visibility set. Hallam (1985b) also describes how, in the case of stationary objects, primitive geometric surfaces constrain the relationship of view-vectors obtainable from the surface, giving the set of view-vectors peculiar geometric features which can be extracted to deduce a classification of the source surface type.

3. Specular Reflections and Visibility Sets

Active sonar sensing is usually implemented with the transmitter and sensor colocated. Sonar returns detected are mainly specular (from surface patches parallel to the sonar wave front) and possibly, weaker diffused (non-specular) reflections. Specular returns have more consistent characteristics and better signal quality and hence are the prime source of sonar information.

In the underwater world, objects which give rise to specular echoes can be natural (e.g. rocks, the sea-bed, or even a big marine creature) or man-made (pipes, submerged superstructure of oil-rigs, etc). Unlike natural objects, man-made objects generally have a regular surface topology with the local surface shape belonging to a small set of primitive surface types viz. planar, cylindrical, spherical and ellipsoidal. These primitive surface patches can be identified by specular analysis, producing the essential data for object modelling.

Each type of surface constrains the relationship between the view-vectors obtained from it. Assuming that the observer's motion is 3-dimensional, that is the observer positions do not lie on a line or plane, a spherical surface will give rise to view-vectors which intersect at the centre of the sphere (see Figure 1) and hence

are said to form a spherical visibility set. View-vectors from a
cylindrical surface intersect the axis of the cylindrical surface and
are also skewed-parallel (see Figure 2). These view-vectors constitute
a cylindrical visibility set. The ellipsoidal surface has a
"variable" visibility set which is neither spherical nor cylindrical.
In the case of the planar surface view-vectors are constrained to be
mutually parallel (see Figure 3), forming a prismatic visibility set.

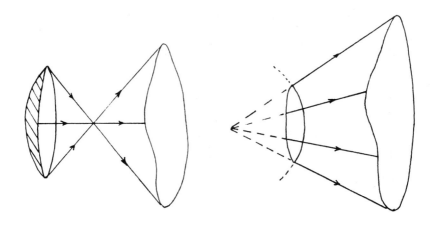

Figure 1. Spherical Visibility Set

　　　　　　Specular reflections can also occur at concave corners and
concave edges (straight and curvilinear). The corner has a spherical
visibility set and can be considered as a degenerate sphere. A
straight concave edge yields a cylindrical visibility set and can be
viewed as a degenerate cylinder. The methods for identifying spherical and cylindrical surfaces are therefore applicable to these two
cases. The curvilinear edge (for instance, formed when two cylindrical parts meet) is an oddity which in general produces a visibility
set which is "variable". It can be interpreted as a curvilinear edge
or an ellipsoidal surface. For simplicity, we shall consider sources
giving rise to "variable" visibility sets as members of the family of
ellipsoidal surfaces and leave the discrimination of a curvilinear
edge to higher level analysis using information from deduced adjacent
surfaces.

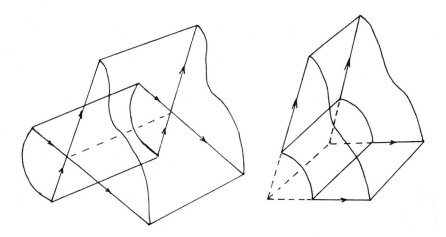

Figure 2. Cylindrical Visibility Set

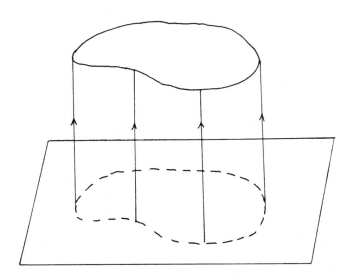

Figure 3. Prismatic Visibility Set

4. Features

For the sake of brevity, we shall adopt the following symbols:

E - the set of the last n view-vectors from a surface, or the body of evidence in the context of the Dempster-Shafer theory (Dempster 1968; Shafer 1976; Gordon & Shortliffe 1985).

α - the very first view-vector from a surface.

δ - the dimension of the observer positions in E. If the observer moves linearly, δ is 1; if its motion is within a plane, then δ is 2, and in the case of general 3-dimensional motion, δ is 3.

R - derived from E, it is the set of resultant vectors from the cross-product of α and each element of E.

ν - a member of the class of visibility sets i.e. {prismatic, cylindrical, spherical, variable}; assumed exhaustive.

P - the 2-tuple {δ ν}.

Classification proceeds by first determining P, the premise of a typical classification rule. This is achieved by extracting the following features from E:

Parallelism in E

If and only if the view-vectors in E are more or less parallel, then the visibility set is prismatic. The method used in measuring parallelism is to compute the variance of the cosine of the angle between each element of E and α. When the view-vectors are roughly parallel the variance will be very small and its order of magnitude will not vary significantly. This method has been found to be more discriminating than the average measure of the cosine values.

Centroid of E

When the visibility set of E has been found to be non-prismatic, the point of nearest approach (called the "centroid".) of the view-vectors is computed by minimising its total square Euclidean distance from the lines. The centroid is a relevant measure because the extent of its deviation as new evidence is gathered from the same source is related to the surface curvature class. For example, a spherical surface will produce view-vectors which tend to meet at its centre and hence the centroid of E will not deviate significantly as E varies. In the case of motion in a skewed direction with respect to the axis of a cylindrical surface, the centroid will be observed to move along the axis in the same sense as

the observer's motion. Significant deviations of the centroid
may also be observed when the surface is ellipsoidal.

Parallelism in R

The purpose of extracting this feature is to enable discrimination between cylindrical and "variable" visibility sets. If
and only if the elements of R are more or less mutually parallel, then the original view-vectors in E are skewed-parallel.
This means that the visibility set is cylindrical.

Observer Dimension of Motion

This is an important parameter because it indicates the degree
of constraint of E, which is least when δ is 1 and greatest
when δ is 3. It is determined by first computing the eigenvalues of the scatter matrix of the observer positions in E
and then counting the number of the eigenvalues which exceed a
certain threshold.

Other Geometric Information

When the surface source is suspected to be either spherical or
cylindrical, the program computes the perceived radius of curvature. The hull type (convex/concave) is also determined if
the surface is non-planar. Although the radius is irrelevant
to classification of surfaces, it is useful information for
object modelling, besides indicating the presence of a degenerate source (near-zero radius).

5. Resolution of Ambiguity

The view-vectors corresponding to 3-dimensional motion of
the observer are sufficiently constrained to enable rather definite
conclusions on the surface source type. When the motion of the
observer is linear or planar, however, the view-vectors are under-
constrained and multiple hypotheses are possible. For example, when
the observer's trajectory is on a plane which passes through the axis
of the cylindrical source, the observed visibility set is prismatic.
This observation could also be due to any planar motion over a planar
surface. In other words, when P = [2 prismatic], the source can be
either cylindrical or planar. However, noting that in the cylindrical
case, the plane of motion is constrained to pass through the axis
whereas the plane is unconstrained in the planar case, one can subjectively assign a measure of belief to the cylindrical hypothesis which
is lower than that assigned to the planar hypothesis. Following a
similar approach, further rules interpreting P can be established by
analysing all possible hypotheses for each P and the underlying motion
constraints, and on the basis of such a critical assessment of the
relative likelihoods, subjectively assign the degrees of belief to the
competing hypotheses.

In this implementation, uncertainty is managed using the Dempster-Shafer theory. Uncertainty is expressed in terms of degrees of belief which take values in the unit interval (0 = total unbelief; 1 = total belief). An example of a rule with uncertain hypotheses is:

IF   observer motion is planar AND
        the visibility set is prismatic
THEN   the surface type is:
            planar with degree of belief 0.6,
            cylindrical with degree of belief 0.2.

Notice that the degrees of belief in the consequent of a rule need not add up to 1 as in probability theory where $P(A) = 1 - P(\text{not } A)$ forces the full unit measure of belief to be divided between the hypothesis A and its negation "not A". In contrast to this, the Dempster-Shafer theory allows for the representation of the effect of incomplete evidence or ignorance in the form of uncommitted belief. In the consequent of the above rule, it is implicit that the amount of uncommitted belief, which is 0.2, represents the extent of ignorance, and one should read the uncertainty of a hypothesis as a numerical interval $[b,d]$ where b, $d \in [0,1]$ and $b \leq d$. The interval $[b,d]$ is also called the belief interval in Dempster-Shafer theory and is interpreted as follows:

"b" represents the degree of belief based on
    evidence which supports the hypothesis.

"d" represents the degree of doubt based on
    evidence which refutes the hypothesis.

"d - b" represents the amount of uncommitted belief
    due to incomplete evidence or ignorance with
    respect to the hypothesis.

The theory hence accommodates two aspects of uncertainty - the uncertainty about the hypothesis itself and the uncertainty about the estimation of this first uncertainty. In other words, first and second order uncertainties can be represented. Having higher order abstraction in this way seems intuitively to be a better model of the way people often subjectively quantify uncertainty.

Given a body of evidence which matches the premise of a rule, the consequent suggests the hypotheses to be believed to varying degrees. This will be taken as the current state of belief pertaining to the source if there are no current hypotheses, as when a new source has been detected. If there is an existing set of hypotheses, then it must be reconciled with the new finding using Dempster's rule of evidence combination.* This updating process is repeated incrementally for each new body of evidence gathered. With consistent bodies of

---

* Gordon & Shortliffe (1985) contains a concise description of the Dempster-Shafer theory. For those with a mathematical penchant, Shafer (1976) has a rigorous development of the original key ideas reported in Dempster (1968).

evidence, the width of the belief intervals will diminish and the
hypothesis with the highest degree of belief can be taken as the classification of the surface source. Alternatively, the ranking procedure can be based on the mid-point of the belief interval.

6. Implementation and Results

        The main phases of the program written in POP-11 are shown
in Figure 4. Classification is performed incrementally after every
new group of 10 view-vectors has been analysed, and the belief state
updated accordingly.
        A point to note is that a record of previous visibility
sets found (the historical component) may be used to influence the
evidential reasoning. This is done by using heuristic rules which
interpret all evidence gathered so far instead of just the most recent
body of evidence. For example:

        IF   (the visibility set is spherical OR cylindrical)
                                AND
                there is a history of prismatic visibility sets
        THEN   the surface type is:
                cylindrical with degree of belief 0.8.

        The idea here is to exploit the consistency constraint
whenever possible to yield more definite conclusions quickly, since
current evidence viewed in conjunction with previous evidence may
strongly support a particular hypothesis. The consistency constraint
requires that different visibility sets from the same source must be
explanable. For example, if prismatic and non-prismatic visibility
sets were observed from the same source, the former can be attributed
to the flat or straight parts of the source and the latter to the
curved parts. Of the four primitive surfaces, only the cylindrical
surface can best account for these observations since it has both
straight and curved parts.
        Test runs using simulated data with Gaussian noise up to
0.3m standard deviation in each dimension and ranges up to about 40m
have been able to correctly identify all the surface types. Table 1
summarises the results from 4 test runs. The best current hypothesis
and its degree of belief are shown after analysing each body of evidence gathered along a V-shaped observer trajectory. Although initial
classifications may be incorrect, in all cases the program begins to
produce correct classifications after the fourth update. Its performance improves with additional updates. In another test run (see
table 2), we used a V-shaped observer trajectory in which the first
straight leg was parallel to the axis of a cylindrical source. Along
this leg, the view-vectors appeared parallel and the most plausible
hypothesis was a planar source. Later, as the observer proceeded
along the second leg in a skewed direction with respect to the axis of
the source, it began to perceive a curved surface. From a global view,
the only possible source which can account consistently for the
behaviour observed is the cylindrical source. The program was able to
take the more sensible global view in this case and invoke one of the

heuristic rules which strongly biased the cylindrical hypothesis. Consequently, it corrected its belief state almost immediately.

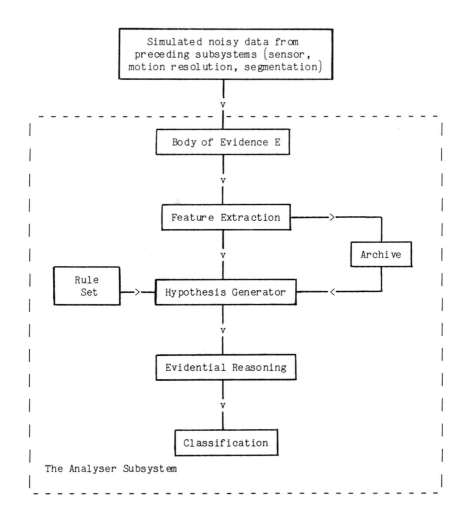

Figure 4. Schematic of Analyser

No. of	Object (surface type)			
updates	Spherical(S)	Cylindrical(C)	Ellipsoidal(E)	Planar(P)
1	S 0.3	S 0.3	C 0.5	P 0.5
2	S 0.4	C 0.48	C 0.69	P 0.69
3	S 0.67	C 0.66	C 0.56	P 0.8
4	S 0.71	C 0.78	E 0.67	P 0.87
5	S 0.74	C 0.86	E 0.86	P 0.93
6	S 0.77	C 0.91	E 0.95	P 0.95

Table 1. Most Plausible Classification

┌─ 2nd leg begins

1	2	3	4	5	6	7	8
P 0.5	P 0.69	P 0.8	P 0.87	P 0.93	C 0.8	C 0.8	C 0.88

Table 2. Results from cylindrical source (special trajectory)

7. Further Work

Further investigation could be carried out in the following areas:

- Off-line test with real sonar data.

- Use of interim results to construct a navigation plan aimed at minimising additional efforts to enable conclusive classification.

- Use of the results from specular analysis for object modelling.

8. Conclusion

Sets of specular sonar reflections considered in isolation are inherently ambiguous, but when analysed in conjunction with previous results can gradually produce correct classification of the surface source. The incremental approach towards resolving ambiguity answers the real-time requirement of a sonar interpreter system.

Acknowledgements

This work was funded by SERC grant GR/C/44730, using facilities provided by the University of Edinburgh.

References

Dempster, A. R.(1968). A generalisation of Bayesian Inference. J. of the Royal Statistical Society, Series B, 30, pp 205-47.

Gordon, J. & Shortliffe, E. H. (1985). A method for managing evidential reasoning in a hierarchical hypothesis space. Artificial Intelligence, 26, no. 3, pp 323-59.

Hallam, J. C. T. (1985a). Intelligent automatic interpretation of active marine sonar. PhD thesis, University of Edinburgh.

Hallam, J. C. T. (1985b). Analysing specular echoes in active acoustic range data. Proceedings of the AISB-85 Conference, Warwick.

Shafer, G. (1976). A mathematical theory of evidence. Princeton: Princeton University Press.

SECOND GENERATION EXPERT SYSTEMS

LUC STEELS
ARTIFICIAL INTELLIGENCE LABORATORY
VRIJE UNIVERSITEIT BRUSSEL
Pleinlaan 2. 1050 Brussels Belgium

Abstract

Second generation expert systems are able to combine heuristic reasoning based on rules, with deep reasoning based on a model of the problem domain. This solves a number of major problems of current expert systems, most importantly the problem of knowledge acquisition: second generation expert systems can learn new rules by examining the results of deep reasoning. The paper outlines the components of second generation expert systems and gives an example.

1. Introduction

In the last decade significant advances in the study of Artificial Intelligence have given rise to a new class of computer programs called expert systems. Expert systems are programs capable of expert level performance in specialised fields. They constitute an important development in computer usage because they make a whole new class of problems amenable to computational treatment.

The scientific, technological and business opportunities caused by this development are enormous. Many existing industrial and governmental organisations are now applying this new technology to their own aims, new businesses have sprung up, and expert systems have formed the subject of substantial national and international research programs all over the world.

What we see emerging today is a substantial jump forward in expert systems technology. The development is substantial because it touches on all aspects of an expert system: The nature of the potential problem domains, the type of reasoning being performed, the explanation capabilities, and most importantly the way knowledge acquisition is performed.

In brief, whereas first generation systems rely purely on heuristic knowledge in the form of rules, second generation systems have an additional component in the form of a deeper model which gives them an understanding of the complete search space over which the heuristics operate. This makes two forms of reasoning possible: (1) the application of heuristic rules in a style similar to the classical expert systems, (2) the generation and examination of a deeper search space following classical search techniques, if there are no heuristics.

A number of fundamental problems of current expert systems are solved using this extra complexity.

+ First generation expert systems are brittle, in the sense that as soon as situations occur which fall outside the scope of the heuristic rules, they are unable to function at all. In such a situation, second generation system fall back on search which is not knowledge-driven and therefore potentially very inefficient. However, because these traditional search techniques can theoretically solve a wider class of problems, there is a graceful degradation of performance instead of an abrupt failure.

+ First generation systems base their explanations purely on a backtrace of the heuristic rules that were needed to find a solution. It is well known however that the path followed to find a solution usually differs from a convincing rational argument why the solution is valuable, particularly if a lot of heuristic knowledge entered into the reasoning process. Because second generation systems have access to a deeper understanding of the search space, they are capable to formulate a deeper and more convincing explanation which goes beyond the mere recall of which rules fired.

+ The most important advantage lies however in knowledge acquisition. Finding heuristic rules has turned out to be extremely difficult. Experts typically take a long time to come up with solid rules, the ruleset seems never complete, is continously changing and shows inconsistencies across experts (and even within the same expert). These inconsistencies are apparently due to different experiences which are the source of heuristic rule discovery. Second generation expert systems constitute a major jump forward in current technology because they exhibit learning behavior in the sense that they are capable to acquire new heuristic rules.

The need for a new generation of expert systems has been felt for quite a while by various authors. An important milestone paper in this respect was Davis (1982) who discussed the strengths and weaknesses of first generation expert systems. But evolutions in expert systems technology are by necessity slow because it takes at least five years to construct a serious system.

Second generation expert systems draw on a lot of recent work in A.I.. One source is the work on qualitative causal reasoning which provides ways to handle deep reasoning (see Bobrow and Hayes (1985) for a recent overview.) Another source is recent work on learning such as reported in the collection put together by Mitchell, Michalski and Carbonell (1984). Recent advances in the design and implementation of knowledge representation systems which have an open-ended set of formalisms and are capable of meta-representation and meta-reasoning are another enabling factor.

The objective of this paper is to outline the components of a second generation expert system and to illustrate briefly how each of them works. The examples are drawn from one important application area, namely expert systems for repair and maintenance of technical systems.

Technical systems, such as trains, computers, airplanes, power plants, or cars, are artefacts constructed to perform a particular function. In contrast to biological or natural systems which formed the domain of most first generation expert systems, they are in principle completely understood. All components are known and the behavior of the whole can theoretically be predicted from the behavior of the parts. Maintaining technical systems involves diagnosing possible failures (or the potential for future failures) and planning and executing a sequence of repairs that will lead again to a functioning system.

The repair and maintenance of technical systems is a skill that relatively few people possess. Skill is needed because technical systems are very complex. An exhaustive search of all possible things that could go wrong is typically out of the question. Also, because not every component is observable, reasoning has to proceed on the basis of weak and very partial information.

The trouble-shooting of an ordinary car is taken here as specific application because many people have intuitions about it. Unfortunately, the exposition of the examples (which have all been implemented) has to be brief. Steels and Van De Velde (1985) contain more details.

2. Components of a second generation expert system

The kernel of an expert system consists of two components: A representational component and a problem solving component. Other components for communicating with the user, constructing explanations, gathering data, etc. are constructed around this kernel and will not be discussed in this paper.

THE REPRESENTATIONAL COMPONENT

The representational component has two subcomponents: A conceptual model and one or more factual models. The conceptual model delineates the basic entities in the universe of discourse, their possible properties and relations, as well as associated information like defaults, ways to compute certain properties, ways to communicate with the user, etc. The factual model contains all the facts, intermediate hypotheses and final conclusions for a specific problem instance using the conceptualisations provided by the conceptual model.

The representational component is typically frame-based. Information is structured in units with various slots that hold information about the concept described by the unit. This information can be in the form of defaults, rules, procedures to compute information, etc. and is inherited by more specific units.

PROBLEM SOLVING COMPONENT

In first generation expert systems, the problem solving component consists solely of a collection of rules. A rule contains conditions (the IF-part) and inferences which can be drawn if the conditions are satisfied in the factual model under investigation (the THEN-part). Rules are typically structured in rule sets and their activation is guided by a control structure which selects what rule to explore in case more than one rule is applicable. Recently there has been a trend to let the components of a rule be richer in structure, so that the various functions of the conditions or the conclusions become explicit. Thus a diagnostic rule might have preconditions, typical symptoms, impossible symptoms, probable symptoms and necessary symptoms. See Clancey(1984) or Breuker and Wielinga (1985) for motivations and more examples. This finer structuring of a rule is also important for learning.

In second generation expert systems there is an additional problem solving component which performs deep reasoning. In comparison to the heuristic rules, this component explores a much larger search space because the primitive operators reflect a more fundamental and deeper description of the domain.

For many application domains a deep model is available. For example the anatomy and internal working of many technical devices is entirely known because it has been designed. Therefore it is possible in principle to perform a thorough investigation. However such an investigation will be virtually impossible if a complex device is involved or if the cost of certain observations is very large. Hence a graceful performance degradation.

THE LEARNING COMPONENT

The discovery of heuristic rules as an outcome of deep reasoning requires a third component, the learning component. It has two important subcomponents: one that extracts rules from deep reasoning (the rule-extractor) and one that incorporates the rules in the existing rule-set (the rule-integrator). Other learning operations can be performed on rule-sets to derive new concepts or optimise the rule-set.

TOOLS

There is a growing number of commercially available tools to construct expert systems (see the overview in Kinnucan, 1985). These tools range from relatively simple expert system shells which support a particular rule formalism (such as the IF/THEN rules of OPS-5, Forgy (1981)), to sophisticated knowledge engineering environments. Second generation expert systems require the more sophisticated class of tools to implement and integrate their various components.

First of all a variety of formalisms needs to be supported: Frame-structured representations to represent the models, rule formalisms to represent the heuristic knowledge, constraints to drive deep reasoning, etc. Moreover it must be possible to represent knowledge ABOUT each of these items, requiring the capacity for meta-representation and meta-reasoning. For example, it must not only be possible to represent and use heuristic rules, but also to represent facts or rules about the rules and reason explicitly over their structure. In addition, it must be possible to represent and reason explicitly over deductions that have been made, new concepts that have been introduced, or questions that have been asked.

Various knowledge representation systems now have the capability to perform these functions. In our own experiments we use the knowledge representation system KRS (Steels, 1984).

KRS is designed to support the definition and manipulation of concepts. Systems based on KRS (and indeed KRS itself) consist of nothing but concepts. Concepts are structured in inheritance hierarchies and have a number of associated concepts (called subjects). There is a graphical interface to browse through networks of concepts and to interactively construct or edit them (cfr. Figure 1).

The construction of a specific application requires the introduction of domain concepts. But KRS also supports the definition and use of formal concepts. These are concepts about knowledge representation although defined and used in the same way as domain concepts. Thus there are formal concepts for keeping information, such as a relation-formalism, or a set-formalism. There are computational concepts to describe algorithms, and concepts defining knowledge representation formalisms like a rule, a logical implication, or a constraint. Control-structures and inheritence schemata are also described explicitly as concepts.

3. The problem solving component

3.1. The task

A causal model consists of a set of properties of components which are causally related in the sense that the value of one property is determined by the values of one or more other properties. Some of these properties are observable, most of them are not or only with difficulty. Causal relations can easily be represented in a network where the nodes represent the properties of the components.

Figure 1 shows a causal network which is part of the system for starting a car. There are three requirements for an engine start. The starter must turn the engine, the two sparkplugs must fire and the starter-transmission must be okay. Each of these has a number of further enabling causes.

The following task will be taken as example application: Given a technical device described as a network of causal relations between properties of components, given a state of the device and an anomalous property, i.e. a property whose observed value differs from the expected value, find an explanation either in terms of malfunctioning components or in terms of external controls that need to be changed.

The task assumes a human (or computer) capable of observing properties and judging whether the property is supposed to be the way it should be based on a functional model.

3.2. Heuristic rules

It is easy to envisage heuristic rules for this task. For example, there might be rules like "if the headlights are not on, check whether they have been turned on", or "if the lights cannot burn, the batteries are not charged". Most user's manuals contain such rules and even non-experts know at least some of them.

3.3. Deep reasoning

Alternatively it is possible to look at the detailed causal network of the car. We will give one example but other deep reasoning mechanisms would work equally well. Deep reasoning can be done using the following principles:

1. If the effect of a property is normal, then there is reason to believe that it is itself normal.

2. If the effect of a property is anomalous, it may itself be anomalous too.

Thus if the engine is not starting and one of its causes is the presence of gas, then this property becomes suspect.

A possible deep reasoning algorithm starts from an anomalous property and investigates the causes of this property until observable properties are arrived at. The user is queried for these properties and if they are anomalous (i.e. different from his expectation), an explanation has been found. If they are normal (i.e. matching with the expectation) then the explanation for the original anomaly lies elsewhere.

When none of the observed properties which ultimately caused the anomalous property were anomalous, the cause of the anomaly must lie somewhere in between. In other words, one of the internal components must be faulty.

The number of faulty components can often be reduced if there are other observables who also were caused by the same properties. Consider for example, the following network which depicts the causes emanating from x, and y.

Y X

  A B C

  D

 E F

X is anomalous and needs to be explained. E, F, B, and C are observable properties and they are all normal. So the explanation why X is anomalous must be because there is a faulty component in between. But if Y is also normal, it can be deduced that its cause, namely D must also be normal, and therefore the only possible explanation for the anomaly of X is that A is anomalous, i.e. the component of which A is a property must be malfunctioning.

Let us consider an example where the network given earlier is examined because the starter is not turning. The other relevant observations are:

Starter = Turning Is Anomalous
Battery = Charged is Normal
Contact = On is Anomalous

Backward examination of the causes of Starter = Turning leads to Starter = Powered. This is not observable so the reasoner descends further in the network. The causes of Starter = powered are Battery = Charged and Contact = On. Battery = Charged is normal so that cannot provide the explanation for the original anomaly. On the other hand, Contact = On is anomalous, therefore an explanation has been found.

3.4. Differences between heuristic rules and deep reasoning

Based on the above discussion the differences between heuristic and deep causal reasoning become clearer. Thus, there could be a heuristic rule that says "when the headlights are not on, check whether they have been turned on". A deep reasoning system would follow the causal connections starting from the headlights and would eventually arrive at the switch to turn them on, but it would possibly check many other things on the way or start wandering around in the causal network in directions that have little to do with the initial problem.

So we see the following differences:

Heuristic rules make shortcuts: intermediate steps are skipped because those steps are unlikely to lead to a quick solution of the problem.

Heuristic reasoning does not refer to the working of the internals of the system but associates a number of easy to make external observations with a plausible conclusion.

A deeper causal model will be able to come to the same conclusion, but would in principle also examine many other things. Some of which might not be easy to answer without extra measuring apparatus.

On the other hand the set of heuristic rules is necessarily incomplete because it would require a rule for every possible failure in the system and thus the power (in terms of efficiency in problem solving) obtained from heuristic rules would be lost.

What we want of course is the best of both: use heuristic rules for common cases to get a quick solution to the problem but fall back on deep reasoning when the case is not covered by heuristic rules. This is precisely what a second generation expert system does. It makes it also possible to extract heuristic rules after a deep reasoning sequence has been done. The next section shows how.

4. The learning component

A deep reasoning sequence potentially investigates many causal connections and queries the user for a lot of observations. To be worthwhile, heuristic rules must do the opposite: They should be as simple as possible, leaving out all the details and all the observations that did not directly contribute to a solution of the problem. Extracting rules from deep reasoning is difficult because it is not obvious which details are irrelevant. Steels and Van De Velde (1985) describe a technique, called rule-learning by PROGRESSIVE REFINEMENT, which addresses this issue.

Initially a new rule makes as much abstraction as possible using circumscriptive reasoning (McCarthy, 1983): Everything which is not mentioned in a rule is supposed to be irrelevant or normal. Later the conditions of a rule are progressively refined to discriminate with a new rule whose conditions overlap but whose conclusions are different. Interestingly enough, this technique is monotonic. A learned rule never becomes invalid, although its applicability is restricted.

We consider learning a particular type of rules (called solution rules) which have primary symptoms, secondary symptoms and corrected properties. The rule becomes active when all its primary symptoms are present. Then the secondary symptoms are checked and when they are present as well, a number of properties are to be corrected. (Other construction procedures are needed for other types of rules although the principles remain the same).

A rule can be extracted from a deep reasoning sequence as follows:

1. The primary-symptoms of the rule are equal to the anomalous property that triggered the deep reasoning sequence.

2. The corrected-properties are equal to the conclusions of the deep reasoning sequence, i.e. the list of properties which deep reasoning deemed ultimately responsible for the anomaly. It is assumed that a change of these properties either directly or indirectly causes the anomaly to disappear.

3. The secondary-symptoms are initially empty.

For example, after the first deep reasoning sequence discussed in the previous section, the following rule can be extracted:
Rule-1
  Primary-symptoms: Not Starter=turning
  Secondary-symptoms: -
  Corrected-properties: Contact=on

Clearly this is an extreme form of abstraction. It assumes that the encountered situation is the only situation that can ever go wrong! The triggering symptom is therefore linked directly with the corrections that worked.

New rules need to be integrated with already existing rules to make sure that they remain mutually exclusive, i.e. no two rules should fire and propose a different solution for the same primary-symptom.

Rule-integration is trivial if the rules are orthogonal, otherwise the following procedure is used:

1. The corrected-properties of the new rule are added as necessary symptoms of the old rules, unless the property is one of the corrected-properties of the old rule.

2. The negation of the corrected-properties of the new rule is added as a secondary symptom of the new rule.

The intuition behind this integration procedure is that symptoms are added from other rules to make sure that the rules remain mutually exclusive. The refinement process is monotonic and works also for rule chaining.

For example, suppose we have a rule which says that the car should be put in parking mode when it does not start:
RULE-2
  primary-symptoms: Not car=starts
  secondary-symptoms: -
  corrected-properties: mode=parking
Suppose there is now a new rule which says that there should be gas put in the car when the car does not start:
RULE-3
  primary-symptoms: Not car=Starts
  secondary-symptoms: -
  corrected-properties: gas=present
then the ruleset after integration looks as follows:
  RULE-2
    primary-symptoms: not Car=Starts
    secondary-symptoms: gas=present
    corrected-properties: mode=parking

  RULE-3
    primary-symptoms: not car=starts
    secondary-symptoms: not gas=present
    corrected-properties: gas=present
The rules now say: if the car does not start and there is gas present, put the car in parking mode. If the car does not start and there is no gas present, make gas be present.

If a new problem is posed to the system, The rules constructed following the above procedure are tried before any deep reasoning is done. If a rule fires because the primary-symptom and the secondary-symptoms have been observed, then the corrected-properties are tested out in the model and it is investigated whether their correction indeed resolves the initial anomaly. If this is the case then the rule is confirmed and no changes need to be made. If not, deep reasoning is started again to perform a more thorough diagnosis. From the result a new rule can then be extracted and incorporated.

FURTHER LEARNING

Although the ruleset obtained through the above construction process will progressively solve more and more problems, it is far from efficient. Rules that partially overlap remain independent, the same conditions will be checked many times over, etc. Therefore other construction procedures are introduced that operate once the initial rulesets have been formed. Here are some example:

+ LEARNING THROUGH RULE COMBINATION

Rules that have structure in common can be combined. For example, if two rules have the same set of corrected-properties, then a new rule may be generated with a combination of primary symptoms and secondary symptoms.

+ LEARNING THROUGH GENERALISATION

Deep reasoning typically takes place over a small part of a complex system. Often there are other portions of the same device (or different devices) which have the same causal structure. By making abstraction of the specific area for which it was discovered, rules get a wider applicability. If the causal structures are not equal but similar, then further learning through adaptation can refine the ruleset acquired elsewhere.

+ LEARNING NEW CONCEPTS

A subset of the necessary symptoms may be common to many rules. In such cases it is possible to introduce a new concept which can be used to formulate an intermediate conclusion. It will be more efficient to first establish this intermediate conclusion, instead of reconsidering all of its components. The new concept can also be used to enrich the model of the device.

+ LEARNING THROUGH RULE-ORDENING

The ruleset needs to be restructured so that rules are ordered. This leads to greater efficiency because symptoms present in more than one rule are not investigated more than once. The ordening itself again depends on experience, so that rules covering situations which are more frequent get priority.

+ GROUPING OF RULES

Another important form of learning is the division of rules in smaller sets and the learning of rules that lead from one set to another set. This division can often be based on the underlying model.

5. Conclusions

A second generation expert system not only uses heuristic rules, but has also a model of the domain so that deeper reasoning is possible if the rules are inadequate. This leads to a graceful performance degradation instead of an abrupt failure if there is no rule covering a particular situation. It also leads to a new way of doing knowledge acquisition by extracting rules from experience in solving a particular problem.

The state of the art in Artificial Intelligence is sufficiently advanced to realise second generation expert systems. Our own experiments in the domain of diagnosis of technical systems have confirmed the feasibility.

ACKNOWLEDGEMENT

Many people at the VUB AI lab, and particularly Walter Van De Velde, have in one way or another contributed to the ideas presented in this paper or to their implementation. The KRS-system is a team effort with Peter Van Damme and Kris Van Marcke as prime implementers of the LISP-machine version used for the experiments reported here. Leo De Wael and Patrick Backx are other members of the team involved in technical expert systems. They have been instrumental in the development of models for deep and heuristic reasoning in this domain. Van De Velde has developed and implemented the learning experiments. This research is partially sponsored by the Belgian Ministry of Scientific Planning.

REFERENCES

Bobrow, D. and P. Hayes (1984) Special Issues On Qualitative Reasoning. In Artificial Intelligence Journal. North-holland Pub. Co.

Bobrow, D. and T. Winograd (1977) KRL, A Knowledge Representation Language. Cognitive Science, Vol 1, 1. Lawrence Erlbaum. New Haven.

Breuker, J. and B. Wielinga (1985)

Clancey, W. (1982) The epistemology of rule-based systems. Artificial Intelligence Journal. North-Holland Pub. Co. Amsterdam.

Davis, R. (1983) Expert Systems: Where Are We And Where Are We Going. The AI Magazine. winter 1983.

Greiner, R. and D. LENAT (1982) RLL, A Representation Language Language. Proceedings Of Aaai-82. Kaufman. Los Angeles.

Michalski, R., J. Carbonell and T. Mitchell. (1984). Machine Learning. An Artificial Intelligence Approach. Springer-Verlag. Berlin.

Steels, L. (1984) The Object-Oriented Knowledge Representation System KRS. In T. O'Shea (ed.) proceedings of ECAI-84. North-Holland Pub. Amsterdam.

Steels, L. And W. Van De Velde (1985) Learning In Second Generation Expert Systems. Chapter 10 In Kowalik (ed.) Knowledge-based Problem Solving. Prentice-Hall, Englewood Cliffs. New Jersey.

MANY SORTED LOGIC = UNSORTED LOGIC + CONTROL?

Anthony G Cohn
Department of Computer Science
University of Warwick
Coventry CV4 7AL
England

Abstract

Many sorted logics can allow an increase in deductive efficiency by eliminating useless branches of the search space. This is achieved by factoring out taxonomic and certain related knowledge out of an axiomatisation and by modifying the inference rules. The purpose of this paper is to discuss the relationship of many sorted logic to unsorted logic. Although it is well known how to transform a many sorted axiomatisation to an unsorted one through a *relativisation* , the relationship of the search spaces and the proofs in the two logics is not well understood. The main aim of this paper is to show how we might attempt to simulate the reduction in the search space achieved in a many sorted logic by specifying certain control constraints on the inference machinery of an unsorted logic.

1.0 Introduction

One technique which has recently been shown (Walther, 1985; Cohn, 1985) to be able to dramatically cut down the search space of a mechanised inference system is the use of a many sorted logic (msl). In a many sorted logic the individuals in the intended interpretation are divided into subsets (called sorts). Moreover the sorts of the arguments of all the non-logical symbols in the language are specified, for few functions are naturally applicable to the entire universe of discourse (equality being perhaps the only obvious exception). The result sort of a function symbol is also given.

Inference rules can be devised for such a logic so that many inferences which are obviously 'pointless' (to the human observer) can easily be detected to be such by the system because functions or predicates are being applied to arguments of inappropriate sorts. Expressions containing such sort violations are said to be "ill sorted". Eg if the predicate PRIME is only defined when its argument is of sort NATURALNUMBER, then PRIME[3.142] can be detected as being unsatisfiable without resort to general inference. Msls thus provide a simple syntactic way of specifying semantic information.

Early investigations into many sorted logic include (Oberschelp, 1962; Herbrand, 1971; Wang, 1952; Schmidt, 1938, 1951; Hailperin, 1957). Several mechanised msls have been proposed or built: eg (Reiter,1981; Minker & Mcskimin, 1977; Walther, 1983; Weyhrauch, 1978; de Champeaux, 1978; Cohn, 1983a, 1983b; Schmidt-Schauss, 1985b).

The purpose of this paper is to provide a brief introduction to many sorted logic and to give an insight into its relationship with ordinary logic. The major question which this paper addresses is "Can many sorted logic be viewed as just a clever implementation of ordinary logic; ie is it just ordinary logic but with special control rules to give a more efficient search space?". Hence the title of this paper: "Many Sorted Logic = Unsorted Logic + Control?".

First we will review many sorted logic and then show how it can be "translated" into ordinary logic. Then we will try to translate the mechanisms and inference procedures of many sorted logic into unsorted logic mechanisms and inferences. The paper is deliberately informal in order to present the ideas without getting lost in a welter of technicalities. In particular, the equivalences between many sorted logic and unsorted logic are demonstrated via examples rather than proved. In some cases the proofs do exist elsewhere; in other cases they do not, though they should not be difficult to produce.

2.0 Technical Preliminaries

We will assume the reader is familiar with the first order predicate calculus, with clausal form and with resolution (Robinson, 1979) . We shall use upper case roman for predicate symbols, lower case roman for function symbols, lower case italic for individual variables. We shall use square brackets [ ] as object language parentheses and the usual logical symbols ($\forall$, $\exists$, $\wedge$, $\vee$, $\rightarrow$, $\neg$). We shall be assuming a clausal based resolution logic throughout, although for notational convenience we shall sometimes write formulae in non clausal form. All formulae are quantifier free with all variables assumed to be universally quantified.

Throughout the paper we will be assuming the use of the set of support restriction (Pirotte, 1974) with the set of support initially containing the clausal form of the negated formulae to be proved.

3.0 A Brief Description of Many Sorted Logic

There have been many formulations of many sorted logic, varying in expressive power and the amount of sortal information which may be represented specially. In this section we shall briefly describe a very simple but perhaps the most common formulation of many sorted logic. This is essentially the logic to be found in, for example, (Walther, 1983).

Although it is important that a logic has a formal specification, semantics and inference procedure and possesses proofs of soundness and completeness (it is to be lamented that few many sorted logics in the AI literature are so rigorously defined), our presentation here need only be informal.

As already mentioned, the main difference between a many sorted logic and an ordinary logic is that the universe of discourse is divided into subsets, called *sorts*. These sorts need not be disjoint and in general form a partial order, ordered by the set inclusion relation. We will write $\tau 1 \subset \tau 2$ when the sort $\tau 1$ is a *subsort* of $\tau 2$. Note that $\subset$ is transitive. If $\exists \, \tau 3 \neq \perp$ s.t. $\tau 3 \subset \tau 1$ and $\tau 3 \subset \tau 2$ then $\tau 1$ and $\tau 2$ are *compatible*.

Predicate symbols and functions symbols are only defined on particular argument sorts. We will use the syntax

type $\alpha(\tau 1, ..., \tau 2)$ **type** $\beta(\tau 1, ..., \tau 2)$: τ

to indicate that the predicate symbol α and the function symbol β are only defined when their arguments are of sort $\tau 1, ..., \tau 2$ respectively and to indicate that the result sort of a term $\beta[...]$ is τ. The sort τ of a constant β is given by the notation:

type β: τ

Variables also have a sort associated with them. We shall indicate the sort of a variable α with a declaration of the form

var α: τ

This notation is equivalent to the practice of subscripting quantifiers with sort symbols[1].

The effect of the sort machinery is felt primarily in two places. First, formulae must be *well sorted*: the sort of every term must match the sort of its argument position. To keep the logic simple, match will mean "be a subsort of". Secondly, substitutions performed during unification must also obey certain sort constraints. As is usual, we will insist that the sorts of two variables being unified must be compatible and the sort of a non variable term must be a subsort of the variable it is being substituted for.

<u>4.0 The Relationship of Many Sorted Logic to Standard Logic</u>

A standard technique to relate a many sorted logic to an unsorted logic is to give rules to translate a many sorted axiomatisation into[2] an unsorted axiomatisation. We will call the unsorted translation of a many sorted axiomatisation **A,** its *relativisation*, denoted by **A** . The relativisation of a many sorted formula **C** is

$$[\tau1[x1] \land ... \land \tau n[xn]] \rightarrow C$$

where the free variables of **C** are $x1$,...,xn and $\tau1$,..., τn are their respective sorts.

It is also necessary to include a set of sort axioms in the relativisation which encode the sort structure and the information concerning the sortal behaviour of all the non logical symbols. We will denote the sort axioms for a set of formulae **A** by **A$_S$**

Definition

$C \in$ **A$_S$** iff **C** is not a variant of any other clause in **A$_S$** and is an

instantiation of one of the axiom schemas Σi below.

$\Sigma1)$ $\tau[\alpha]$ where α is a constant symbol of sort τ

$\Sigma2)$ $[\tau1[x1] \land ... \land \tau n[xn]] \rightarrow \tau[\alpha[x1 ,..., xn]]$

where α is a function symbol declared as **type** $\alpha(\tau1,..., \tau n)$: τ

$\Sigma3)$ $\tau1[x] \rightarrow \tau2[x]$ where $\tau1$ and $\tau2$ are sorts such that $\tau1 \subset \tau2$.

Axioms of type $\Sigma1$ and $\Sigma2$ give the sortal behaviour of the non logical symbols. Note that, since sorts are interpreted as non empty sets, it is required that there is a constant symbol of every[3] sort. Axioms of type $\Sigma3$ define the sort structure. Note that **A$_S$** is always finite provided the set of sorts is also finite.

Note how much larger the unsorted axiomatisation is, both because there are more formulae (because of the sort axioms) but also because there are extra literals expressing sortal preconditions on the original formulae. Some of the computational efficiency of many sorted logics comes from this, as is discussed in (Walther, 1985; Cohn, 1985).

It might seem that the sort axioms ($\Sigma1$ - $\Sigma3$) above do not constitute a sufficient translation for all the information expressed by the **type** declarations. In particular one might intuitively expect the following additional axioms.

$\Sigma4)$ $\alpha[x1 ,..., xn] \rightarrow [\tau1[x1] \land ... \land \tau n[xn]]$

where α is a predicate symbol and we have **type** $\alpha(\tau1 ,..., \tau n)$

$\Sigma5)$ $\tau[\alpha[x1 ,..., xn]] \rightarrow [\tau1[x1] \land ... \land \tau n[xn]]$

where α is a function symbol declared as **type** α $(\tau1 ,... \tau n)$: τ

$\Sigma6)$ $\tau1[x] \rightarrow \neg \tau2[x]$ whenever $\tau1$ and $\tau2$ are incompatible.

However these axioms are not needed in order to prove the sort theorem below. We will return to the possible uses of these axioms later.

A many sorted axiomatisation can be related to its relativisation by the *Sort Theorem* . This theorem is most easily stated with the aid of a diagram (adapted from Walther (1983)).

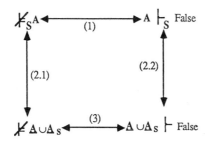

The horizontal connections (1) and (3) represent the soundness and completeness of the many sorted calculus and the unsorted logic respectively. The vertical arrows (2.1) and (2.2) represent the Sort Theorem. (2.1) is the model theoretic part and (2.2) its proof theoretic part.The former states that a set of many sorted clauses is unsatisfiable iff its relativisation is also unsatisfiable. The latter states that a refutation for a set of many sorted clauses exists iff a refutation for its relativisation exists. The Sort Theorem is usually proved by showing the soundness and completeness of each of the logics and then proving (2.1). The commutativity of the diagram then gives the other part of the Sort Theorem "for free". The model theoretic part of the Sort Theorem is usually proved because this is easier. Unfortunately this fails to give us any insights into the relationship between a many sorted proof and an unsorted one. By contrast, a constructive proof of (2.2) might yield some such insights.

5.0 Simulating Many Sorted Logic

5.1 Well Sortedness

A key notion in a many sorted logic is that of a formula being well sorted. Intuitively, this means that, for every formula, the sorts of all the constituent terms match the sorts of their argument positions. In the many sorted logic we are presently considering this means that the sort of every term must be a subsort of its argument position. Formulae which are not well sorted are ignored by the inference machinery thus reducing the search space.

The question is, can we perform inferences in unsorted logic on the relativisation of a formula[4] which have the effect of computing well sortedness?

The simplest case is a ground atom containing only constant symbols. An obvious technique is to attempt to derive a contradiction by resolutions involving the ground atom and the sort axioms alone. Such a contradiction would indicate that the atom was inconsistent with the sort axioms and thus "ill sorted". The sort axioms of type ($\Sigma1 - \Sigma3$) are not sufficient however, since there are no literals involving non logical predicate symbols. We could remedy this however, by adding sort axioms of type $\Sigma4$ above. Consider an example. Suppose we have the following declarations.

    sort S1 $\subset$ S3 **sort** S2 $\subset$ S3
    type c1:S1   **type** c2:S2   **type** c3:S3   **type** Q(S1)
The sort structure can be represented diagramatically thus:

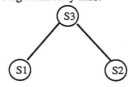

The sort axioms that these declarations induce are

1) $S1[x] \rightarrow S3[x]$ 2) $S2[x] \rightarrow S3[x]$ 3) $S1[c1]$ 4) $S2[c2]$

5) $S3[c3]$ 6) $Q[x] \rightarrow S1[x]$

If the ground atom under consideration is $Q[c2]$ then we can resolve this against (6) to obtain $S1[c2]$. If we also have sort axioms of type $\Sigma6$ then we would have the additional axiom

7) $S1[x] \rightarrow \neg S2[x]$

which would then enable us to quickly derive the desired contradiction.

However if the ground atom is $Q[c3]$ then we no longer can obtain a contradiction but our many sorted logic would regard this as ill sorted because the sort S3 of c3 is a supersort of (ie it is more general than) the sort of the argument place of Q. However it is not surprising that we do not get a contradiction because a possible interpretation is that c3 is interpreted as a member of the set denoted by the sort S1. (The logic in Cohn(1983a, 1983b) would regard $Q[c3]$ as being well sorted for this reason). In order to be able to simulate a definition of well sortedness that makes $Q[c3]$ ill sorted it would seem necessary to take the opposite approach and try and prove well sortedness rather than ill sortedness. Thus, having used (7) to infer $S1[c3]$ we will then negate this before continuing. A refutation would now indicate that $S1[c3]$ is a theorem. However, we fail to find a refutation, indicating that $S1[c3]$ is not well sorted according to the definition we have in mind. Attempting to prove $S1[c2]$ similarly fails, while a proof of $S1[c1]$ succeeds, reflecting the respective ill and well sortedness of $Q[c2]$ and $Q[c1]$.

If the clause which we wish to determine the well sortedness of is not ground then we need to elaborate the technique a little. The formula must be in the form of a relativised many sorted formula - ie each variable must be predicated by a negative characteristic literal. Thus for each variable α in the clause there must be a literal $\neg\tau[\alpha]$ in the clause for some sort τ. Each such characteristic literal must be resolved away against sort axioms of type $\Sigma1$ yielding a set of ground literals to which we may individually apply the above technique (ie we must prove that each top level argument of each atom is of the appropriate sort as defined by axioms of type $\Sigma4$).

This procedure will work for any clause including one containing function symbols of rank greater than zero as we can demonstrate informally by means of an example. We will add the declarations

type $f(S1):S1$ **var** $x1 : S1$ **var** $x2 : S2$

to the declarations in the example above. The additional sort axiom we obtain is

8) $S1[x] \rightarrow S1[f[x]]$

To show that the relativisation

$\neg S1[x1] \vee Q[f[x1]]$

of

$Q[f[x1]]$

is well sorted we first resolve the characteristic literal $\neg S1[x1]$ with (3) to obtain $Q[f[c1]]$ and then resolve this against the appropriate instance of $\Sigma4$, (6) to obtain $S1[f[c1]]$. A proof of $S1[f[c1]]$ can easily be obtained via (8) and (3). Conversely, given the ill sorted formula $Q[f[x2]]$ and its "relativisation" $[\neg S1[x2] \vee Q[f[x2]]]$, we attempt to refute $\neg S1[f[c2]]$ but ultimately fail because we cannot resolve away $\neg S1[c2]$.

It is not difficult to see that these "proofs of well sortedness" as outlined above will always terminate. This follows straightforwardly from the finite number of sort axioms and the use of the set of support restriction which effectively ensures that sort axioms of type $\Sigma2$ can only be used "backwards" to decompose complex terms rather than in an "runaway" forwards manner. It is also not difficult to see that this procedure really is equivalent to the notion of a well sorted formula. Thus we have a decision procedure for "well sortedness" in unsorted logic. The axiom schemas needed are Σ1, Σ2, Σ3, Σ4 and Σ6. The technique may seem to be a little inelegant and unwieldy but it is difficult to see how to do better.

5.2 Unification

In a many sorted logic the unification algorithm is modified so that every substitution has to obey certain sort restrictions. Consider the case where two variables $x1$ and $x2$ are being unified, and their sorts are τ1 and τ2 respectively. τ1 and τ2 must be compatible otherwise the unification fails. If τ1 ⊂ τ2 then we can substitute $x1/x2$ and similarly if τ2 ⊂ τ1 . Otherwise we must introduce a new variable $x3$ of sort τ3 = τ1 ∩ τ2 and make two substitutions: $x3/x1$ and $x3/x2$. If a constant or functional term is being substituted for a variable then the unification succeeds provided the sort of the former matches the sort of the latter. As with well sortedness, many sorted logics differ as to whether the sort of the former must be a subsort of the latter or whether the two sorts must merely not be disjoint.

These restrictions act as a pruning mechanism to restrict the search space of a many sorted logic in a very effective manner. The question we now ask is whether we can simulate this pruning mechanism in an unsorted logic?

To simulate the restriction when unifying two variables, the basic mechanism we shall employ is to check whether any newly generated clause is logically implied by the sort axioms of type Σ6 which express the disjointness of incompatible sorts. If it is so subsumed then the clause can be deleted. The following example shows how a resolvent can be deleted because it is subsumed by a disjointness axiom.

Consider the many sorted axiomatisation:

sort S1 ⊂ S4 **sort** S2 ⊂ S4   **sort** S3 ⊂ S1   **sort** S3 ⊂ S2
var $x1$: S1   **var** $x2$: S2   **var** $x3$: S3   **type** P(S4)   **type** R(S1)
[P[$x1$] ∨ R[$x1$]]   ¬P[$x2$]

The sort structure can be represented diagramatically thus:

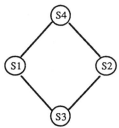

The two clauses resolve to give the clause R[$x3$]. Now consider the relativisation:

1) ¬S1[$x1$] ∨ P[$x1$] ∨ R[$x1$]   2) ¬S2[$x2$] ∨ ¬P[$x2$]
3) S3[x] → S1[x]   4) S3[x] → S2[x]
5) S1[c1]   6) S2[c2]
7) S3[c3]   8) S4[c4]
9) S1[x] → S4[x]   10) S2[x] → S4[x]
11) P[x] → S4[x]   12) R[x] → S1[x]

We can resolve (1) and (2) to obtain
¬S1[x] ∨ ¬S2[x] ∨ R[x].

Resolving with (3) and (4) gives us the clause

$$S3[x] \rightarrow R[x]$$

which is the relativisation of the previous many sorted resolvent.

However if S1 and S2 are disjoint (ie if sort S3 does not exist) then a many sorted logic will refuse to make any inference from the two many sorted clauses. Again, consider the relativisation.

1) $\neg S1[x1] \lor P[x1] \lor R[x1]$ 2) $S1[c1]$
3) $S2[c2]$ 4) $S4[c4]$
5) $S1[x] \rightarrow S4[x]$ 6) $S2[x] \rightarrow S4[x]$
7) $S1[x] \rightarrow \neg S2[x]$ 8) $P[x] \rightarrow S4[x]$
9) $R[x] \rightarrow S1[x]$

We can resolve (1) and (2) to obtain

$$\neg S1[x] \lor \neg S2[x] \lor R[x]$$

However further inference is futile because we can never resolve both $\neg S1[x]$ and $\neg S2[x]$ away. This can be detected immediately by noticing that the resolvent of (1) and (2) is subsumed by the instance of $\Sigma 6$, (7).

The subsumption technique just described is however not appropriate when the unification involves substituting a non variable term for a variable. For example, $\neg P[c2]$ cannot be resolved with the many sorted clause $P[x1] \lor R[x1]$ when S1 and S2 are incompatible because c2 does not unify with $x1$. The relativisation of $\neg P[c2]$ is just itself. Resolving this against (1) gives $\neg S1[c2] \lor R[c2]$.

How can we make the unsorted inference machine realise quickly that this is "ill sorted" and not waste time trying to find a refutation of R[c2]? Obviously we must insist that instantiated negative characteristic literals (ie negative characteristic literals whose top level argument is not a variable) must be always be chosen as top priority literals for resolving away. Ie we must prove that an instantiated variable is of the correct sort by resolving against a sort axioms of type $\Sigma 1 - \Sigma 3$. In the current example no such inference is possible and therefore the search space is immediately pruned as required.

In summary therefore, the control we must impose on the inference engine of an unsorted logic in order to simulate the unification check of a many sorted logic is of two types: a subsumption check and an ordering on the selection of literals for resolution; if a clause is subsumed by a sort axiom of type $\Sigma 6$ then the clause should be deleted; secondly, if a clause ever contains a negative "sort literal" predicating a non variable then it must be resolved away against a sort axiom of type $\Sigma 1 - \Sigma 3$ as appropriate. Negative "sort literals" predicating variables may only ever be selected for resolution if there are no other literals in the clause. Resolving such literals against sort axioms of type $\Sigma 1$ or $\Sigma 2$ simply generates objects of the appropriate "sort" as instantiations for the variable in question. As Frisch (1985) has observed, one of the advantages of a many sorted logic is that variables are not instantiated unless absolutely necessary. The proof is kept at a more general level than generally the case in an unsorted logic.

6.0 Final Remarks

Some discussion concerning the inclusion and use of sort axioms of type $\Sigma 6$ is in order. In effect, these assert that incompatible sorts are disjoint - ie their interpretations are non intersecting sets. This seems to be a stronger assumption than is warranted by the partial ordering of the sort structure. However we never use these axioms as part of the proof but merely to prune the search space by using them in a subsumption check and in the well sortedness check. Thus a proof produced by the system will not have relied on the axiom expressing the disjointness of incompatible sorts although we will have used the fact to help us find the proof in a shorter time owing to the pruning of the search space. Moreover if a formula has an interpretation where incompatible sorts are given interpretations which intersect, then it is also satisfiable by an interpretation in which their interpretations do not intersect.

It is also worth pointing out that this appears to be another case where adding knowledge (the disjointness axioms of axiom schema $\Sigma 6$) can decrease the combinatorial explosion rather than increase it (cf Waltz's experience in adding knowledge about shadows to his linelabelling program (Waltz, 1972)).

Some care is in fact required when formulating the set of sort axioms schemas. It might seem very tempting to add the schemas

$\Sigma 7$) $\tau 1[x] \lor ... \lor \tau n[x]$ where $\tau 1 ,..., \tau n$ are the set of (maximal) sorts

$\Sigma 8$) $\neg \tau 1[\alpha[x1 ,..., xn]]$

whenever we have **type** $\alpha (...) : \tau 2$ and $\tau 1$ is incompatible with $\tau 1$
in order to express the facts that every individual is of some sort and that functions only every deliver objects of the declared type. However ($\Sigma 1$ - $\Sigma 8$) are inconsistent! To see this consider the following many sorted declarations:
sort S1   **sort** S2   **type** f(S1):S1
The instances of ($\Sigma 1$ - $\Sigma 8$) obtained from these declarations are

1) $S1[x] \rightarrow \neg S2[x]$ 2) $S1[c1]$ 3) $S2[c2]$
4) $\neg S2[f[x]]$ 5) $S1[x] \rightarrow S1[f[x]]$ 6) $S1[f[x]] \rightarrow S1[x]$
7) $S1[x] \lor S2[x]$

If we resolve (1) and (3) together and then successively resolve the result against (6), (7) and (4) then we obtain the null clause. The problem is due mainly to the fact that we are trying to express the fact that f is a partial function but the unsorted calculus interprets every function symbol as a total function and hence the contradiction. Thus the relativisation can only ever approximate to the many sorted axiomatisation. One possible solution to this problem of partial functions might be to add an "error sort" and amend $\Sigma 7$ appropriately.

The relativisation technique is not the only way to translate a many sorted logic into unsorted logic. If we have a very simple many sorted logic, where the sort hierarchy is restricted to a tree structure, then we can gain much of the effect of a many sorted logic by creating a rank one function symbol $\tau i'$ for each sort τi, and then replace every term β of sort τn by $\tau 1'[\tau 2'[... \tau n'[\beta]...]]$ where $\tau 1,..., \tau n$ is the maximal sequence of sorts such that $\tau n \subset ... \subset \tau 2 \subset \tau 1$. A generalisation of this technique is described in (Bundy, Byrd and Mellish, 1982) who attribute the idea originally to Dahl(1977); their generalisation allows a set of tree structured sort hierarchies and each term has a sort in each of the hierarchies (eg one hierarchy might break up a universe of discourse of all humans by virtue of professions whilst another might simply divide humans into the two sexes).

Providing the sort structure is tree structured this technique provides a very simple way to get much of the computational advantage of a many sorted logic since terms of incompatible sorts will fail to unify because one of the rank one function symbols representing a sort will be different in the two terms. However the technique seems to be rather adhoc: what do these function symbols mean? A particular term will still denote the same individual in an interpretation, so the rank one function symbols representing sorts can only be interpreted as the identity function; their sole purpose is syntactic - to prevent the unification of certain terms. Moreover, given any depth of hierarchy, formulae will be almost unreadable because terms will be very deeply nested. Of course this technique does not provide any obvious way to check the "well sortedness" of a formula.

Finally, we return to our original question: is Many Sorted Logic = Unsorted Logic + Control? The sort theorem tells us that anything we can prove in msl can be relativised and proved in unsorted logic as well. However the msl will enable us to find a proof much quicker. We have sketched some techniques which would allow the usnsorted inference machine to produce much the same search space as the msl although of course in the msl the well sortedness check and unification checks can be specially coded rather than computed via unwieldy inference chains. Moreover, the proofs themselves are shorter in the msl because we never have to prove that terms are of the right sort as we do in the unsorted logic where we have to resolve away the additional characteristic literals in the relativisation of each clause against axioms of type $\Sigma 1$ - $\Sigma 3$.

To conclude: we have sketched a way in which we might change the control mechanism of an unsorted inference machine in order to obtain the effect of a simple many sorted logic. Our treatment has not been rigorous nor have we considered the more complex many sorted logics of, for example, Cohn(1983a, 1983b) and Schmidt-Schauss(1985b) which allow polymorphic sortal descriptions for the non logical symbols. The former has a number of additional features; for example it allows the sort of a term to be more general than the argument position it occupies and this necessitates not only the introduction of characteristic literals into the many sorted logic but also some additional inference rules (for example we need a rule to resolve characteristic literals predicating the same term so that we can resolve $S1[x\ ]$ against $S2[x\ ]$ even though the predicate names differ. However extending[5] the techniques developed here to such logics would only really be of value if we actually wanted to implement these logics via a specially controlled unsorted inference machine. The purpose of the development here is more as an exercise to explore the relationship between many sorted logic and unsorted logic rather than as a serious proposal that many sorted logics should be implemented in this way, though it might be interesting to design an architecture for an unsorted inference engine which would allow the control rules we have sketched here to be formally represented and acted upon.

One possible use which such an implementation might have concerns the representation of "default sortal knowledge". In a conventional many sorted logic, the sort structure is built into the logic, and although there might be a reason maintenance system (eg Doyle 1979) available in the object language, since the sort axioms are not explicitly represented, default sortal knowledge cannot be represented. If parts of the sort hierarchy need a default operator for their representation then we would have to represent the sort lattice (or at least part of it) explicitly as first order axioms. However, by employing the control rules we have sketched here, some of the computational advantages of a many sorted logic could still be retained.

Acknowledgements

I have had useful discussions with many people including Alan Frisch, Manfred Schmidt-Schauss and Christoph Walther. I am grateful to Bob Kowalski for providing the inspiration to write this paper when he suggested that it might be interesting to see if a many sorted logic could be simulated in unsorted logic by "running" the sort axioms "intelligently". I also wish to thank Felix Hovsepian and an anonymous referee for their comments on a draft of this paper. The financial support of the SERC on grant GR/C/65148 is gratefully acknowledged.

Footnotes

        <1> It is also possible for variables to be sorted implicitly by the sorts of the argument positions they occur in (eg (Cohn, 1983)).

        <2> Given the computational advantages of many sorted logic, rules to translate in the other direction would clearly be very desirable. However this problem is much harder since the sort information has to be extracted and this may not be trivial. It would obviously be desirable to produce an "optimal" many sorted axiomatisation. However it is not immediately obvious how precisely to define optimality or how to test for it. Schmidt-Schauss (1985a) has conducted some investigations on this subject.

        <3> It is only really necessary to have a constant symbol for every minimal sort (ie of every sort $\tau 1$ for which $\neg \exists \tau 2$ s.t. $\tau 2 \subset \tau 1$).

        <4> Relativisations are usually only defined on well sorted formulae but we will ignore this.

        <5> Extending the techniques described here to these more complex msls may not be entirely trivial or even possible in any straightforward way. For example the well sortedness calculation of the logic in (Cohn, 1983a, 1983b) is very complex. I am currently investigating how the ideas in this paper might be extended to other many sorted logics and what effect different or additional inference rules (such as paramodulation) may have. It is also planned to give a formal account of the ideas here and give a proof of correctness for the control regime.

References

Bundy A, Byrd L & Mellish M (1982) Special Purpose, but Domain Independent, Inference Mechanisms, Proc ECAI.

de Champeaux D, (1978), A Theorem Prover Dating a Semantic Network, Proc AISB/GI Conf on AI, Hamburg.

Cohn A G, (1983a) Improving the Expressiveness of Many Sorted Logic," Proc AAAI, Washington DC, Morgan Kaufmann, Los Altos.

Cohn A G (1983b) Mechanising a Particularly Expressive Many Sorted Logic, PhD Thesis, University of Essex.

Cohn A G (1985) On the Solution of Schubert's Steamroller in Many Sorted Logic," Proc IJCAI 9, Morgan Kaufmann, Los Altos.

Dahl V (1977), Un System Deductif d'Interrogation de Banques de Donnes en Espagnol, Technical Report,. Groupe d'Intelligence Artificielle, Univ of Marseille-Luminy.

Doyle J (1979), A Truth Maintenance System, Artificial Intelligence *12 (3)*.

Frisch A M (1985), An Investigation into Inference with Restricted Quantification and a Taxonomic Representation," SIGART Newsletter *91*.

Hailperin T (1957), A Theory of Restricted Quantification II," J Symbolic Logic *22(2)*.

Herbrand J (1971), Logical Writings, Havard University Press.

McSkimin J & Minker J (1977), The Use of a Semantic Network in a Deductive Question Answering System, Proc IJCAI 5, Cambridge.

Oberschelp A (1962), Untersuchungen zur Mehrsortigen Quantorenlogik, Math. Annalen *145* , pp. 297-333.

Pirotte A (1974), Automatic Theorem Proving Based on Resolution, Annual Review *in* Automatic Programming 7.

Reiter R (1981), On the Integrity of Typed First Order Data Bases, *in* Advances in Data Base Theory, Volume 1, ed. H Gallaire, J Minker & J M Nicolas, Plenum Press.

Robinson J A (1979), Logic: Form and Function, Edinburgh University Press.

Schmidt-Schauss M (1985a), Mechanical Generation of sorts in Clause Sets, Interner Bericht, Fachber Informatik, Univ. Kaiserslautern.

Schmidt-Schauss M (1985b), A Many Sorted Calculus with Polymorphic Functions Based on Resolution and Paramodulation, Proc IJCAI 9, Morgan Kaufmann, Los Altos.

Schmidt A (1938), Uber deduktive Theorien mit mehreren Sorten von Grunddingen, Math. Annalen 115.

Schmidt A (1951), Die Zulassigkeit der Behandlung Mehrsortiger Theorien Mittels der Ublichen Einsortigen Pradikatenlogik, Math Annalen *123*.

Walther Ch (1983), A Many Sorted Calculus Based on Resolution and Paramodulation, Proc IJCAI 8, Morgan Kaufmann, Los Altos.

Walther Ch (1985), A Mechanical Solution of Schubert's Steamroller by Many Sorted Resolution, Artificial Intelligence 26.

Waltz D (1972), Understanding Line Drawings of Scenes with Shadows, *in* The Psychology of Computer Vision, ed Winston P, McGraw Hill, New York.

Wang H(1952), Logic of Many Sorted Theories, J Symbolic Logic *17(2)*.

Weyhrauch R (1978), Lecture Notes for a Summer School, Istituto di Elaborazione dell'Informazione, Pisa.

SPACES - A SYSTEM FOR THE REPRESENTATION OF
COMMONSENSE KNOWLEDGE ABOUT SPACE FOR DESIGN

Sue Green
CAD Centre, University of Strathclyde,
131 Rottenrow, Glasgow.

Abstract

In the design of spatial arrangements, a great deal of
commonsense awareness and understanding of space is used.
However, most computer based approaches supporting this type
of design focus on the geometric aspects of an arrangement.
The aim of the work presented in this paper is to explore the
possibilities for representing and manipulating commonsense
spatial knowledge for arrangement design. The paper
outlines a calculus for describing arrangements and describes
and illustrates a system called SPACES which implements the
calculus.

1. Introduction

Computer Aided Design (CAD) provides the designer with
the opportunity to build descriptions of hypothetical
solutions to design problems. These descriptions may be
used for many processes during design, such as analysis,
production of detailed drawings and production planning.
One area in which the computer can play a major role during
design is that of defining the "space taking" aspects of that
object. Many systems, (1,2), have been developed which
allow the creation of a geometric model of an object during
the design process. A geometric model provides a specific
definition of the geometry of the object, with the system
acting primarily as a sophisticated draughting aid and data
manager (3). The system has no knowledge of the real-world
objects that are being represented by the geometric model,
and cannot use the relationships between them or the
additional functional, production or parts information which
is a natural specification of the user's problem and method
of working.
Techniques for representing knowledge about objects
which allow the integration of graphical and textual
descriptions have been investigated (4). The MOLE system
implements the link between a drawing of a building and a
textual description of it. Other work (5) which
investigates the representation and use for reasoning about
topological relationships, geometric entities and attributes
of building, allows general statements about the components
of a building (rooms), and relationships among them, to be
made. Specific statements about the object under design can
also be represented, and reasoning about those objects takes
place to allow help to be given during the design process.
Bierre (6) has described knowledge representation as the
problem of mapping from the external world to a discrete
symbol system inside the computer. Very often, facts

pertinent to a specialised domain may be represented without referring to commonsense world knowledge; but the symbol system employed to perform the task does not allow the implications of those facts to be understood.   A representation of commonsense world knowledge is needed as a basis on which to build the more specialised knowledge. Lenet et al (7) is building a large knowledge base of real world facts, heuristics and reasoning so that by having commonsense knowledge, the system can better acquire additional knowledge, and solve problems that cannot be solved by existing expert systems.

Any object which is being designed has associated with it (at least in the mind of the designer) knowledge which may generally be regarded as commonsense.   In the case of spatial layout design, this includes knowledge about the relationships which exist between the objects in terms of their relative positions, their functions, and other attributes.   Without this "commonsense spatial knowledge" other domain knowledge will not be able to be represented, because the concepts necessary to express the domain knowledge do not exist for the computer.

This paper presents a method of representing commonsense spatial knowledge for design.   The entities and relationships which are used in this knowledge will be described and examples of their use given.   A system called SPACES provides operators to create a spatial layout in terms of these basic components.   The use of commonsense knowledge for the design task will be discussed.

2. Commonsense Spatial Knowledge

A major problem in building a system for commonsense spatial knowledge is to find a suitable representation which describes the scope of the problem area with adequate richness.   It is therefore important that the way in which the knowledge will be used is defined to provide limits to the scope.

2.1 Purpose of the Knowledge

In this work the aim of establishing the body of commonsense spatial knowledge is to allow a commonsense spatial description of an object to be represented within a CAD system.   Commonsense spatial knowledge is used in the early stages of design where some constraints are expressed in non-numerical terms, and decisions are reached about the arrangement of blocks of space before their precise dimensions have been established.   Throughout the design process, many spatial constraints are expressed not as a series of geometric parameters, but in terms of objects and the relationships between them.

Criteria influencing the definition of a body of commonsense spatial knowledge have been:
* basic entities and relationships which designers might use to describe a spatial layout should be available;
* the entities and relationships must be able to be manipulated to allow construction of a model of an

object by the designer.   Knowledge about the changes
which occur to the entities and relationships when a
spatial arrangement is modified must be available in
the system;
* the definitions used should not rely on points, lines
  or shapes defined by Euclidean co-ordinate space –
  i.e. a non-geometric definition of elements for
  spatial arrangement description is required.
A commonsense spatial model may be used throughout the
design process to allow:
* the evaluation of constraints contained in the
  specification with respect to the partial or full
  design solution;
* a numerically uncertain model of the object to be
  represented;
* design expertise to be used to advise the designer
  about how to improve the design.

2.2 A Calculus for Commonsense Spatial Knowledge

It was decided that the problem should be approached by
defining a calculus which is independent from a geometric
description of space.   The calculus defines a set of
primitive entities, attributes used to describe them more
fully and relationships which may exist between them.   The
type of entities are spaces with attributes such as
boundaries and area, boundaries with attributes such as
length and orientation, and relationships such as next-to and
colinear.

Each entity has a set of attributes which are necessary
to define it.   For example, a space is defined as a set of
points [P] (infinite) which are inside a set of boundaries
[B], where [B] is a closed set.   A boundary is a straight
line which connects two endpoints, p1 and p2.   Relationships
such as closed and inside are defined independently from
entity definitions, so that circular arguments do not occur.

Other relationships and attributes are defined in terms
of each other.   For example, the relationship next-to
between two spaces is defined by saying:
>   A is next-to B
>   if there is a boundary of A
>   and a boundary of B
>   and the two boundaries are colinear
>   and A is outside B

or
>   A is next-to B
>   if B is next-to A

At the lowest level in the definitions, the relationships are
defined in terms of whether one set of points is a member of
another set.   For example:
>   space A is inside space B
>   if [pA] is the point set of A
>   and [pB] is the point set of B
>   and all the members of [pA] are also members of [pB].

2.3 Construction Operators

The design process is one of taking a specification and

building an object description.   A set of operators are
necessary to allow a designer to define a spatial arrangement
in terms of the elements of the commonsense spatial knowledge
defined by the calculus.   These are called "construction"
operators.   A designer might require operators to:
  * create a space or boundary
  * divide a space
  * place a space or boundary
  * move a space or boundary
  * join two spaces
  * remove a boundary.
A construction operator causes a change to the
description of the object.   The result of using an operator
is to initiate the assertion of new entities and to infer
relationships among them such that the arrangement remains
consistent.   For example, the arrangement illustrated below
in (a),

            (a)   (b)
                        Figure 1

can be represented by the fact that space A is next to space
B.   If space C is placed between space A and space B, as in
(b), new facts, "A is next to C' and "C is next to B" must be
added to the description and the fact that A is next to B
must be removed.   A full description of the new space C must
also be established.
    The calculus and constructive operators for spatial
arrangements provide a foundation for building commonsense
knowledge of space in a computer aided design system.
However, not all aspects of the calculus are able to be
implemented.   The next sections describe a partial
implementation and evaluations of the calculus in a system
called SPACES.

3. The SPACES System

    The aim of the SPACES system is to implement the
calculus described in 2.2 and to use the system to evaluate:
  * the representation of a model of a design object in
    commonsense terms
  * the representation of the necessary operators
  * the use to which this type of model could be put
    during design
The SPACES system is implemented in Prolog on a SUN
Workstation.

3.1 System Description

    The system provides the user with a set of functions
which allow a spatial arrangement to be constructed (the
construction operators).   The user provides dimensions of an
initial rectangle which is then subdivided into smaller
rectangles following user instructions.   The elements

defined in the system are shown in table 1.

The construction operators which the user has available
are those of creating a space and dividing it.   In addition,
functions which report on the state of the object model are
available to provide any information that the user requires.

entities	relationship	attributes
space	next-to above below left-of right-of	dimensions area boundary subspace
boundary	colinear parallel right-angles	length orientation point sub-boundary
point	coincident	

Table 1

Three assumptions are made in the system which affect
the type of spatial arrangement which may be described in the
SPACES system.   These are:

(i) Spaces are Rectangular

A number of implications result from this assumption.
First, each space has exactly four boundaries which have the
attribute that they are either horizontal or vertical.
Secondly, any dividing boundary must start and finish on the
opposite boundaries of a space to maintain rectangularity.

The rectangular assumption allows the relative
positional relationships above, below, left-of and right-of
to be defined unambiguously, and for only one of them to be
true between any two spaces.   In addition it reduces the
complexity involved in manipulating the model for any
construction operation.

(ii) Subspace Hierarchy

In order to reflect a designer's view of an arrangement
through the design process, all spaces created by the SPACES
system are retained, no matter how much they are subsequently
divided.   A hierarchy has been implemented to structure and
manage the spaces.   When a space is divided, the resulting
spaces are created as subspaces of it.   The form of
hierarchy is fixed; the system decides at what point in the
hierarchy a new space shall be placed.   However, the
hierarchy has been chosen so that it is not intrusive to the
designer and reflects the order of division of the enveloping
space.

(iii) Use of Numerical Values

Minimum use is made of numerical attributes of the
objects in SPACES, the emphasis in this representation being
on the non-numerical attributes.   In the SPACES system the

user provides dimensions for the rectangle which envelops the arrangement, after which no further input of actual size is required, and the user states the position of a division as a proportion of the size of the space being divided.   The system calculates the dimensions of all subsequently created spaces but stores the position of boundary intersections as proportions of the boundary lengths.   In this way there is minimal use and representation of geometry.

3.2 Representation of Knowledge within the System

The SPACES system has three main components:
* a set of definitions for the entities, attributes and relationships which are within the system;
* a set of predicates which act as operators to allow the user to create and modify a model of the spatial arrangement;
* a "database" which holds statements which form the model of the spatial arrangement.

3.2.1 Entity, attribute and relationship definitions

Three entities are defined within the system:
spaces, boundaries, points.
Sets of attributes which more fully describe these entities, and relationships which may exist between them are also defined.   The entity definitions are stored in atomic clauses such as
class (space),
class (boundary),
attrib (space, boundary),
attrib (boundary, length),
rel (space, next-to),
rel (boundary, right-angles).
These state which entities are valid in the system and which relationships (rel) and attributes (attrib) are valid for each entity class.
Definitions which state the interactions between attributes and relationships allow new instances of them to be inferred.   For example:
pdata (area, space, X,A)
:- pdata (dims, space, X, [L,H]),
A is L*H.
states that if the dimensions of a space X (following the Prolog convention, variables are denoted by capital letters) are L by H, then the area (A) is L*H.   Similarly:
pdata (above, space, X,Y)
:- pdata (below, space, Y,X).
states that if space Y is above space X then X is below space Y.

3.2.2 User Commands

The SPACES system has two types of commands at the user level - those which allow the user to create and modify the model of the spatial arrangement and those which allow information to be displayed about this model.

The construction operators, which create and modify the database, are divided into two parts – the first checks the state of the current arrangement, the second performs the actions necessary to modify the database.

The knowledge about the entities contained in the construction operators is of a different type to that in the definitions (see section 3.2.1). The definitions say which attributes and relationships are valid to describe an entity. Procedural knowledge is used in the construction operators to define how to create or modify a member of a clas of entities, and what the effects of a particular action on the entity will be. It is here that the rectangular and subspace hierarchy assumptions are expressed, and the consequences of those assumptions put into action. For example, in order to modify arrangement (i) to get arrangement (ii) shown below,

arrangement (i)   arrangement (ii)

Figure 2

the user specifies that the whole arrangement is divided with a horizontal line at say two-thirds of the total height. The construction operator first checks the current state of the arrangement and identifies the spaces which are affected. The system then (in this case) creates 4 new rectangular spaces (rectangular assumption), Au, Al, Bu, Bl, establishing their correct dimensions, creates Au and Al subspaces of A, and Bu and Bl subspaces of B (subspace hierarchy assumption), and determines the correct positional relationships between the new spaces. Appropriate boundary and point definitions and relationships are also inferred.

3.2.3 The Database

The database containing facts about the object model consists of two sets of multi-argument atomic predicates. One predicate "data" holds all information about which entities belong to which class. For example:

        data (space, room307).
        data (boundary, wall32).
        data (point, w-32).

The second predicate "pdata" holds the information about the attributes and relationships which exist for the entities belonging to a class. For example:

        pdata (boundary, space, room27, wall32).
        pdata (area, space, room27, 208).
        pdata (dims, space, room27, [4,52]).
        pdata (length, boundary, wall19,24).
        pdata (right-angles, boundary, wall19, wall20).

The same predicate pdata is used here as for the definition of the relationships and attributes so that if a fact may not be found it may be inferred. The mechanisms that Prolog uses to prove any goal must be considered when relationship and attribute definitions are made.

4. Example of Use

An illustration of the type of information the system uses and requires, and the type of model manipulation that the user may perform is now given.   In the example, the user divides the outer rectangle into three horizontal layers, split with a common vertical division.   A written description combined with diagrams is used to illustrate the example.

step (i) – Create an enveloping rectangle with name s1, dimensions 200 by 50 units,

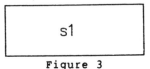

Figure 3

step (ii) – The user asks for facts about the space s1.   The system will provide the following,
        space s1
           boundaries are b1, b2, b3, b4
           dimensions are 200 by 50 units
           area is 10000 units sq

step (iii) – The user asks for facts about the boundary b1. The information provided will be
        boundary b1
           space it was created for : s1
           type of boundary : lower
           length : 200 units
           orientation : horizontal
           relationships with other boundaries :
               right angles with b2
               right angles with b4

step (iv) – The user divides the space s1 using a horizontal division at a position 40% from the lower boundary

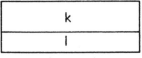

Figure 4

step (v) – Asking for facts about the space k returns the following:
        space K
           boundaries are : kb1, kb2, kb3, kb4
           dimensions are : 200 by 20 units
           area is : 4000 units sq
           relationships with other spaces
               k is above 1
               k is subspace of s1
        s1 now contains the additional information
        subspaces of s1 : k and 1

step (vi) - The user divides space s1 using a horizontal
division at a position 60% from the lower
boundary

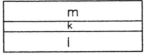

Figure 5

step (vii) - The user divides s1 with a vertical division 30%
from the forward boundary

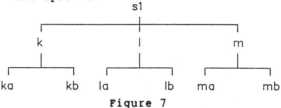

Figure 6

step (viii) - Display the subspace hierarchy starting from
the space s1

```
                          s1
          ┌───────────────┼───────────────┐
          k               l               m
      ┌───┴───┐       ┌───┴───┐       ┌───┴───┐
     ka      kb      la      lb      ma      mb
```

Figure 7

At each construction step (i), (iv), (vi), (vii) the
system has created the necessary data structure to represent
the spatial arrangement using the attributes and
relationships defined, and is able to infer many of the
details of each of the objects. In the example given above
it
* creates names for the new spaces and boundaries
* infers the dimensions of the spaces and length of the
  boundaries which have been created or modified, in
  accordance with numerical value assumptions
* infers the relationships such as "above" and "right
  angles" which are created
* establishes the changes which had to be made to the
  subspace hierarchy, in accordance with the systems
  hierarchy structure, fully described in (8)

The display commands (ii), (iii), (v), (viii), show the
information available about the arrangement that is being
created in the system. The definitions of relationships and
attributes are used by these commands to infer new facts
about the arrangement if they are not already stated.

5. Discussion

The development of the SPACES system is a step towards
producing a system which can act as an intelligent design

assistant.   This will have knowledge about aspects of the
domain in which a design is being carried out, and about the
design process so that it can assist in forming the design
solution, both in terms of how to reach design goals and in
providing information about the design domain.   Central to
these facilities is a good model of the object being designed
which will contain many types of knowledge.   This paper
describes the incorporation of a limited amount of
commonsense knowledge to be used during the design of a
spatial layout.

5.1 Use of Commonsense Spatial Knowledge for Design

(i) What is Commonsense Spatial Knowledge?
      The development of a body of commonsense spatial
knowledge for spatial layout design has highlighted the fact
that "commonsense spatial knowledge" is associated with the
specific domain for which it will be used.   The entities,
their attributes and the relationships between them are not
domain specific.   The operators which act on them however,
make some implicit assumptions about what the user (in this
case a designer of a layout) intends with an action, which
may affect the resulting object description.   For example,
when a designer divides a space, is the intention to slot a
new space between two existing spaces, or to split the
existing space?
      The above example is fundamental in the creation of a
subspace hierarchy.   A "commonsense" hierarchy could not be
agreed upon and it is felt that, ideally, the user should be
able to dictate the criteria by which spaces should be
grouped.   The grouping of individual spaces during the
design process reflects the way in which the designer thinks
about them.   For example, the rooms on one floor of a house
may be required as a special group at one time, while at
others, a grouping of all the rooms which have water running
to them may be required.
      Assumptions are made in the SPACES system where these
issues have arisen, but more investigation is needed to allow
the creation of a model with a form which is close to the
conceptual model of the designer.

(ii) Is a Commonsense Spatial Model Useful?
      Discussions with consulting engineers have indicated
that some level of commonsense knowledge is desirable within
an intelligent CAD system.   They were able to see advantages
in expressing constraints about the spatial arrangement in
commonsense terms.   The SPACES system has been informally
assessed by two designers who accepted the entities used as
the basic elements of knowledge and the flexibility with
which it could be accessed.   They suggested that the system
should be able to represent approximate positions of
boundaries and statements such as "there is an area which
must provide function X and should be near space Z".
Although boundary lengths have a numerical value in SPACES,
the method of representation of intersection position
divorces the size of a space or boundary from its position
relative to other spaces or boundaries.   This
representation, with additional knowledge about how to handle

approximate position, should allow the representation to be extended to handle that type of knowledge.

5.2 Implementation of the Calculus

To simplify the implementation of the calculus, assumptions about the entities in the calculus were made. They allow a reduced number of relationships and attribute definitions to be sufficient for layout design, and simplify the recognition of that state of the arrangement during construction of the layout.

A major problem in the definition of the construction operators is in the recognition of the state of the current arrangement i.e. what it actually looks like. Evaluation of the state is necessary to decide how the spatial hierarchy should be modified, and is required if the model of the spatial arrangement is to be used for a function such as pipe routing. The designer, by using sketches knows exactly the state of the arrangement. The model contained by the system has many relationships expressing a local view, such as space A is above space B, and space B is left-of space C. The space affected by the placement of a new division has to be searched for in the model representation – the human user can see exactly what they are. This problem highlighted the need for the use of "analogous" representations as described by Sloman (9). In this case, a representation which may be used in the same way as a diagram would be ideal. This well demonstrates Sloman's focus on the need for different types of representations.

At present the construction operators hold the knowledge about the changes to attributes of an entity, and changes to relationships between entities which occur due to a modification or development of the spatial layout. This knowledge must be contained as part of the definition of the entities separately from the construction operators. This will allow more generality to be built into the system.

The calculus does not emphasise the numerical values for any attribute. The numerical parameters of the design themselves form a model of an object. The manipulation of this numerical model has been investigated (10), and a body of commonsense numerical knowledge found to be used for the creation and manipulation of the model. Interaction between these two models occurs, which the SPACES system investigates by the use of numerical values for some attributes of the spatial model, for example, lengths of boundaries, dimensions and area of spaces.

6. Conclusion

* The implementation has emphasised the need to include in the representation of the entities not only a declarative description, but also a procedural description which states what happens when a change is made to the spatial arrangement.
* The representation which has been used is satisfactory for much of the reasoning which occurs in design of spatial layout. It allows access to the main

entities in the layout, and allows them to be more
fully described in the system. The representation of
commonsense spatial knowledge for design allows deeper
knowledge of the object to be represented and used in
a system which will act as an intelligent design
assistant.
* Experience has been gained by implementing a system
using commonsense spatial knowledge for spatial
design. The assumptions made simplified the
implementation, but do not affect the generality of
the underlying representation which can be used to
represent the knowledge without including the existing
assumptions. The implementation has highlighted the
need for further investigation of the operators which
act to use the knowledge during the design.

References

(1) Boyse, John W; Gilchrist, Jack E; GMSolid : Interactive
Modelling for Design and Analysis of Solids. In IEEE
Computer Graphics and Applications, Vol 2, no.2, March
1982.
(2) Hillyard, Robin; The Build Group of Solid Modellers.
In IEEE Computer Graphics and Applications, Vol 2, no.2,
March 1982.
(3) Requicha, A.A.G; Voelcker, H.B; Solid Modelling : A
Historical Summary and Contemporary Assessment. In
IEEE Computer Graphics and Applications, Vol 2, no.2,
March 1982.
(4) Szalapaj, P.J; Bijl, A; Knowing Where to Draw the Line.
IFIP WG 5.2, Working Conference on Knowledge Engineering
in Computer-Aided Design, Budapest, 1984.
(5) Gero, John S; Akiner, V. Tuncer; Radford, Antony D;
Whats What and What Where ; Knowledge Engineering in
the Representation of Buildings by Computer.
Proceedings PARC 1983.
(6) Biere, Pierre; The Professors Challenge. In AI
Magazine, Vol 5, no. 4, Winter 1985.
(7) Lenat, Doug; Prakash, Mayanti; Shepherd, Mary; CYC :
Using Commonsense Knowledge to Overcome Brittleness and
Knowledge Acquisition Bottlenecks. In AI Magazine,
Vol 6, no. 4, Winter 1986.
(8) Green, Sue; The Hierarchy Report. Internal Report
ESG/29/TN, CAD Centre, University of Strathclyde, Nov
1985.
(9) Sloman, Aaron; Why We Need Many Knowledge
Representation Formalism In Research and Development in
Expert Systems, ed. M.A. Bramer, 1984.
(10) MacCallum, K.J; Duffy, A; An Expert System for
Preliminary Numerical Design Modelling In Engineering
Software IV. Proceedings of 4th International
Conference, ed. R.A. Adey, June 1985.

BERT - AN EXPERT SYSTEM FOR BRICKWORK DESIGN

J A Bowen, T C Cornick and S P Bull
Departments of Computer Science and Construction Management
University of Reading, Reading, RG6 2AX, England

Abstract

This paper describes an expert system called BERT (Brickwork expERT) which functions in the domain of brickwork design. BERT is one of the first expert systems to involve the use of a graphics interface and a textual knowledge-base. The user provides BERT with a set of drawings which represent a proposed design for the brickwork cladding of a building. BERT examines this proposed design, makes comments on the quality of the design and, where appropriate, makes suggestions for improvement. The knowledge base in BERT is implemented in MUFL, a multiformalism language for building expert systems.

1. Introduction

This paper describes an expert system called BERT (Brickwork expERT) which functions in the domain of brickwork cladding design. As in other areas of building design, although it is appropriate to represent some information in this domain textually, graphical representation is usually more convenient. Thus, since BERT is an interactive design aid, it must allow the user to express himself using graphics where appropriate. BERT, therefore, is one of the first expert systems to involve the use both of a graphics interface and a textual knowledge-base.

Brickwork cladding refers to the use of brick as a medium for providing an external surface coat to a building whose main structural function is performed by a skeleton constructed using some other material, such as reinforced concrete. This contrasts with the more traditional usage of brick in the construction of external walls which perform both a cladding and a structural role. The use of brick purely as a cladding medium requires great care in several detailed aspects, for example in the provision and location of movement joints to cope with thermal expansion. The task is sufficiently difficult that architects usually need to avail of the expertise of specialist brickwork cladding designers. It is this detailed expert design knowledge which is incorporated in BERT.

The user provides BERT with a set of drawings which represent a proposed design for the brickwork cladding of a building. BERT examines this proposed design, makes comments on the quality of the design and, where appropriate, makes suggestions for improvement. The user can then, if he wishes, edit the drawings to take account of BERT's comments and suggestions, before re-submission. This cycle continues until either BERT is unable to find anything wrong with the drawings or the user decides that BERT's comments and suggestions are too pedantic.

BERT comprises three parts (Figure 1): a graphics interface, a textual knowledge base and a program which converts information from graphics files into a form suitable for examination by the program in the knowledge base.

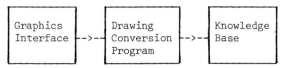

Figure 1: Top-level view of BERT's architecture

The graphics interface, which allows drawings to be input using a mouse
and a menu of pre-defined symbols, is based on an off-the-shelf computer
aided drafting package called AUTOCAD (Autodesk, 1985); the program which
converts information in drawing files into a format suitable for
examination by the knowledge based program is written in C; the knowledge
base contains a group of specialised "consultants" written in MUFL
(Bowen, 1986), a multi-formalism programming language for building expert
systems.
        BERT is being built in conjunction with a major brick
manufacturer. The manufacturer has a number of design offices throughout
the country, which provide design advice to architects on the appropriate
use of the company's products in the construction of brickwork cladding.
The staff who provide the advice may call upon the knowledge of different
specialist consultants, each of whom is concerned with a different aspect
of brickwork. These specialist aspects are as follows:
        * verifying layouts for a brickwork dimensional discipline
        * proposing/verifying movement joint locations
        * verifying the durability and structural aspects of the
          proposed brickwork
        * proposing/verifying elevational layouts for complex
          brickwork elements
        * the design and production of one-off, special shaped brick
          components.
        When BERT is completed, there will be a knowledge-based
consultant corresponding to each of the specialist areas mentioned above.
At the time of writing, however, BERT contains expertise on only two of
these areas, dimensional discipline and movement joint locations.

2. Input to BERT: Graphical Descriptions of Brickwork Cladding

        The input to BERT is a set of elevational drawings, each of
which describes the proposed brickwork cladding for one face of the
building under consideration. Consider, for example, the building whose
plan view is shown in Figure 2. There are sixteen faces to this building,
but of these only fourteen are brick clad, the other two being clad with
another material. The input to BERT would in this case comprise fourteen
drawings, one each for faces 1 to 14 (the plan drawing is not needed).
        Each elevational drawing provides the following types of
information:
        * the outline geometry of the face
        * the position, shape, size and classification of each opening
          in the face
        * the position of vertical and horizontal movement joints
        * the position of other relevant building features,

including downpipes, internal structural framework, parapets and floors

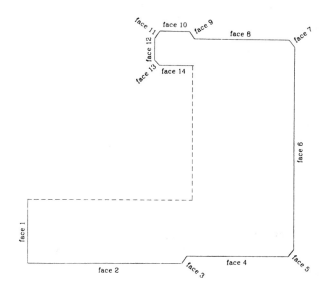

Figure 2: Plan view of the Fulham Building

Consider, for example, the elevation drawing in Figure 3, which shows face 6 of the building whose plan is shown in Figure 2. This drawing shows the face, including the information that the left- and right-hand sides of the face are external edges. (What constitutes an internal and an external edge can be seen from the plan view in Figure 2: the edge between face 5 and face 6, for example, is an external edge; that between face 8 and face 9, for example, is an internal edge.)

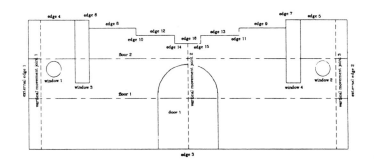

Figure 3: Elevation of face 6 of the Fulham Building

Figure 3 also shows that there are five openings in face 6, a semi-
circular arched doorway, two round windows and two rectangular windows.
There are three vertical movement joints but no horizontal joints. The
only other relevant building features shown are two internal floors; these
floors are cantilevered from beams inside the building: notice that no
supporting columns are shown behind the brick cladding.

3. Output from BERT: Comments and Suggestions

When a set of drawings are submitted to BERT, the drawing files
are transformed into a format suitable for examination by the knowledge-
based program. This program is organised as a collection of consultants,
each of which specialises in one aspect of brickwork cladding. Currently,
there are only two consultants, one for each of the following areas:

* proposing/verifying movement joint locations

* verifying layouts for a brickwork dimensional discipline

Each consultant examines the drawings to see how the proposed
design conforms to its notions of good practice. For example, the
movement joint consultant determines whether there are sufficient movement
joints and whether these are correctly positioned. A consultant comments
on·each aspect of the proposed design which is relevant to its own area of
expertise. These comments can be favourable or unfavourable depending on
whether the particular aspect of the design is deemed to be satisfactory.
If a consultant notices that particular aspects of the design may be
improved, then it makes relevant suggestions.

Consider, for example, the remarks made by the movement joint
consultant on the design of the building face which was shown in Figure 3.
Some of these remarks are shown in Figure 4.

> Face: 6 Name: vertical_joint_1
> Position: 1000 mms right of external_edge_1
>
> Comments:
>   12625 mms left of vertical_joint_2
>   The gap of 12625 mms between vertical_joint_1 and
>   vertical_joint_2 exceeds the maximum permitted
>   separation (12000 mms). A vertical joint is required
>   within this area. However, if a brick type with a
>   smaller coefficient of expansion were selected, this
>   problem would not arise.
> Suggestion:
>   New position: 3150 mms right of external_edge_1
>   Reason:
>   This location is at the middle of a pier.
>   Placing a movement joint at such a position
>   is usually aesthetically pleasing.
>   Reason:
>   No further joints are required to
>   protect adjacent areas of brickwork.

Figure 4: BERT's remarks on vertical joint 1 of face 6.

Consider the remarks shown in Figure 4; these refer to
vertical joint 1 in face 6, which is 1000 mms. from the left hand side of
the face. These remarks include the comment that the distance between
vertical joint 1 and vertical joint 2 exceeds the maximum joint spacing
allowed for the type of brick currently being used: either an extra joint
must be inserted or a brick with a smaller coefficient of expansion should
be used. BERT is programmed to take account of aesthetic factors when
deciding on the exact location for a movement joint and this causes BERT
to suggest that, for reasons of symmetry, the joint should be moved to
the right, to the centre of an adjacent brickwork pier. Before making
this suggestion, BERT will have checked around the corner of the building,
to ensure that this projected move will not introduce problems in face 5
or face 4. Having suggested the move to the middle of the pier for
aesthetic reasons, BERT notes that the new position also has the advantage
of removing the need for an extra joint to protect the area of brickwork
to the right of the joint.

4.   The MUFL Programming Language

Programming languages intended to support the high programmer
productivity required for the prototyping methodology used in building
expert systems (Sheil, 1983) must provide something approaching the
flexibility of expression which is provided by natural language.

MUFL (Bowen, 1986), the language used to implement BERT,
attempts to go some way towards this goal. Although MUFL is a formal
language, and certainly cannot support directly the complete range of
expressive forms used in human communication, it can support a wide range
of formalisms as can be seen in Figure 5. In order to illustrate the
ease with which tokens representing domain-specific concepts can be used
in MUFL, different fonts have been used in Figure 5 to distinguish between
user-defined tokens and MUFL tokens (this font distinction would not, of
course, be present in a MUFL program file). User-defined tokens in
Figure 5 are in roman font and MUFL tokens are underlined. Note that
tokens with an initial capital letter are variables.

```
temperature(kitchen,63).

too_cold(Room) if
temperature(Room,Temperature) and Temperature < 68.

the volume of X is
        width of X * depth of X * height of X if cubic (X).

when too_cold(Room) and heater_in(Room,off)
then replace heater_in(Room,off) by heater_in(Room,on).

repeatedly do (retrieve bag_contains(List) and
               make Item = head of List and
               store on_table(Item) and
               make Newlist = tail of List and
               replace bag_contains(List)
                   by bag_contains(Newlist)  )
until length of Newlist = 2.

to enumerate List do (for all Item in List do output Item).
```

Figure 5: A selection of utterances in MUFL.

MUFL is a multi-formalism programming environment which supports a range of declarative and procedural paradigms, as follows:

* demons, or forward-chaining procedural productions

* backward- and forward-chaining declarative productions

* block-structured imperative programming

* functional programming

The top-level architecture of MUFL is that of a demon-based, or forward-chaining procedural production, language. This means that, like programs written in other forward chaining procedural production languages (Forgy, 1981), the top-level view of a program written in MUFL is that it consists of a set of facts (stored in a Fact Base), which describe an initial state, and a set of demons, which specify the legal transitions between states. A demon is an entity which is continually awaiting an opportunity to "muscle in on" the process of solving a problem. Each demon consists of a condition part and an action part; the conditions describe the kind of situation in which it would be appropriate to per the actions.

The other programming paradigms are supported as follows. The condition part of a demon may invoke backward-chaining through declarative productions; a demon may also be written to perform forward-chaining through declarative productions. The action part of a demon may be a sequence of simple actions or it may involve the use of procedural calls and (possibly nested) looping and conditional constructs like those found in traditional block-structured imperative programming languages. Both the conditions and the actions in demons may evaluate functions; these functions may be pre-defined in MUFL or they may be user-written, either declaratively (i.e., in a pure functional style) or procedurally.

5. Converting Graphical Descriptions into MUFL Facts

When the user describes a proposed design by using a mouse to input a series of drawings, these drawings are stored on disk as binary files. BERT's knowledge, however, is implemented as a set of MUFL demons designed to inspect the Fact Base. The information provided by the user must be copied from the binary drawing files and converted into a text file, in a format suitable for loading into the MUFL Fact Base.

The information in a binary file describes a face as a set of straight lines, rectangles and circles. The drawing conversion program (Figure 1) converts this type of description into a set of MUFL structured facts which describe the face in terms of more meaningful concepts, such as openings, movement joints, floors, brickwork columns and courses. For example, a total of 79 facts are produced by this program to represent the building face drawn in Figure 3. In Figure 6, we present a selection of these facts.

The first fact shown in Figure 6 declares the existence of a horizontal "course" of brickwork which represents, roughly, the bottom half of the face, from the base of the wall to a horizontal line which would pass through the bottom of windows 3 and 4. The "course" starts at a height of zero millimetres above the base of face 6; it comprises two runs of brick, from external edge 1 to the left side of door 1 and from the right side of door 1 to external edge 2. The second fact shown in Figure 6 declares the existence of a vertical "column" of brick which represents the brickwork above and below window 1. The column starts a distance of 1500 millimetres in from the left side of face 6; the "column" is composed of two "cols", one from the base of the wall to the bottom of window 1, the other from the top of window 1 to the top of the wall.

course(6,0,[run(from 0 to 11062, external_edge_1, door_1),
            run(from 16270 to 27375, door_1, external_edge_2)]).

column(6,1500,[col(from 0 to 6000, edge_3, window_1),
               col(from 7200 to 10725, window_1, edge_4)]).

opening(circular, 1500, 6000, 6, window_1).

joint(1000, 10725, 1000, 0, 6, vertical_joint_1).

mid_pier(6, 3150, window_1, window_3).

>Figure 6: A selection of the MUFL facts which describe the
>face drawn in Figure 3.

The third fact shown in Figure 6 declares that a circular window, called window 1, exists in a square whose bottom left hand corner is 1500 millimetres from the left side of face 6 and 6000 millimetres from the bottom of the face. The fourth fact declares the existence of a movement joint, called vertical joint 1, the coordinates of whose end points are (1000,10725) and (1000,0) on face 6. The final fact declares that there is a brickwork pier between windows 1 and 3 and that its middle is 3150 millimetres in from the left side of face 6.

This selection covered just a few of the many different facts, of several different types, which are required to represent the face which is drawn in Figure 3. The sheer size of this body of facts, in all about 4000 characters, and their complexity, means that it would be very difficult for a user to enter them correctly in text form. It is much quicker, and much less likely to introduce errors, as well as being more natural, for the user to describe building faces using graphics; the routine, albeit complex, task of "compiling" graphic representations into text form can be automated.

6. The Movement Joint Consultant

Each of BERT's constituent "consultants" is implemented as a body of demons. To illustrate this, we will consider the movement joint consultant in a little detail.

The movement joint consultant comprises three main groups of demons. Firstly, there is a group of demons whose purpose is to make some overview remarks on the complete set of movement joints in the current design. Next, there is a group of demons which examine, in turn, each vertical movement joint in the current design and make detailed remarks of the type shown in Figure 4. Finally, there is a group of demons which make similarly detailed remarks about each horizontal movement joint.

Let us consider further the task of making detailed remarks on an individual vertical movement joint. This task is broken down into four sub-tasks, each with its own group of specialised demons; these tasks are:

>* detecting the relationship of the joint to neighbouring
> features

     * identifying alternative positions for the joint

     * ranking these alternative positions and choosing the best

     * printing the remarks about the joint

The first group of demons store in the Fact Base a body of facts which
describe important relationships between the current position of the
joint and neighbouring features of the building. The second group of
demons use this information to identify alternative, possibly better,
positions for the joint, and to store facts describing these alternatives
in the Fact Base. The third group of demons examine these suggested
alternatives, ranking them in order of preference and comparing the most
preferred one with the current position, to choose the best overall
position for the joint. The last group of demons print out the remarks
which BERT wishes to make about the joint.

     We present (Figure 7) an example demon from the movement joint
consultant. This demon, which is concerned with the task of identifying
alternative positions for a joint, contributed to the thinking behind the
remarks (Figure 4) made by BERT on vertical joint 1 in the building face
shown in Figure 3.

```
when doing_task identify_posns_for_vertical_joint(Fname,Jname) and
        joint(Jxposn,_,_,_,Fname,Jname) and
        further_joints_required(right:middle,Nxposn) and
        max_allowed_right_movement(Fname,Jname,Rtol) and
        max_allowed_joint_seperation(Sep) and
        Nxposn - Jxposn - Rtol =< Sep
then make Position = Start + Rtol and
        store store_suggestion(Fname,Position,Jname).
```

Figure 7: A demon from the movement joint consultant.

     The demon in Figure 7 is concerned with the case where the
distance between the current position of a joint and a neighbouring joint
to the right is such that further joint(s) are required to protect the
brickwork between these joints. If it is possible to move this joint
far enough to the right to remove the need for further joints, then this
new location is suggested by the demon as an alternative position for the
joint. The demon may be read as follows:

> WHEN you are identifying alternative positions for
> vertical joint Jname which is at a distance Jxposn
> from the left edge of face Fname, and you know
> that further joints are required between this
> joint and its neighbour to the right which is at
> position Nxposn, and you know the maximum distance
> to the right which this joint may be moved, and
> moving the joint this distance would reduce the
> separation between the joint and its neighbour to
> less than the maximum separation allowed THEN
> store this new location as a suggested alternative
> position for the joint.

     Consider how this demon contributed to the thinking behind the
remarks (Figure 4) made by BERT on vertical joint 1 in the building face
shown in Figure 3. It happens that the maximum distance to the right
which this joint may be moved is 2000 millimetres, so the demon in

Figure 7 would have suggested placing the joint at position 3000. As it happens, a further demon in the program would have suggested that the joint be moved to position 3150, that is, at a brick joint near the mid-point of the pier which exists between windows 1 and 3. These suggested positions would then have been compared, by the ranking demons, with each other and with the current position of the joint. Position 3150 would have been favoured both because it is at a pier mid-point and because it removes the need for an extra joint between vertical joint 1 and vertical joint 2.

It is worth observing how the demon in Figure 7 makes use of some of the various programming paradigms supported by MUFL. The action part of the demon involves a user-defined verb, store suggestion. The procedural definition of this verb is shown in Figure 8. There are several features worthy of note in this procedural definition. It involves the use of a rather unusual repetitive construct, a for-loop which iterates through the Fact Base; this is used to access all posn descriptions of this location.

```
to store_suggestion(Fname,Loc,Jname)
    do (store suggested_joint_at(Fname,Loc,Jname) and
            for all posn_description(Fname,Loc,Description) in face base
                do store positional_description(Fname,Loc,Description)  ).

posn_description(Fname,Loc,
    'at the middle of a pier between'(Opening1
                                        and Opening2)  ) if
    mid_pier(Fname,Mid,Opening1,Opening2) and
    closest_brick_joint_position(Fname,Mid,both,Loc).

posn_description(Fname,Loc,
    'overcomes requirement for additional vertical
    movement joints to the right') if
    further_joints_required(right:middle,Nxposn) and
    max_allowed_joint_separation(Sep) and
    Nxposn - Loc =< Sep.

posn_description(Fname,Loc,'at a change of building height') if
    change_of_height(Fname,Loc,Height1,Height2) and
    difference of (Height1 and Height2) >= 1500.

the difference of (H1 and H2) is
        H1 - H2 if H1 > H2
    else H2 - H1.
```

Figure 8: Some MUFL statements which support the demon shown in Figure 7.

Note that the posn descriptions are actually found by backward chaining though a set of declarative productions. Some of these productions are presented in Figure 8; note that the third one involves the evaluation of a function called difference of. This is actually a user-defined function, the definition of which is also presented in Figure 8. So, in this short extract from BERT, there can be found the natural mixed usage of several formalisms: demons, procedures, declarative productions and functions.

7. Conclusions

To achieve high programmer productivity when building expert systems, and to build systems which are acceptable to users and to domain experts, we need to construct programs which process information encoded in a variety of representations. The representations required may be both graphical and textual; a wide range of textual formalisms may be required, encompassing different types of declarative and procedural representation.

We have investigated this problem by building an expert system for brickwork cladding design, a domain where practitioners have long been accustomed to mixing the use of graphical and textual information, and where the textual knowledge covers a broad band of topics, requiring a variety of representations. Our approach has been based on the use of text as the canonical representation medium and on the use of a high level AI programming language which supports a variety of declarative and procedural formalisms.

The development of BERT has been greatly facilitated by the multi-formalism nature of MUFL, the programming language used. Not only has it been easy to "compile" drawings into declarative statements in the language, but the language has been flexible enough to allow us to represent different types of textual domain knowledge in a natural way.

So far, BERT has received favourable comments from members of its intended user community. The main criticism that is levelled concerns its speed of execution. This problem is being addressed on two fronts. Firstly, the speed of the MUFL run-time support system is being improved. Secondly, the production version of BERT will be run on a faster machine - the development version is currently running on an IBM PC/AT but the company for which BERT is being developed will be using minicomputers as their CAD machines.

References

1. Autodesk, (1985), AUTOCAD User Reference, Autodesk, Inc.

2. Bowen J A, (1986), MUFL: A Multi-Formalism Language for Knowledge Engineering Applications, Department of Computer Science, University of Reading, England.

3. Forgy C L, (1981), OPS5 User's Manual, Department of Computer Science, Carnegie-Mellon University, Technical Report No. CMU-CS-81-135.

4. Sheil B, (1983), Power Tools for Programmers, Datamation, pp. 131-144, February.

WHAT <u>IS</u> INFORMATION?*

Tom Stonier
School of Science and Society
University of Bradford
BRADFORD
Yorkshire BD7 1DP

Abstract

This paper is the first in a series of explorations to develop a general theory of information. It focuses on the physical aspects of information -- in particular, it considers information as a property of the universe. Information is <u>not</u> merely a human construct, although like matter and energy, it is perceived by the human senses (and their extensions), then transformed into models of the universe inside the human brain (and its extensions).

A physical system contains information if it exhibits organisation. The information content of physical systems is a function which varies directly with organisation, and inversely with probability and entropy. Equations in physics which contains reference to time and distance, or to some physical constant, refer to some organisational property of the universe, hence to its information content. Energy and information are readily interconvertible. A quantum of light possesses both energy and information. The equation for the "relativistic momentum" of particles is consistent with the hypothesis that there may exist particles (infons) which possess neither mass nor momentum -- instead consist of pure information. Information therefore is not only a property of the universe, but like matter and energy may appear in particulate form.

1. Introduction.

We live in an age of information. Modern economies are largely preoccupied with processing information: The majority of the workforce spends most of its time creating, duplicating, storing, retrieving, dissemination, organising, or applying information. Yet we have no quantitative measures to determine the economic value of these activities. There exists no <u>reliable</u> method for evaluating the economic worth of the output of a teacher, a manager, or a programmer (Stonier 1983).

The machine processing of information via computers is invading virtually all areas of industry and commerce. Not only our economy, but out entire civilisation is undergoing change as information technology begins to dominate the media, our schools and other institutions, and even our homes (Stonier & Conlin 1985).

So far, much of the information processing by computers has involved relatively low levels of information -- information which may consist of either raw data, or information capable of being reduced by means of relatively simple algorithms. With the shift from simple data

---

bases to intelligent knowledge based systems (IKBS), and expert
systems, there has emerged an entirely new set of problems -- and to
help solve them, a new profession -- the knowledge engineer (Stonier
1984).

The knowledge engineer is the technician who is trying to apply
what philosophers have attempted to elucidate for at least two
millenia. The relationship of the knowledge engineer to the
epistemologist may therefore become likened to the relationship between
the mechanical engineer and the physicist.

The present paper is the first in a series of epistemological
explorations of the nature of information, meaning, and intelligence
with a view to creating a general theory of information. Its purpose
here, is to examine the proposition that "information" is as much a
part of the physical universe as is matter and energy, and that like
matter and energy, "information" may be considered a physical entity in
its own right.

Matter and energy is what we interface with physically. It is
what we have come to recognise from earliest childhood on. It must
also have been part of our instinctual heritage from the time of our
earliest proto-human ancestors.

Matter is the ground we walk on, the rocks we throw, the objects
we stub our toes or bang our heads on. Matter is what we manipulate
with our hands.

Energy is what we perceive when we blink in the light or bask in
the sun. Energy can be painful or frightening when we burn our
fingers, are tossed about in a ship, or are jolted by lightning.

Information is more subtle. It's true that it is also part of
our daily experience. Every time we talk, read a newspaper, or watch
television, we are busy absorbing or exchanging information. But we
have always associated information with activities inside ourselves --
inside our heads -- not something that is 'real' the way matter and
energy are.

2. Can information exist outside the human brain?

Information created or accumulated by human beings can be stored
outside the human brain. Our civilisation has created whole
institutions to store information outside our brains: libraries, art
galleries, museums. We say a book contains information. We do not
consider a book to be a human being. Therefore we must concede that
information may exist apart from human beings.

We may argue that a book, and the information contained therein,
is of no use if it is not read by a human being. That is true. But
that does not negate the fact that the information is there, on tap, as
it were. The matter is similar to the old question: "If a tree falls,
and no one is there to hear it, does it produce sound?" The answer is
no if one insists that sound exists only if it causes vibrations in a
human eardrum. The answer is yes if one defines sound as patterns of
compressed air produced by the crashing tree.

The former interpretation is egocentric and obstructs any
intelligent analysis of the world outside. If a tree falls and a bird
nearby hears it and is frightened by it, has the tree not produced

sound? Or does one argue that hearing is a human property and that
animals don't hear? Or suppose there is an instrument which detects
and records the sound, such as a microphone hooked up to a tape
recorder? When that tape is subsequently replayed for human ears, have
we satisfied the criterion that a human ear has detected the crashing
tree? What if that happens only many generations later? Today we
study fossil records of geological ages which passed by long ago: The
Carboniferous period, for example, where we find the remains of giant
fern trees which crashed long before the first hominids appeared to
grace this planet.

The whole idea that a tree does not produce sound unless there is
someone there to hear it, is typical of the kind of egocentric conceit
with which human beings enter into an analysis of the universe. The
question may have been a hot philosophical subject for debate a couple
of centuries ago. It should no longer be of great interest now. To be
consistent, the modern equivalent of the "human ear drum"
interpretation would imply that as soon as we shut off our radio, the
room is no longer filled with radio waves.

The radio illustrates an important point. The electromagnetic
radiation comprising the radio waves carries a lot of information.
However, we cannot perceive that information until we have a detector
-- a radio, and then, and only then, can our eardrums detect the
information. Here is a paradigm for understanding information systems:
information may be stored or communicated in a form not detectable by
humans until a special detector/translator converts the information
into a form both detectable and comprehensible to human beings. A
radio picking up morse code signals or a foreign language broadcast
would provide information in a detectable, but not necessarily in a
comprehensible form.

Thus we must not confuse the detection and/or interpretation of
information with information itself. Patterns of electromagnetic
radiation in the room, or the print on the page contain information
irrespective of whether we turn on our radio or open the book.

3. Can information be processed outside the human brain? -

Computers, like books and gramophone records, can store
information. However, they can also process information. The
information which comes out of a computer may be entirely different
from what went in. At the most primitive level of computation, the
human operator puts in two numbers, let's say "2" and "3", plus the
instruction to add them. The computer will process this information
and come out with "5", a symbol not entered by the human operator. In
this age of the pocket calculator, we are no longer impressed by such a
feat. Not even when the calculator, in a twinkling, gives us the
square root of 14,379. "It is merely following a program" is our
platitudinal explanation. What is overlooked in our anthropocentric
eagerness to avoid the possibility that computers think, is that the
information which went into the computer, is different from what came
out. The computer engaged in information processing. This is very
different from a book or a gramophone which merely regurgitates the
information which went in.

Our perception of the world is the product of our historical
experience. Historically, it was not until we had significant
experience with energy devices, in particular the steam engine, that
the science of thermodynamics appeared. It was the experience with an
energy engine which forced a much clearer definition of the concept
"energy". Similarly, our concept of time did not crystallise until we
had substantial experience with time machines -- mechanical clocks. As
Professor Whitrow has pointed out, most civilisations prior to
post-seventeenth century Western civilisation, tended to regard time in
a rather diffuse manner, and then as cyclic rather than linear
(Whitrow, 1975 pp 11, 21-22). Clocks dissociated time from human
event. Christian Huygens' invention of a successful pendulum clock in
the middle of the seventeenth century provided the world with a device
which could define time in terms of small, even and repetitious units.
Furthermore, for all practical purposes grandfather's clock could go on
ticking for ever. Thus Western culture became permeated with a sense
of time passing, minute by minute, with time exhibiting the properties
of homogeneity and continuity -- a force in its own right.

We are in a parallel historical situation today. Until recently
we have had very little general experience with information machines.
We have now had a new experience: computers -- electronic devices
capable of processing information in a manner which previously could be
accomplished only <u>inside</u> our heads. Gordon Scarrott (1986) has
championed the need for a "science of information" which should
investigate the "natural properties of information such as function,
structure, dynamic behaviour and statistical features ..." Such an
effort should "... lead to a conceptual framework to guide systems
design." Not only does the need of systems designers, computer
scientists, librarians and other specialists lead to an increasing
preoccupation with the technology of information, but our outlook, as a
civilization, is being affected by the advent of machine information
processors. The wider impact of computers on our culture has been
explored with great sensitivity by Sherry Turkle (1984).

4. Biological molecules -

One of the great insights to emerge over the past few decades in
the biological sciences has been the decoding of DNA (deoxyribonucleic
acid). That is, not only has it been possible to establish beyond a
reasonable doubt that DNA can carry the information which is
transmitted from one generation to the next, it has been possible to
decode the manner in which these messages are being communicated. The
DNA story, among other interesting findings, uncovered the fact that
the messages transmitted by this information system are apparently
understood by all forms of extant life on this planet -- bacteria and
sunflowers, mice and men. The amount and the nature of the information
contained in the DNA may vary from one organism to the next, but the
method of coding it into a DNA molecule is the same.

As it has become apparent that the structure of DNA contains
information which can be transmitted, so has it become apparent that
other macromolecules and cellular structures such as RNA (ribosenucleic
acid), structural proteins, and membranes also possess transmissible
information. That is, these substances either can be replicated in the

cell (thereby transferring the information to the next generation of molecules), or may be important in their own growth by acting as templates which mold the future organisation of atoms and molecules.

The non-random distribution of atoms and molecules in living systems, that is, the intricate organisation of matter and energy which makes possible that phenomenon which we call life, is itself a product of the vast store of information contained within the system itself.

4. Inorganic systems –

Is it possible to apply these considerations to simpler, non-living forms of organisation? Let us consider the growth of crystals. Again, parenthetically, the entire chip industry is based on the insight that it is possible to obtain a highly purified form of silicon by letting crystals of silicon 'grow' in the appropriate solutions. The organisation, ie, the spatial arrangement of the atoms in such a crystal, acts as a template for other atoms being added on, resulting in a non-random arrangement -- bringing order out of chaos (Prigogine & Stengers 1985).

If it is beyond a reasonable doubt that DNA molecules contain, and are able to transmit, large amounts of information (sufficient to program a single cell so that it can grow into a human being), and if a crystal of silicon contains sufficient information to create more of itself, is it not reasonable to extend this idea to a broad generalisation: All organised structures contain information. No organised structure can exist without containing some form of information. Further, the addition of information to a system manifests itself by causing a system to become more organised, or reorganised.

Conversely, the best test of a 'no information' state is that the system is so random that it is not possible to make any prediction about its organisation. In a gas without a boundary (all boundaries or containers possess information), there is no pattern in the position of the molecules: knowing the position of ten molecules does not allow one to predict where the eleventh one will be. In contrast, in the regularly defined lattice of a crystal, prediction becomes possible. Knowing the position of only a few atoms or molecules allows one to predict the rest of the structure.

5. Information and prediction –

The predictive element is an important property of systems which contain information. This may be true not only for a physical system such as a crystal, but it may also be true for a system of abstract symbols such as a sequence of numbers: Contrast the sequence
"5, 3, 6, 7, 4, 8, 2"
with the same arranged as
"2, 3, 4, 5, 6, 7, 8"
It would be difficult to answer the question: "Which number is likely to precede the series?" or "Which number is likely to follow the sequence?" in the first instance, but rather obvious in the second.

It may be said axiomatically: <u>If it is possible to produce an algorithm describing a system, then the system exhibits organisation, hence contains information.</u> It is important to emphasize that the conceptualisation of the term "information" in this paper is diametrically opposed to the concept proposed by the early communications engineers. Claude Shannon and Warren Weaver (1964) define information as "a measure of one's freedom of choice .... Thus greater freedom of choice, greater uncertainty, greater information go hand in hand." They therefore equate information to entropy.

If a crystal possesses a lot more information than a gas, it is still low in information content because it is homogeneous. In evaluating the information content of a system, the biological concept of 'differentiation' is helpful. That is, the organisational complexity of a mouse is vastly greater than that of a sponge. A sponge consists simply of two layers of cells so loosely organised that it is possible to squeeze a living sponge through a fine mesh so as to separate the sponge into thousands of individual cells, which then rapidly reaggregate to form a new sponge.

Needless to say, the organisation of a mouse is much too complex to squeeze through a mesh. Biologists consider a mouse to be a much more highly 'differentiated' creature than a sponge. This concept of 'differentiation' is applicable to all systems and it would seem axiomatic that the more highly differentiated a system is, the greater the store of information within it. For these reasons, a simple crystal which exhibits no differentiation, possesses relatively little information.

In contrast, the information contained in a biological molecule such as a DNA molecule must be enormous. Here, using the nucleotide base pairs as the basic unit, one can measure the probability of having any one specific sequence characterising a particular DNA. If information content is directly related to improbability, then the number of possible combinations for a given DNA becomes astronomical. The number of combinations increases still more if, instead of using nucleotide combinations as the basis for information content, one uses the number and types of atoms possible in such a molecule. Considering the fact that atoms, in turn, are made up of nucleons, which themselves are made up of more fundamental particles, it must become apparent that in order to describe the probability of biological systems, it will become necessary to invent new forms of mathematics.

6. An Introduction to Information Physics

The task of information physics is to reinterpret classical physics by introducing information as a parameter in the analysis of phenomena previously described purely in terms of matter and energy. Historically there was a time when "energy" was also not recognised as a separate entity. Heat was a property of matter: Some things felt hot, others cold. Matter could change states. Water could solidify into ice, or vaporise into steam. The idea that these different states reflected variations in the energy content of matter is relatively recent in human thought.

7. Information and Work

"Work" is a process; it is a transient phenomenon. Work cannot be stored as such. Work acting upon a system, upon completion of the process, manifests itself in one of two ways: Either the system exhibits a change in energy content, or it exhibits a change in organisation -- hence information. Usually it is a mixture of both.

8. The relationship between heat and information

To understand the relationship between work and information, we need to clarify the relationship between heat and information. Heat constitutes pure energy acting on matter. The application of heat, by itself, constitutes no input of information. Heat causes molecules or other particles to move more randomly. It causes a crystal to melt -- then vapourises a liquid into gas. At each stage, the system becomes less organised, its structure shows less certainty. The application of heat brings about a randomisation of the universe -- it produces disorder in the universe. The converse, withdrawing heat from a system such as condensing a gas, or freezing a liquid, brings about an increase in organisation. Such cooling processes therefore are associated with an increase in information and a concomitant decrease in entropy: As temperatures approach $0°$ K, the entropy of a system also approaches 0.

In this sense, heat is the antithesis of information.

If heat comprises pure energy (acting on matter) and contains virtually no information, all other forms of energy do: Mechanical energy involves motion, which, in turn, involves distance, time and direction, all three of which, represent information. Sound energy is dependent on the organisation of the medium which propagates it. Chemical energy is dependent on the electronic structures of the atoms and molecules involved as reactants. Osmotic work depends on the organisation of semi-permeable membranes. Electrical energy is dependent on structures which allow non-random charges to build up. Atomic energy relates to the structure of the atom.

The idea that different forms of energy may contain different amounts of information may seem strange at first glance: Energy is energy, and one form may be readily converted into another: Not only is there a great body of experimental and practical experience attesting to the fact that one form of energy may be converted to another, but theory has established the precise formulae for describing (and predicting) such interconversions.

However such an argument is specious: Water is water irrespective of whether it is ice or steam; the one may be converted into the other. But this interconvertibility of water cannot be used as an argument to deny that water may contain different amounts of energy, and that in fact, it is the added energy component which determines its physical state. Similarly with energy. Surely it makes intuitive sense that a beam of coherent light contains more information than a beam of incoherent light of equal energy content.

Engineers have traditionally considered that heat constitutes a form of low grade energy while mechanical energy is a higher form. The information physicist would scrap these imprecise terms and instead analyse the various forms of energy in terms of their information content. That is, just as ice, liquid water, and steam represent matter whose form is determined by the amount of energy contained within it, so may the various forms of energy reflect the nature and amount of information contained within them.

9. The basic propositions of information physics

Without attempting to prove all of them, the following comprise the basic propositions of information physics:

1 The structure of the universe consists of at least three components: matter, energy, and information; information is as intrinsic a part of the universe as is matter and energy.

2 Physical information is related to at least three factors: First, and foremost, it is reflected by organisation. Second, it is a function of improbability. Third, the information content of a system is a function of the amount of work required to create it.

    2A Any system which possesses organisation, either in temporal or in spatial terms, manifest or inherent, contains information. What mass is to the manifestation of matter, and momentum is to energy, organisation is to information.

    2B Information (I) is the reciprocal of Boltzmann's probability function W, and thereby is related to the negative of entropy (S). Changes in entropy measure both changes in probability and changes in organisation. The relation between entropy and information is provided by the equation: $S = k \ln(c/I)$.

    2C Other things being equal, the information content of a system is determined by the amount of work required to produce the information or organisation exhibited by the system.

3 The organisation of the universe involves two kinds of information: structural information which reflects the organisation of matter, and kinetic information which reflects the organisation of energy*.

4 Energy and information are interconvertible. Potential energy and kinetic information are synonymous terms.

5 Heat is a form of energy lacking information. The application of heat to a system requires a further input of information in order to obtain useful work out of the system. The output of work in any process is a function of the mathematical product of energy times information.

6 The increase in entropy associated with energetic processes reflects the degradation of the applied (kinetic) information into heat.

7 All forms of energy other than heat, contain an information component.

8 Physical constants reflect nature's algorithms. They reflect an ordering of physical systems or events. The human perception of that natural order is reflected in how such constants are expressed mathematically.

---

* In the future, we may be able to prove an additional proposition: The greater is the relevant structural information contained by an energy-transducing system (such as a membrane, or a steam engine), the greater is its potential for generating kinetic information.

    The above laws imply that every existing equation describing the
interaction between matter and energy, the relationship between various
forms of energy, or between various forms of matter (e.g. sub-atomic
particles), needs to be re-examined and reinterpreted.
    There are many implications derived from the above. Let us
consider axiom 2B:
The equation $S = k \ln(c/I)$ means that
    $I = ce^{-S/k}$. Its graph is shown in Figure 1.

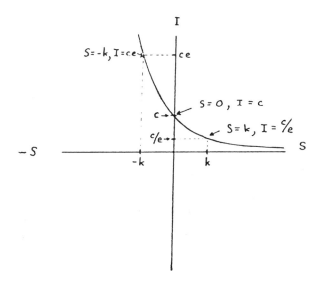

Figure 1. The relationship between information (I) and entropy (S)

    In the light of the above, one would expect the "zero
information/infinite entropy" state to be approached when the system
consists of a plasma of pure fundamental particles containing no
organisation whatsoever (at neither the inter- nor at the
intra-particle level). The "zero information/infinite entropy" state
would be achieved when even the fundamental particles are transformed
(evaporate?) into pure energy. At this point the addition of further
energy would have no further impact on the organisation of matter,
since matter would no longer exist. In other words, the "infinite
entropy" state not only would comprise a zero information state, but
also a zero matter state. One can envision two phenomena in the
universe which could fulfil such a condition: 1) At time zero inside
the big bang, and 2) inside a black hole. The implications for
cosmology will be considered elsewhere.

Shifting our attention from the positive entropy quadrant of Figure 1 to the curve as a whole, note that information always remains positive, and once it crosses over to the negative entropy quadrant, becomes positive very rapidly in an exponential manner. That is, a slight increase in negative entropy (ie, a further decrease in entropy), leads to an enormous increase in information.

This leads to the question: What is negative entropy?

The Third Law of Thermodynamics states that the entropy of a perfect crystal at absolute zero equals zero. Therefore, a system may be said to possess negative entropy if it is more organised than a perfect crystal at $0°K$. Alternatively, negative entropy implies that the system is more improbable than such a perfect crystal at $0°K$.

What might be more improbable than such a crystal? For one thing a perfect crystal at room temperature. Although the matter has not been properly investigated, organic molecules and systems exhibit properties which would be associated with inorganic crystals near absolute zero. First, the covalent bonds and other linkages such as pi electrons stabilise interatomic linkages of highly organised and complex matter into tightly bound structures. That is, at temperatures well above $0°K$, the restriction of the freedom of movement of atoms in an organic molecule is equal to that of an inorganic crystal at $0°K$. This restriction of movement in an organised organic crystal such as a protein molecule accounts for the large changes in entropy upon its disorganisation.

The second phenomenon encountered at $300°K$ in organic systems, which is encountered only near absolute zero in inorganic systems, is superconductivity. Again, the matter has not been properly investigated, but Albert Szent-Györgyi (1968 p 23) has suggested that the function of a molecule such as carotene is to facilitate the movement of electrons with a minimum of energy loss.

Certainly, if one looks at the electronic resonance structures not only of the carotenoids, but also of phenolics, chlorophyll, haemoglobin, membranes, and other such systems, found in abundance in all cells, coupled to the insights biochemists have achieved in elucidating a myriad of metabolic electron transport systems, it would seem highly probable that many organic molecules and systems behave like superconducting systems.

Even more improbable and highly organised than organic molecules and systems are living cells. Returning to Figure 1, as we move along the curve from right to left, as we cross the I-axis, we move from the realm of traditional thermodynamics to the realms of biology and information physics. As we move up the curve in the left quadrant, we trace the evolution of ever more complex and improbable arrangements of matter and energy.

10. Information and electromagnetic radiation

The energy of light is dependent on its wavelength. One measures wavelength in terms of distance. Conversely, one may assess the energy of light in terms of frequency which one measures as pulses per unit time. But any arrangement within space and time implies some pattern of organisation, hence information. Therefore light must contain information.

Information must be a key element in organising the atom, its
nucleus, its sub-nuclear components, and its electronic shell
structure. When light is absorbed by an atom, there is a
reorganisation in its electronic shell as an electron is moved out into
a higher energy level. Such reorganisation implies not only a changed
energy state, but also a changed information state.

If the absorption of light leads to a change in the atom's
information state, then either, light contains information or
alternatively, the energy of light may be converted into information.

In the interactions between electromagnetic radiation and matter,
the photo-electric effect demonstrates that energy may be absorbed in
discrete packets (photons). Similarly, might it not be possible that
the interactions between information, matter and energy, also involves
information as discrete packets?

If a photon contains information then perhaps a photon is not a
fundamental particle after all. Rather, it may be made up of two
components: first, an energy component which might be called an
"energon", and second an "infon". Eddington's descriptive term
"wavicle" refers to the dual nature of light quanta. A wavicle may be
viewed as a combination of energy and information states, with energons
and infons alternately being transformed from one into the other as
part of an oscillating system.

The frequency of an oscillating system such as a musical
instrument producing sound, or an electronic system producing pulses of
electricity, is determined by the resonance of the system. Resonance,
is a function of the organisation of the system -- in other words, of
its structural information content. Thus the frequency of oscillation
reflects an input of information rather than an input of energy.

The frequency of a photon reflects the structural information of
the resonating system which acted as a transmitter. When light acts as
a particle, as in the photoelectric effect, it is the energy component
(the energon) which is responsible for ejecting the electron, although
the energon can act only on "vulnerable" electrons which are part of a
resonance system in tune with the resonance of the infon. When light
acts wave-like, as when producing interference patterns, it is the
information which interacts to produce such patterns. Although energy
and information are readily interconvertible in a quantum, it is the
energy which relates to the particulate nature of light, while the
information is responsible for its wave nature.

11. Infons

Infons are hypothetical particles which consist of only
information. They would not show up in any traditional physical
experiment since such particles would possess neither mass nor energy
-- they would, however, manifest their effect by changes in
organisation.

To explore the interconvertibility of energy and information we might begin by examining the relationship between energy and matter in a moving particle:

1) $E = m_0 c^2 / \sqrt{1 - v^2/c^2}$

If a particle is massless, ie, $m_0 = 0$, then equation (1) implies that unless the particle is travelling at the speed of light (c), its energy must be zero. That is, if $m_0 = 0$:

2) $E = (0)c^2 / \sqrt{1 - v^2/c^2} = 0$

However, if the particle is travelling at the speed of light (v=c), then $v^2/c^2 = 1$.

If $v^2/c^2 = 1$, then E in equation (1) becomes indeterminate, ie:

3) $E = (0)c^2 / \sqrt{1-1} = 0/0$

This means E can have a value, but it cannot be determined by means of equation (1).

A similar argument can be made for "relativistic momentum" (p) which is given by the following equation:

4) $p = m_0 v / \sqrt{1 - v^2/c^2}$

It is apparent, therefore, that a massless particle moving at a speed less than that of light (c), can possess neither energy nor momentum. Yet, in theory, such a particle could exist. Like a photon, it would possess no rest mass; unlike a photon, however, it would not travel with a velocity of c, and therefore possess no momentum either. Nevertheless, it would possess both direction and velocity; therefore it would represent a moving unit consisting of pure information.

Let us explore the properties of such a hypothetical particle further. The linear momentum of a photon, as given in equation (4), may also be expressed as:

5) $p = \dfrac{h\nu}{c}$

where h = Planck's constant
and ν = frequency of the photon

The relationship between frequency (ν) and the wavelength (λ) is given by the equation:

6) $\nu = \dfrac{c}{\lambda}$

or

7) $\dfrac{\nu}{c} = \dfrac{1}{\lambda}$

therefore, by substituting (7) in (5), we obtain

8) $p = \dfrac{h}{\lambda}$

or

9) $\lambda = \dfrac{h}{p}$

Substituting (4) in (9), we obtain:

10) $\lambda = h \div [m_0 v/\sqrt{1 - v^2/c^2}]$

$\qquad = \dfrac{h\sqrt{1 - v^2/c^2}}{m_0 v}$

The same kind of argument made in respect to equations (2-4) holds here. Since both a photon and an infon are massless ($m_0 = 0$), then λ becomes infinite, except when the particle travels at the speed of light ($v = c$), at which point one obtains an indeterminate quantity (0/0).

This leads to two interesting postulates:

1 An infon is a photon whose wavelength has been stretched to infinity.

And conversely,

2 A photon is an infon travelling at the speed of light.

Once as infon is accelerated to the speed of light, it crosses a threshold which allows it to be perceived as having energy. When that does happen, the energy (E) is a function of its frequency ($\mathcal{V}$), ie:

11) $E = h\mathcal{V}$

Conversely, at velocities less than c, the particle exhibits neither energy nor momentum, its apparent wavelength becomes infinite, and its frequency zero -- yet it retains at least two information properties -- velocity and direction.

In other words, at velocities less than c, a quantum of energy becomes converted into a quantum of information.

12) References

Prigogine, I. & Stengers, I. (1985). Order out of Chaos. London: Fontana.

Scarrott, G. (1986). The need for a 'science' of information. J. Inform. Technol., 1 no 2, 33-38.

Shannon, C.E. & Weaver, W. (1964). The Mathematical Theory of Communication. Urbana: University of Illinois Press.

Stonier, T. (1983). The Wealth of Information. London: Thames-Methuen.

Stonier, T. (1984). The knowledge industry. In Expert Systems, ed. R. Forsyth, pp. 211-26. London: Chapman & Hall.

Stonier, T. & Conlin, C. (1985). The Three Cs: Children, Computers, and Communication. Chichester: John Wiley & Sons.

Szent-Györgyi, A. (1968). Bioelectronics. New York: Academic Press.

Turkle, S. (1984). The Second Self: Computers and the Human Spirit. New York: Simon and Schuster.

Whitrow, G.J. (1975). The Nature of Time. Harmondsworth, Mddx: Penguin Books.

EXPERT SYSTEMS: PRACTICAL APPLICATIONS IN A TRADITIONAL
INDUSTRY

R M G Perkin, M Pitt and A E Price
Communications and Control Division, British Coal,
Headquarters Technical Department, Burton-on-Trent,
Staffordshire, England.

Abstract

Well documented examples of practical expert systems are
scarce; this paper describes the progress and success which can be
achieved with expert systems technology in a traditional industry. The
development strategy is outlined, and examples are given of consultative
expert systems: UFEL, a large multi-disciplinary system for predicting
the risk of unusual emissions of methane; SHEARER, a classical fault
diagnosis system for coal cutting equipment; and GATEPLAN, a system for
selecting the best method of roof support for underground roadways. Real
time systems are acknowledged to be considerably more complex, and the
paper describes current progress in building an expert system for the
prediction, detection, location and control of spontaneous combustion of
coal during mining operations. With on line access to a data base
updated in real time from a process monitoring system, this expert system
will combine both algorithmic and heuristic knowledge.

1. Introduction

Headquarters Technical Department (HQTD) at Burton-on-Trent,
Staffordshire, England is responsible for conducting mining research and
development for British Coal, the nationalised industry which operates
all deep mines in the United Kingdom. HQTD has had a team investigating
potential applications of expert systems technology, performing
feasibility studies, and building prototype systems for two years. There
are many areas of application in mining and so far investigations have
concentrated on mine safety, mining engineering and machine breakdown
problems.

The capital investment required for mining is higher than is
often appreciated, and equipment costs at a single coal face will exceed
£3 million. Indeed, it is this concentration of high cost mechanical
equipment operating under difficult conditions which is the spur to many
of the expert systems developments. Other heavy areas of investment are
in the fields of process monitoring and control, with some one hundred
and eighty real time systems installed, with a further forty information
systems installed for mining and production management, linked to the
real time systems.

Two distinct strands of expert systems development are now in
progress:
- consultative systems, built using commercially available expert system
  shells, and attacking applications where benefits have been positively
  identified.
- real time systems, built using lower level tools and designed to
  perform intelligent analysis on data from process monitoring systems.

Consultative systems are, by their very nature, more straightforward to construct, and this paper describes three systems which are in practical use or installed at field test sites. These systems are

UFEL :   a large multi-disciplinary system for predicting the risk of unusually high emissions of methane.

SHEARER :   a classical fault diagnosis system for coal cutting equipment.

GATEPLAN : a system for selecting the best method of roof support for underground roadways.

Real time systems are considerably more complex, and this paper describes current progress in defining and building an expert system for the prediction, detection, location and control of spontaneous combustion of coal during mining operations.

2. Development Strategy

In early 1984, a small team was set up to investigate the potential applications for artificial intelligence (AI) and expert systems in British Coal. Because of the considerable AI effort in academic and specialist research institutes throughout the world, it was decided at an early stage that HQTD should not undertake fundamental research, but apply the new ideas and techniques as they became available. This decision to tackle real industrial problems using available techniques underpins many of the decisions leading to the current strategy.

A comprehensive programme has been set up with three major tasks:

- Collaborative work with other disciplines outside the expert system development team, with the objective of spreading the use of expert system technology.
- Work within our Communications and Control Division to provide real time and embedded systems.
- Liaison with other research programmes outside British Coal.

It is normally accepted that the development of knowledge based systems consumes large resources, and that such systems are characterised by being difficult to build and require the efforts of highly skilled staff. The development team and technical management were convinced that the technology offered significant benefits to the mining industry; how were we to demonstrate these benefits to senior management without committing major resources and scarce skills to an unproven technology?

It was decided to identify a number of modest problems which would be suitable for knowledge based solution, that is problems where the development risk was low, which could be readily built, and which would show benefits in a relatively short time. These systems would be consultative systems based on commercially available software tools. For such systems, the following strategy has been adopted:

- Investigate and purchase a range of software products to form an 'expert system building toolkit'.
- Select and purchase suitable development systems and target systems on which to deliver the expert systems.

- Identify problems which might be amenable to solution by knowledge based techniques, and select those problems which are both feasible and practical.
- Implement a concept proving model and one or more prototypes in collaboration with the domain expert and system users.
- Hand over the system to the domain expert for further development as required.

This strategy has worked well, and is demonstrated by the three consultative systems described later in the paper, together with further systems under active development.

The use of an 'expert system building toolkit' has both advantages and disadvantages. Available tools can be broadly classified into two types: high level, and low level. High level tools can be further classified as: expert system shells, and high level programming language environments. Low level tools can be considered to be procedural programming languages, and fundamental AI languages such as PROLOG and LISP.

The distinction between the two types of high level tool is the provision of an inference engine. While shells may be restrictive (Alvey, 1983) in that they provide a single inference engine and a constrained knowledge representation scheme, we have had considerable success in building practical systems using some of the more flexible products.

Our toolkit contains a range of both shells and low level languages; it does not (yet) contain high level AI environments such as KEE, ART, KnowledgeCraft or object oriented languages such as LOOPS. References to and review descriptions of many of these approaches are given in Hayes-Roth (1985), Genesereth (1985) and Fikes & Kehler (1985). Most of these environments are not only very expensive, but present the user with a rich, possibly bewildering array of tools with which to build systems - including purpose designed inference engines. Reichgelt & van Harmelen (1985) give a valuable guide to the selection of logic and knowledge criteria, although our experience would show that expert system shells are not as restrictive as other workers have found.

For real time systems, we have adopted a different strategy. This technology is much less well advanced, and there are few published, working examples of industrial real time expert systems. A decision was made to adopt the following strategy:
- To identify lower level software tools capable of operating at real time or near real time speed.
- To acquire expertise from the body of academic research.
- To identify problems which could be solved by intelligent analysis of information available in existing real time systems.

This strategy is in operation now, and progress towards our first real time knowledge based system is reported later.

3. Methane Risk Prediction : UFEL

All coal seams contain methane (CH_4) which is released during mining. The emissions from normal coal cutting operations can be predicted using algorithmic techniques, and this method has been in use for some years within British Coal.

However, the problem of predicting if mining operations on a new coal face or in driving a new underground roadway would give rise to an emission of methane well beyond the 'normal' volume has never been successfully addressed. The information needed for the prediction is complex, specialised and extensive. Expertise is required from both geologists and ventilation experts, as well as reference to historical data and case histories which indicate where problem areas may arise. Much of the information could be uncertain and some information may not be available for every site.

This type of application which combines knowledge from several experts is ideal for the expert system approach. The expert system is called UFEL (Unexpected Firedamp Emission Levels), firedamp being the mining term for methane. UFEL was developed in conjunction with Methane Group at HQTD, who provided the domain expertise. UFEL is implemented in the SAGE expert system shell; it is some 6000 lines long, approximating to 700 rules.

The program is based on statistical weightings given to replies from specific questions. From these an overall weighting is derived, which together with production rules is used to give an overall risk assessment.

A consultation with UFEL is a thorough process and can take some 20 minutes, which gives an idea of the level of detailed information involved, and indeed why knowledge of this kind is not available except through a knowledge based system.

UFEL starts by making an assessment of the gassiness of the coal mine being considered. Actual measurements can be used if available, otherwise a prediction is made from the geographical location of the mine (within the UK) or by using coal rank and moisture content.

UFEL asks questions on the type, thickness and proximity of nearby coal seams, type and proximity of nearby competent rock beds, fault information and permeability aspects of the strata above and below the workings. Other questions relate to borehole data, nearby old workings, production factors such as coalcutting methods, face stoppages and previous emission data.

UFEL is an expert system which contains 'deep knowledge', that is it contains a detailed model of the causal mechanisms of unusually high methane emissions (to the extent that these are understood and defined by the domain expert). However, it is perhaps in this area that the limitations imposed by representing knowledge within the constraints of an expert system shell are most apparent. The underlying knowledge of the geological processes is only available to solve one specific problem - that of methane emission risk. The knowledge base can only readily be queried for this purpose, so confining the knowledge to this single application, rather than open to a variety of uses.

One of the important features of UFEL is its use as a teaching or tutoring aid. The user gains valuable knowledge from the questions asked by the system, but as we have discussed, the knowledge representation mechanisms of the SAGE shell provide only a limited query facility and explanation system.

UFEL is successfully installed and in use (August 1986) at one coalfield Area. It is undergoing validation against specific occurrences, and has to date confirmed increased risk factors following three unexpected methane emissions.

Quantifiable benefits are of course what determine the usefulness or otherwise of a system. Provisional estimates indicate that

£2 million of coal production can be lost per year in a single Area through unexpected methane emissions. British Coal operates ten Areas, so the potential cost savings are high indeed.

4. Fault Diagnosis : SHEARER

Fault diagnosis is the classic expert system application. Perhaps the best known is MYCIN (Shortcliffe, 1976) for assisting in the diagnosis and treatment of bacterial blood infections - that is, fault diagnosis in humans.

On a longwall coal face, the coal is cut from the coal seam by a machine called a shearer. The shearer is a very expensive and complex combination of mechanical, hydraulic and electrical systems. If the shearer stops, coal production stops and at a modest production rate of 300 tonnes/hour at £30 per tonne, even short delays are very expensive.

Reducing the time taken to diagnose a fault or breakdown condition on the shearer has the potential to reduce the cost of lost production, and in repair costs if engineering staff with appropriate skills (and replacement parts) are directed to the location. Two types of diagnostic system were considered:
- An embedded system to perform machine health monitoring by the intelligent assessment of trends recorded by embedded transducers.
- A breakdown diagnosis system interrogated by an operator by keying in fault symptoms.

The embedded on-board system is the goal, but the present state of transducer technology and lack of intrinsically safe computer systems (the electronics have to operate in flammable atmospheres) have precluded its development. It is possible to use a computer system installed at the surface, with data acquisition over a communications link, and this is the approach which will be taken for the time being.

SHEARER is a breakdown fault diagnosis system for the Anderson Strathclyde AM500 range of coal cutting machines. SHEARER was developed in conjunction with both design and service staff from the manufacturer, and embodies their expertise together with practical operational experience and field expertise from within British Coal. SHEARER is implemented in the SAVOIR expert system shell; it is some 10000 lines long, approximating to 750 rules (1100 SAVOIR 'items', that is questions, variables, actions). There is extensive explanatory and advisory text.

SHEARER diagnoses both hydraulic and electrical faults, caters for chain hauled and self hauled machines and radio control systems.

The program is based on a fault tree analysis of faults and their underlying causes. This fault tree is traversed by forward chaining from the symptom of the fault to the cause with the extensive use of demons which are fired as soon as a particular set of symptoms is satisfied. Knowledge acquisition took place by repeated discussions with Anderson Strathclyde staff and with British Coal engineering staff.

SHEARER (in common with most other fault diagnosis systems) is a system which contains 'shallow knowledge'. The knowledge base does not contain any understanding of the underlying causes; it simply contains relationships between observed symptoms and known faults. This is not a limitation of the shell but of the knowledge itself, and this

limitation shows most clearly in an explanation mechanism effectively
restricted to a trace of shallow rules.

To overcome this limitation, and the known shortcomings of
such systems as tutoring aids (Clancey & Letsinger, 1981) extensive
amplification, advisory and help text has been added. Although such text
is canned, it provides a positive framework of explanation within which
the rule firing sequence is given meaning.

SHEARER is currently (August 1986) installed and in use at
three British Coal mines, and has been well received by engineering
staff.

5. Roof Support Selection : GATEPLAN

Access to the coal seams from the base of the vertical shafts
which provide entry to a mine is along underground roadways. Typically
some 2.5 metres in height, these roadways are usually supported by steel
arches. As the stresses in the surrounding strata are relieved, this
steelwork supporting the roof is deformed and the floor rises causing
access problems for men, materials and equipment, and a reduction in
ventilation.

British Coal spends some £120 million per year on repairs to
underground roadways, therefore any system which provides better design
of equipment and reduced repair costs has the potential to provide large
savings in cost.

GATEPLAN is an expert system for planning roof support
selection in underground gate roadways (that is, the roadways leading
directly to the face). GATEPLAN is implemented in the SAVOIR expert
system shell; it is some 1600 lines long, approximating to 30 rules (500
SAVOIR 'items').

While GATEPLAN has a smaller knowledge base than the other
applications described, it is interesting in that it uses a combination
of techniques. The system is iterative; it allows repeated consultations
to achieve improvements in design. The system incorporates algorithms
for arithmetic calculations, implemented as Pascal procedures external to
the SAVOIR shell. The system incorporates access to an external database
of case histories, again accessed by Pascal procedures. And GATEPLAN
provides intelligent design decisions.

6. Real Time Systems : HEATINGS

HEATINGS is a real-time expert system to interpret the data
from an underground monitoring system to determine the location of
spontaneous combustion. The systems elicits further data from colliery
staff and presents its results and recommended actions as a display.

The use of expert systems operating in real time is confused.
Although the literature contains a number of references to such
applications, on closer examination these turn out to be demonstration
systems, feasibility studies or simulations. There are of course a
number of examples in the military and defence fields, but in industrial
applications only one commercially available system claimed to operate in
true real time has been identified - PICON, Process Intelligent Control
(Moore, 1986). Some work has come out of the UK Alvey Programme, but
this is as yet unpublished.

Description of Spontaneous Combustion

Spontaneous combustion is the self heating of coal caused by oxidation which takes place wherever coal is exposed to air. The process produces heat, carbon monoxide (CO) and carbon dioxide (CO_2). Under most conditions an equilibrium is reached where all the heat is removed and the carbon monoxide remains at a low level. However, if the heat of oxidation is not removed, then the combustion process speeds up and eventually smouldering or even open fire results. This 'heating' threatens the health and safety of the men and can cause serious damage to the colliery. Many millions of pounds worth of coal reserves may be made unworkable, effectively sterilising large productive areas of the mine.

The control of spontaneous combustion can be split into five distinct areas. Note that the following descriptions are a simplification of the problem statement for the purposes of this paper.

Prevention
The risk is reduced by minimising the flow of air through coal or material containing coal. This requires careful design of roadways and faces together with appropriate precautions during mining operations.

Detection
If a heating does start then it is essential to detect it as soon as possible. The best available form of detection is to measure CO concentrations at selected locations. All faces and roadways are regularly inspected and CO is sampled manually.

Automatic monitoring systems provide alarms in the control room when carbon monoxide levels exceed a specified value. The most widely used environmental monitoring system is the tube bundle system which draws samples of gas from underground and analyses them on the surface. MINOS (Mine Operating System) is British Coal's real time process monitoring and control system which can monitor either discrete underground transducers or the output from a tube bundle system to provide alarms. MDA (Multi Discriminating Alarm) is an algorithmic technique which can filter out temporary changes in CO caused by shot firing or diesel fumes. Detection involves two criteria. The first is the absolute level of CO. Small amounts of CO are produced under normal conditions in mining but high values suggest a heating. The second criterion is the trend. An increasing trend, even at a low absolute value, also suggests a possible heating.

Interpretation
The data from detection (alarms etc) and from other sources is analysed to confirm the presence of a heating and to indicate its approximate location. Appropriate action is then taken to ensure the health and safety of men and to limit possible damage.

Analysis
Determine the precise location of the heating and its source of oxygen. This is a difficult and highly skilled activity.

Control
Reduce the supply of air to the heating location using various techniques such as sealing the pack, building pressure chambers, and injecting nitrogen. If the heating cannot be controlled then the district must be closed down and sealed, with the consequent loss of production, reserves of coal and often coal face equipment.

Lord (1986) and Morris & Atkinson (1986) give recent summaries of the factors underlying spontaneous combustion.

Scope for Expert Systems

Spontaneous combustion becomes a serious mining problem when it causes a heating underground. Computer systems are used with considerable success for the detection of heatings but there is scope for the application of AI techniques. Two specific applications have been identified:
- A real-time expert system to interpret the data from a monitoring system and determine the location of heatings.
- A diagnostic expert system to provide support for the analysis and control of heatings.

These systems will provide both operational and financial benefits. In the first case, heatings will be identified and located more quickly, with a reduced number of false alarms. In the second case, it is possible to use skills and expertise gained from previous incidents.
Both these systems are difficult though for different reasons. Real time expert systems are still at the research stage and few systems have been implemented. However, there is considerable interest in this field of work, new computer architectures are being developed and real time software tools are becoming available. In the case of diagnostic expert systems the knowledge itself is spread over a wide range of people and is poorly documented. It will require considerable effort to analyse this knowledge in detail.

HEATINGS Expert System

HEATINGS is a real time expert system which interprets data from a monitoring system and determines the location of heating incidents. It has the following characteristics:
- real time, because it must respond to changes in the data. In advisory expert systems, 'real time' means 'fast enough to give the operator information when he needs it'. Here the system is driven by the arrival of data, but the operator only needs information at low frequency intervals, say minutes.
- some of the knowledge is deterministic (calculation of gas flows etc).
- some of the data is heuristic (local knowledge of conditions where there is a risk of a heating).
- linked to a database which is continuously updated as monitoring proceeds.
- operation is automatic under normal conditions but it may be necessary to hold a dialogue with colliery staff to elicit further knowledge when a heating is being interpreted.
- goal driven system. The top goal is the health of men and safety of the colliery, which involves proving subsidiary goals concerned with

particular aspects of safety.

HEATINGS performs the following functions:
- confirmation or rejection of alarms from the monitoring system
- checking the consistency of measured CO concentrations
- determination of the location of a heating
- checking that levels of CO are safe
- provision of a status display showing active heatings

The system is being written in PROLOG as this offers the most suitable way of representing and manipulating the knowledge. In a simplified form, the knowledge structure can be represented as:

Safe_situation in colliery IF
  Possible heating incidents have been interpreted AND
  Appropriate actions have been taken AND
  Ventilation is OK

  Possible heating incidents have been interpreted IF
    Generate list of possible incidents AND
    Check incidents using monitored data AND
    Hold dialogue with user

  Appropriate actions have been taken IF
    Advise on actions required AND
    Display heatings status

  Ventilation is OK IF
    There is sufficient oxygen AND
    CO levels are low AND
    Methane levels are low

Much of the knowledge appears to be available in a 'frame' format, where a frame is a group of pieces of knowledge which forms a pattern of activities or measurements. An example is the trend of increasing CO at the start of a heating with other, related symptoms.
The project is being developed in three stages:
- Prototype System - Not real time, not linked to the database. The purpose is to develop a suitable knowledge base to demonstrate the basic principle of interpretation of heating data.
- Database System - Not real time but linked to the database. The system runs on request from a user to interpret heating data.
- Full System - Real time operation and linked to the database.

Hayes-Roth et al (1983) and Fagan et al (1979) have provided much of the necessary background to the initial design of the system.

7. Conclusions

Mining is a traditional industry with a long history of evolutionary and sometimes revolutionary change in the methods and techniques utilised. Within that long history lies a wealth of experience, knowledge, expertise and skill found in few other industries. To capture that knowledge and to apply the best of those skills to every problem is a challenge to expert systems technology.

The mining industry has invested heavily in the engineering technology required to produce coal at a cost which is economic not only to the coal industry but to the industries that consume energy.

This paper has described three consultative expert systems which are in use within British Coal as practical, industrial examples of knowledge based systems. Also described is the development of a real time expert system linked to a process monitoring system.

Expert systems technology is rapidly maturing, and the authors look forward with interest to the day when the mainstream of industry accepts the challenge of this technology with the same determination as the mining industry.

Acknowledgements

The authors wish to thank Mr C T Massey, Head of Mining, British Coal, for permission to present and publish this paper.

Any opinions expressed are the authors' and not necessarily those of British Coal.

Due acknowledgement is given that the names of software systems mentioned in this paper are trademarks and registered trademarks.

References

Alvey, P. (1983). Problems of designing a medical expert system. Proceedings of Expert Systems 83, 30-42.

Clancey, W. J. & Letsinger, R. (1981). Neomycin : Reconfiguring a rule based expert system for application to teaching. Proceedings IJCAI 81, 829-836.

Fagan L. M., Kurz, J. C., Feigenbaum, E. A. & Osborn, J. (1979). Representation of dynamic clinical knowledge: measurement interpretation in the intensive care unit. Proceedings IJCAI 79, 260-262.

Fikes, R. & Kehler, T. (1985). The role of frame - based representation in reasoning. Communications of the ACM, 28, No. 9, Sep., 904-920.

Genesereth, M. R. & Ginsberg, M. L. (1985). Logic programming. Communications of the ACM, 28, No. 9, Sep., 933-941.

Hayes-Roth, F., Waterman, D. A. & Lenat, D. B. (eds) (1983). Building Expert Systems. Cambridge, Mass.: Addison Wesley.

Hayes-Roth, F. (1985). Rule based systems. Communications of the ACM, 28, No. 9, Sep., 921-932.

Lord, S. B. (1986). Some aspects of spontaneous combustion control. Mining Engineer, May, 479-488.

Moore, R. L. (1986). Expert systems in process control : applications experience. Proceedings of Applications of Artificial Intelligence in Engineering Problems, 21-30.

Morris, R. & Atkinson, T. (1986). Geological and other factors affecting spontaneous combustion of coal. Mining Science and Technology, 3, 217-231.

Reichgelt, H. & van Harmelen, F. Relevant criteria for choosing an inference engine in expert systems. Proceedings of Expert Systems 85, 21-30.

Shortcliffe, E. H. (1976). Computer Based Medical Consultations : MYCIN. New York: American Elsevier.

DIAGNOSTIC HEURISTICS AND PERSPECTIVES

Padraig Cunningham.
Trinity College, Dublin. Ireland.
John Gleeson.
Coopers & Lybrand Associates Ltd. Plumtree Court, London EC4A 4HT.*
Simon Hakiel.
Plessey Electronic Systems Research Ltd. Roke Manor, Romsey, Hants.
Mike Wheatley.
The Vanilla Flavor Co. Ltd. 6 St. Clement's Street, Winchester, Hants.*

ABSTRACT.

This paper presents "Perspectives", an architecture for utilisation of diagnostic heuristics within a "deep knowledge" system. The work was carried out whilst developing an electronic circuit fault diagnosis Sample Expert System (SES) for a phase of Esprit Project 96 "Expert System Builder".

The Perspectives paradigm was developed while attempting to design a simple control strategy for a 'deep' knowledge-based Expert System. However, the notion is considered to be applicable to Expert Systems operating in other domains. The presence of an underlying deep model makes the diagnostic system very powerful, but it is not crucial to Perspectives.

Analysis of knowledge harvesting sessions has shown that diagnostic experts tend to hypothesise the existence of a fault within a specific context, e.g. heat-related faults, and concentrate investigation within that context or perspective until no further corroborative information can be obtained. If the fault has not been identified, then a new fault area is hypothesised according to the expert's interpretation of the state of the circuit, and the investigation continues. This method of working can be represented as a conceptual transition network of faults or fault area. Not only does this approximate a diagnostician's operational behaviour, but it also provides a simple and explicit control strategy. The Perspectives formalism is an implementation of this model; it provides a means for constraining an Expert System's investigation by focussing attention on particular aspects of the problem.

* This work was carried out whilst Mike Wheatley was at Plessey Electronic Systems Research Ltd. and John Gleeson was at Trinity College, Dublin.

1. INTRODUCTION

The overall architecture of the Sample Expert System (SES) is a mixture of "deep" and "shallow" knowledge. The deep knowledge is provided by a "deep model" which consists of a series of functional, structural and temporal networks describing the circuit under test. The deep model itself is beyond the scope of this paper, see [Bodington, 1986] for a discussion of these issues. Shallow knowledge comes from the inclusion of diagnostic heuristics; these control the simulation and inference performed on the deep model. Heuristics are included in the SES to provide a short-cut, or set of short-cuts, to the formal diagnostic strategies embodied within the deep model of the circuit. The relationship between the heuristics and the deep model is analagous to that between an expert and an interactive tool: the tool is only consulted when the expert has exhausted his/her current relevant experience. Having gained advice, help or perhaps values from the tool, he/she then continues relying on experience again, incorporating information obtained from the tool into his/her interpretation of the state of the faulty circuit. In a similar way, the heuristics will have recourse to the deep model.

2. A PARADIGM FOR AN EXPERT SYSTEM ARCHITECTURE

2.1 Background

Analysis of material collected during knowledge harvesting exercises [Davies, 1985; Davies, 1986] showed that diagnostic experts tend to hypothesise the existence of a fault within a specific perspective, e.g. heat-related faults, and concentrate investigation within that perspective until no further corroborative information can be obtained. If the fault has not been identified, then a new fault perspective is hypothesised according to the expert's interpretation of the state of the circuit, and the investigation continues. This method of working can be represented as a conceptual transition network of faults or fault perspectives. Not only does this approximate a diagnostician's operational behaviour, but it also provides a simple and explicit control strategy for an Expert System approach.

The perspective formalism is an implementation of this model (hence the name 'perspective'); it provides a means for constraining an Expert System's investigation by focussing attention on particular aspects of the problem. This is achieved by structuring the knowledge base such that a number of distinct rule-sets, or perspectives, are produced, each of specific relevance to a fault or group of faults.

2.2 Definition Of Perspectives

Perspectives are defined as meta-level control structures which explicitly segregate the rule base to suport the following:

- Different levels of detail or abstraction within the diagnostic process:

  Within a particular perspective there are meta-rules which control how the applicable rules are used. These applicable rules may refer to a level of detail or abstraction level within the problem domain. Movement between perspectives may therefore reflect movement between levels of abstraction or generality.

- Independent methods of reasoning at different stages in the diagnosis:

  As the diagnosis progresses from one perspective to another, different inference mechanisms or controls may be applied; for example, forward or backward chaining, statistical weighting of rules, or the imposition of a limit on the number of inferences to attempt before the next perspective is investigated.

- Focussing on separate identifiable groups of faults or logical units of the domain:

  All the rules relating to a particular class of fault or logical part of the fault domain may be applicable within a given perspective. For example, in the electronics domain a perspective may contain the rules relating to heat faults, or faults with the system bus. So the rules may be segregated not only according to the physical area of the system (bus, processor, EPROM etc.) but also according to cause, e.g. heat. Rules may be applicable in one or more perspectives, so a rule dealing with failure of the system bus due to heat damage from an adjacent component may be in the perspective dealing with that component, and in the heat faults perspective, and also in the bus faults perspective.

Each perspective can be considered as a rule-set consisting of a number of subsets:meta-rules, local test rules, product specific test rules, and rules for interfacing to the deep model. Fig 1 below shows an example perspective construction for identifying heat-related faults.

Meta-rules control the application of rules in the other subsets of the perspective.

Local test rules are heuristics which deal with faults in that perspective; for example, if there were a perspective concerned with heat-related faults, then the local test rules would be concerned with looking for indications of such faults

Product specific test (PST) rules are the group of shallow heuristics which relate to a particular board, component, or group of components. In other words, they represent the human expert's comment "Oh yes, IC-5 always fails on boards of this type because of poor design..". In this system, the PST will be grouped together in the same manner as the Local Tests. Within any perspective only a subset of the PST will be applicable. Any perspective may access both the PST and any number or combination of Local Tests. In principle, it is just accessing the subset of rules which are applicable within that perspective, although the rule set level segregation into Local Tests and PST supports control over the manner and order in which these rules are tried.

Rules for interfacing to the deep model control the interactions between it and a perspective. These procedures allow perspectives to query the deep model for values, component names or test results.

2.3 Perspective Control Structure

The perspective architecture is notionally as shown in Fig. 2.

A default schedule of perspectives is generated from analysis of diagnostic requirements. The schedule is held as a list in a controller and determines the order in which perspectives are investigated. During an investigation within a perspective, a fault candidate may be generated by applying appropriate heuristics and/or by requesting information from the deep model. The fault candidate is posted as an hypothesis in the global data-base, which is continually monitored by the controller. When a Perspective's meta-rules have fired all the relevant rules, then a 'change-Perspective ARG' message is posted in the global data-base. If ARG is uninstantiated, then the next default perspective is investigated; otherwise, ARG will have been instantiated as a perspective name which becomes the next perspective to be investigated. The controller maintains the order of perspective investigation by monitoring the data-base and registering the form of the 'change-Perspective' messages. It also registers the appearance of fault candidate hypotheses. When a fault candidate hypothesis has been posted in the data-base, and a sufficient amount of corroborating evidence has been associated with it, then the controller halts the investigation. Finally, the controller either runs a simulation in the deep model in order to prove or disprove the hypothesis, or it notifies the user that a fault has been identified.

PERSPECTIVE NAME: PERSPECTIVE_HEAT_FAULTS

META-KNOWLEDGE

(META-RULE n
  IF has_child C test_being_performed
  AND not pursued C
  THEN pursue_child C)
(META_RULE m
  IF investigative_conditions Z
  THEN inform new_perspective Z)

LOCAL TESTS

(RULE FAULT_ONLY_WHEN_HOT
  IF components_hot_within_physical_area Y
  AND fault_disappears_when_cooled
  THEN assert heat_faults_in physical_area Y)

(RULE GENERATE_HEAT
  IF component_standing_out_from_board X
  THEN component_probably_generating_heat X)

PRODUCT SPECIFIC TESTS

(RULE HEAT_GENERATION
  IF open_circuit_nodes (N23, N17)
  THEN   assert component_blown R17)

DEEP MODEL QUERIES

(RULE GET_PHYSICAL_NEIGHBOURS
  IF asserted component_probably_generating_heat X
  AND run_model_for_physical_neighbours X
  THEN assert candidate_list)

(RULE GET_FUNCTIONAL_NEIGHBOURS
  IF asserted component_probably_generating_heat X
  AND asserted within_damaged_sub-network X Y
  AND run_model_for_functional_neighbours X Y
  THEN assert candidate_list)

Fig. 1   Example Perspective Construction

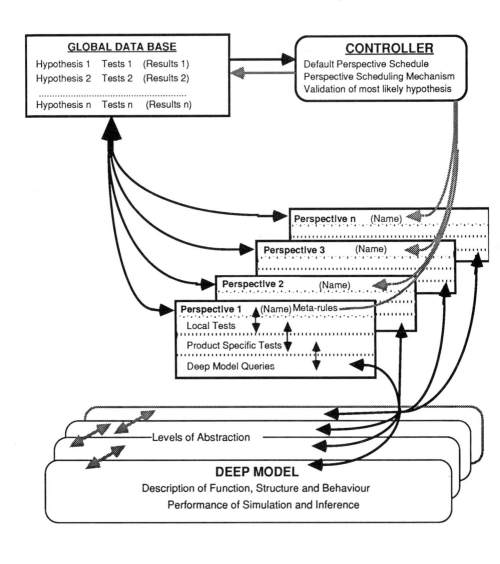

Fig.2 Perspective Architecture

The control strategy is very simple, as shown in Fig. 3.

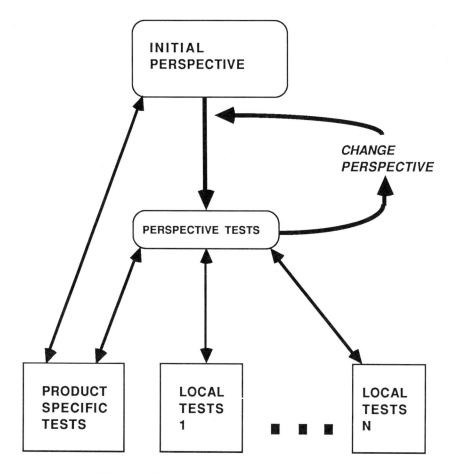

Fig. 3 Perspective Control Strategy

The progression between perspectives during the consultation may be represented in a form of state diagram, as shown in fig. 4 below. perspectives are shown as lettered circles, possible paths between them indicated by lines and arrows. The default perspective schedule is indicated by **bold** arrows.

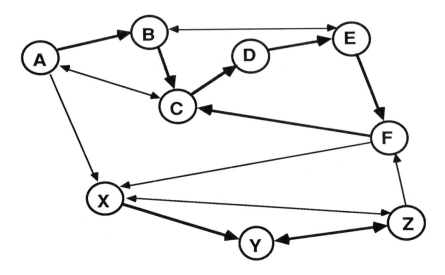

Fig. 4 Perspective Transition Diagram

Movement between perspectives represents changes in levels of abstraction, methods of reasoning, or areas of concentration (groups of faults). A default path through this network is specified, but on the basis of the findings within any perspective this path may be altered.

Within any perspective, only a sub-set of the rules in the rule base will be applicable, as illustrated in fig. 5 below.

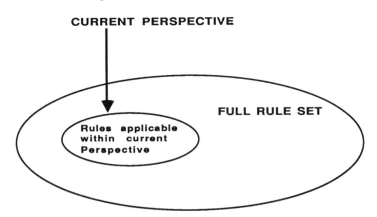

Fig. 5. Rules Applicable Within Current Perspective.

In this manner the rule base is partitioned into rules applicable in various perspectives. Facts and assertions made in previous perspectives will still remain in the data-base, and may be used to make new assertions in the current perspective. This means that a simple notional blackboard mechanism is implied as assertions in the data-base may represent hypotheses from previous perspectives, concerning other levels of abstraction.

This is a characteristic of the perspective mechanism and was not an intentional design feature.

2.4 Perspectives as Knowledge Structures

Various existing knowledge structures exhibit characteristics that are similar to those of perspectives and it is worth examining these similarities in some detail. Perspectives are more than knowledge structures, they are knowledge sources. This implies that new knowledge is produced in perspectives. This would not be claimed for frames or other more passive knowledge structures.

perspectives are similar in some aspects to a diverse set of knowledge structures; the following will be considered:

-Associative Networks
-Frames
-'Levels' in a hierarchical Expert System

2.4.1 Associative Networks

An associative network is a network of nodes and arcs, the nodes represent the objects in the knowledge base and the arcs represent the associations between these objects [Brachman, 1979].

Perspectives can be seen as a large set of knowledge sources which are linked to the extent that control passes from one to another. In order to understand how control passes from one perspective to another in the diagnostic process it is useful to conceive of this set of knowledge sources as an associative network, perspectives being the nodes and the various paths from one perspective to another being the links.

Visualising the set of knowledge sources as an associative network is a useful way of visualising the structure of the shallow knowledge in the SES. At present, however, we are not developing this idea to the extent that the heuristic knowledge be implemented as an associative network; this would require the development of an inference mechanism which would be complicated by the fact that it would have to work over a network of knowledge sources, not a network of knowledge structures.

2.4.2   Frames and Scripts

Perspectives and frames [Minsky, 1975] are similar to the extent that the main motivation for developing the formalisms was to alleviate the problem of combinatorial explosion in knowledge based systems. This is done by efficient knowledge organisation and controlled inference generation.

A frame-based system is a set of stored schemes with the basis of the system centered on three concepts:

-    The 'frame' is the fundamental object.
-    Each frame contains 'slots' that are attributes of that object.
-    Each frame may have 'attached procedures' that may be used to determine further attributes.

Whilst frames are an efficient method of organising knowledge, they are essentially passive in nature. The perspective structure is active by contrast and has a temporal dimension.

An elaboration on the idea of frames are 'scripts'. Scripts were developed to represent stereotypical sequences of actions and events that define a situation [Kobsa, 1984]. As such, scripts are a generalisation of frames incorporating a time dimension. It is precisely this time dimension that prompts the comparison between scripts and perspectives. The important difference is that whilst a script has a time dimension within it, it is the complete set of perspectives that has a time dimension.

2.4.3   'Levels' in Hierarchical Expert Systems

Perhaps the existing knowledge structure that is closest to the idea of perspectives is the concept of 'levels' in hierarchical Expert Systems. The definitive hierarchical Expert System is Hearsay-II [Erman, 1980] so we shall use this as our reference in considering hierarchical Expert Systems. Hierarchical Expert Systems represent a second generation of Expert Systems characterised by a hierarchically structured knowledge base. In Hearsay-II the knowledge base is partitioned into levels and each level is a seperate autonomous knowledge source. Hearsay-II is a speech understanding system and the different levels represent different levels of abstraction. As an example, one level would produce information about syllables and another level would produce information about phrases. The knowledge in these levels is encoded as a set of condition-action clauses so each module can be considered to be anautonomous Expert System. These mini Expert Systems communicate through a blackboard. Each hypothesis generated by the knowledge sources is recorded on the blackboard where it can be accessed by the other knowledge sources.

Evidently, perspectives are similar to these levels in hierarchical Expert Systems, but there are some important differences. perspectives are not hierarchical in structure, they are better represented as a network (as described earlier). Perhaps the most important distinction is that the knowledge sources in Hearsay-II operate concurrently, whereas perspectives operate sequentially; control being passed to the perspective that will investigate the most likely hypothesis.

3. CONCLUSIONS

3.1 Perspectives

Perspectives are a simple way of controlling the behaviour of a diagnostic Expert System. As a consultation proceeds, the perspective within which the diagnosis is being performed changes. Within a given perspective, only a sub-set of the total rule-set will be applicable. Although there is explicit segregation of the rule-set, the applicable rules within any perspective may be in a number of the subdivisions of the rule-set. The rule-set segregation supports control over how and when these rules are applied.

The blackboard mechanism is implicit within perspectives; it is not, as in true blackboard systems, explicitly constructed. Frames are groups of rules, or heuristics, or knowledge, each one of which deals with a specific subject area. This is not the case in the perspective mechanism. In perspectives the rule base is homogeneous, each rule can be used in more than one system state, or perspective.

Perspectives also allow the operational behaviour of human experts to be modelled (to some extent at least). It is important to note that the notion developed from two distinct directions: from the implementation requirements to constrain the deep model's possible exhaustive searches, and from analysis of knowledge harvesting sessions. This 'two-pronged' development implies that perspectives may well prove to be a useful general Expert System design paradigm.

Perspectives therefore represent a new approach to constructing an Expert System, concentrating on providing a simple and flexible control strategy within an intuitively accurate structure for heuristics.

3.2 Adaptive Generation of Perspectives

By organising rules into perspectives, the knowledge engineer builds into the system a "higher" level of knowledge. Each perspective 'tunes' the system to a particular problem area by making available only those rules relevant to a specific problem class. At any one time, therefore, the system has to process fewer rules than would be necessary were this organisation not built into the system. At this level, then, knowledge is implemented in the form of structures defined over the total rule set. The implementation of perspectives adapts the system to a set of distinct problem classes.

A characteristic constraint in the construction of knowledge-based systems is that there can be no guarantee that the set of rules specified during the construction of the system will be appropriate to problems that might be encountered during diagnostic sessions. This constraint applies equally to the specification of perspectives; there can be no guarantee that the set of perspectives derived from knowledge harvesting sessions will be either complete or optimum for the range of problems that might be encountered during diagnostic sessions. Although overall system performance will be enhanced when perspectives match problems, performance might easily be degraded if a problem is encountered for which no appropriate perspective has been defined. A situation could arise in which all perspectives would have to be invoked before sufficient rules would be fired to generated a diagnosis.

A significant enhancement to perspectives, therefore, would be implementation of a facility for automatic generation of new perspectives. Since this would involve only the identification of new collections of rules, and not the identification of new rules, automatic production of perspectives should not be too difficult to implement.

In principle, the procedure might be as follows: Each time the system is run, a log is generated containing the rules invoked in the generation of a successful diagnosis and the number of perspectives involved. After successful diagnosis has been achieved, the set of accumulated rules is then reduced to that subset sufficient for effective diagnosis of the problem. This subset can then constitute a new perspective.

Clearly, however, it would not be desirable to create new perspectives each time a problem class is encountered which requires rules from more than one existing perspective. This could quickly lead to the proliferation of a large number of perspectives with only minimal distinctions between them. In order to prevent excessive proliferation of perspectives some mechanism should be implemented to restrict the circumstances under which new perspectives are created. Even with such a procedure, however, it is still possible that, over time, the system could become overloaded with perspectives, and that some further means for limiting the accumulation of perspectives would be required. This could be achieved by a simple 'housekeeping' procedure based on the frequency of use of system-generated perspectives. Any perspective that has not been of direct use in problem-solving over a predefined period of time should be deleted from the working repertoire of perspectives.

Following these principles, the perspective system would not only be adapted to known problems, but also adaptable to new ones.

REFERENCES:

Balzer R., L. Erman, P. London, C. Williams (1980).
"Hearsay-III: A Domain-independent Framework for Expert Systems"
USC/Information Sciences Institute

Bodington R. (1986)
Forthcoming ESPRIT Project 96 publication.

Brachman R.J. (1979)
"On the Epistemological Status of Semantic Networks". In Findler N.V.
(ed. 1979), "Associative Networks", Academic Press, London, pp. 3-50.

Clancey W.J. (1981)
"NEOMYCIN: Reconfiguring A Rule-Based Expert System For Application To
Teaching", IJCAI-81.

Clancey W.J. (1983)
"The Advantages Of Abstract Control Knowledge In Expert System Design",
Stanford Report No. STAN-CS-83-995 and HPP-83-17.

Davies M.R. (1986)
"A Practical Investigation of Knowledge Acquisition Techniques",
Report 72/86/R147U. Plessey, Roke Manor. 1986.

Davis R. (1977)
"Meta-Level Knowledge: Overview And Applications", IJCAI-77.

Davis R. (1983)
"Diagnosis Based on Causal Reasoning", AAAI-83.

Duda R.O., P.E. Hart, N.J. Nilsson, R. Reboh, J. Slocum, and G.L. Sutherland
(1977)
"Development of a Computer-based Consultation for Mineral Exploration". Annual Rep
SRI Projects 5821 and 6415. SRI Int, Menlo Park, California, USA.

Erman L.D., Hayes-Roth F., Lesser V.R., Reddy D.R. (1980)
"The Hearsay-II Speech-Understanding System: Integrating Knowledge to
Resolve Uncertainty". Computing Surveys, Vol.12, No.2, JJune 1980.

Genesereth M.R. (1982)
"Diagnosis Using Hierarchical Design Models", AAAI-82.

Kobsa A. (1984)
"Knowledge Representation: A survey of its Mechanisms, A sketch of its
Semantics". Cybernetics and Systems: An International Journal, 15:42-89,
1984

Minsky M. (1975)
"A Framework for Representing Knowledge". In Winston P. (ed 1975)
"The Psychology of Computer Vision". New York, McGraw Hill, pp. 211-277

Intelligent Front Ends to Numerical Simulation Programs

Kjell Tangen   *Computas Expert Systems*
Ulf Wretling   *P.O. Box 410, 1322 Høvik, Norway*

Abstract

Programs simulating physical processes is a class of computer programs sharing a number of distinct, common features. It is therefore meaningful to talk about Intelligent Front Ends to numerical simulation programs (IFES) as a separate sub-class of the Intelligent Front End class of knowledge systems. This paper describes common features of numerical simulation programs, and discusses functional demands on the front-end to make it a real engineering tool. Furthermore, various common types of knowledge required to make use of complex numerical simulation programs are identified, and a number of knowledge representation schemes applicable to these types of knowledge are surveyed. Causal models of physical processes are relevant to simulation for several reasons, and integration of causal models into the front end is discussed. A general architecture of an IFES is described. A sample IFES, KIPS (Knowledgebased Interface to Process Simulation), is presented, highlighting and realizing some of the ideas presented in this paper. KIPS is an intelligent front end to a petrochemical process simulation program.

1.   Introduction

In many fields, technological advancement requires deeper understanding of, and ability to predict and control, the underlying physical processes. For complex physical processes, numerical simulation of the process is an invaluable tool for generating this knowledge [1]. Examples of such fields are numerous: Oil reservoir exploration, simulation of nuclear power plants, design of chemical process plants, weather forecasting, etc.

The increasing power of modern computers makes numerical simulation of physical processes interesting as an engineering tool for e.g. design work and safety assessments. Numerical simulation programs are typically batch-oriented, and require extensive input in the form of a text file. The input format is cumbersome, and simple model modifications may require extensive modification of the input file. In addition, numerical simulation programs are often highly specialized , and require, apart from knowledge of the field itself, expert knowledge of several types: How to represent a problem in a way compatible with the solution strategy of the simulation program (*modelling knowledge*), detailed knowledge about the input format of the simulation program, knowledge about how different program options can be utilized to fulfill the user's tasks, and experience on how to tune the simulation program to obtain "good" results (*handicraft knowledge*).

Both the modelling knowledge and the handicraft knowledge comes with experience, and are (almost) never documented. Nevertheless, they are both essential when it comes to problem solving.

Typical for such programs is therefore:

●   *New users need considerable training in running the program due to the complexity of the problem and program.*

●   *Input generation and modification are often elaborate due to obscure input format and large amounts of input data needed to be specified.*

An *intelligent front end* (IFE) [2] is amenable to reduce both these barriers, because an IFE, in addition to letting the user specify the problem in a more convenient way, and automating pertinent operations, incorporates some of the domain knowledge described above. The objective of incorporating domain knowledge into a front-end is to provide extensive expert help and advice in the course of specifying a problem and interpreting results.

IFEs bear promise of becoming practical tools for two reasons:

1) The objective of an IFE is to make a program more accessible and reduce the probability of input errors. This may let the user work more efficiently.

2) An IFE may encourage users to use the program in new, more sophisticated ways, hence supporting the user in making more efficient use of the program. This may increase also the quality of the user's work.

This paper deals specificly with one subclass of IFEs, namely *intelligent front ends to numerical simulation programs* (IFES). The similarities between numerical simulation programs in general make it possible to be highly specific when describing general features of an IFES.

Section 2 gives some characteristics of numerical simulation programs. Section 3 describes some possible functional characteristics of IFES. Section 4 describes various types of knowledge typically required to make proper use of a numerical simulation program. It also accounts for relevant knowledge representation schemes. Section 5 lines up a general IFES architecture. In section 6, a sample IFES is described, a front end to a large petrochemical process simulation program.

2.   Characteristics of Numerical Simulation Programs.

Physical systems are often described in terms of a set of main physical parameters and a corresponding set of partial differential equations, which in general are inferred from basic laws of nature combined with empirical correlations. Inherent in the equations are always a number of assumptions and approximations made with respect to the class of physical systems being described by the equations.

Numerical simulation of a physical system means solving the system's equations numerically on a computer. Boundary conditions are in most cases specified initially, but may also be altered interactively during the calculation (interactive simulation).

Numerical simulation programs can be divided in two categories: *Static* and *dynamic* simulation programs. A static simulation program calculates a static (time-independent) state of the system, while a dynamic simulation program calculates the dynamic behaviour of the system.

Scenario analysis is a key concept in numerical simulation. Numerical simulation programs are mostly used for detailed scenario analysis. A *scenario* is a class of related problems leading to similar system behaviour. Examples of scenarios are: Blow-outs in oil-wells, loss of coolant in nuclear reactors, gas separation in petrochemical process plants, etc. Given a scenario, an expert in the field will always be able to give a brief, qualitative description of the system's behaviour. Numerical simulation of the system will add on to his scenario knowledge detailed information about the system's behaviour.

Problem specification means creating an input to the simulation program in order to simulate the problem. A complete problem specification is done in two stages: The first stage is the *model design stage*. If no model template exists, a simulation model template of the system must be designed on basis of a *task specification*, i.e. a specification of particular goals set by the user which the model should meet. The second stage is the *specification stage*, in which a detailed specification of model parameters is done. Scenario knowledge is in general applied at the second stage of the problem specification.

Representing scenario knowledge is a key to the construction of an IFES capable of assisting the user in the translation from a task specification to a detailed problem specification. In a number of cases, the simulation program is designed to handle only a few, specific scenarios. In such cases, fixed routes to problem specifications exist. In other cases, however, only overall scenario descriptions exist, and detailed problem specifications must be configured in each single case.

Some important characteristics of numerical simulation programs are:

- The equations are mostly solved using finite-difference techniques. The model of the system is therefore divided into sections or "nodes" connected with each other. A typical node diagram, showing how a system is divided into nodes, is shown in figure 1.

- Each section has a set of characteristic parameters. Sections can be of several types (units) (e.g. pumps, valves, pipe-segments, etc.), and each unit has its own individual characteristic parameters in addition to the main physical parameters. (E.g. the pump head is a characteristic parameter of a pump).

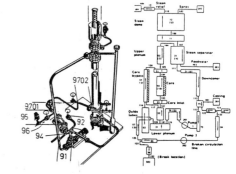

The performance of the simulation program is closely coupled to the skills of the user, and in particular to:

- How the system is divided into units.

Figure 1:   Example of node diagram.

- How well model and program characteristics represent physical characteristics of the system being modeled.

- How well the boundary conditions represent the interaction between the system and the surroundings.

3.   Functional Aspects of IFES

In contrast to most other types of knowledge systems, an IFE is judged solely on the basis of its functional aspects. Because it is a support-system for users of another program, an IFE can only be justified when its user interface is recognized by the users. Therefore, during the design of an IFE, more emphasis must be put on the functional aspects of the system than for most other knowledge systems.

The combination of graphical interfaces with AI techniques offers unique possibilities of creating IFES meeting this requirement.

An IFES should allow the user to build a problem specification incrementally, without any predefined sequence, but supported by knowledge and IFES functionality.

Possible functional aspects of IFES include:

- *Graphical interface.* Since important parts of a numerical simulation model and simulation results consist of visual information (geometric models, graphs, symbols, etc.), a graphical interface lets the user work with computer models closer to his conceptual models than traditional, text-oriented interfaces. When appropriate, the interface should support interactive, graphical model design.

- *Flexible presentation of simulation results* combined with e.g. some *post-processing facilities.*

- *Entry of simulation results back into model.*

- *Advice on different levels of abstraction* (e.g. advice on model design alternatives, advice on parameter setting, advice on how simulated results can be improved, etc).

- *Automatic checks on validity or consistency of model specifications.*

- *Planning and conducting a systematic series of simulations* in order to achieve particular goals set by the user.

- *User-specific model directories.*

- *Easily extendable knowledge-bases.*

- *Model documentation.*

- *Plotting/printing facilities.*

4. Knowledge Aspects of IFES

Numerical simulation of physical systems is a class of problems sharing a number of distinct features. It is therefore possible to single out specific knowledge types typical for this kind of problem solving.

The types of knowledge, as well as how they are applied, are briefly described below.

Depending on what is meant by the notion *modelling*, the notions *model design* and *problem specification* have different meanings. In most cases, modelling means making a computer model of an existing system in order to reproduce the system's properties. In some cases, however, modelling means the actual design of a system fulfilling some specific tasks. An example of the latter is petrochemical process simulation, which is an aid in the design of process plants.

A) Model design knowledge

Model design knowledge applies to the first stage of the problem specification process (see paragraph 2). The result of the model design stage is a model template, i.e. a model of the system which is general enough to encompass each feasible state of the system. Depending on whether the modelling is based on a task description or a system description, the model design knowledge differs in structure. The knowledge is applied in the same way in both cases, however (See figure 2). Optional representation schemes for this knowledge are:

- Production rules generating design alternatives for parts of the system.

- Production rules giving advice on different design alternatives.

- Templates for common design alternatives for parts of the system, represented as e.g. frames.

In KIPS, the sample IFES described in section 6, model design knowledge was represented in the two latter ways. A number of partial models (submodels), implementing existing design knowledge, are available to the user. Based on the user's task specification, KIPS advises on what submodel to be used in a particular situation.

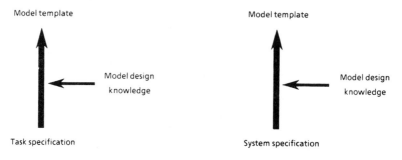

Figure 2 a: Modelling based on task description

Figure 2 b: Modelling based on system description

An example of modelling based on system description would be the modelling of an existing process plant, while an example of modelling based on task description would be the modelling of a non-existing process plant with the intention of designing one.

B)   Scenario knowledge

Scenario knowledge is:

● Knowledge about how a given scenario can be realized in the simulation program (scenario realization knowledge).

● Qualitative knowledge about system behaviour in a scenario.

The former type of scenario knowledge is the most relevant for IFES, but the latter may be valuable in combination with e.g. causal models.

Scenario realization knowledge may either be represented in frames, or, in a more complex case requiring scenario configuring, in the form of production rules.

Scenario knowledge is applied at the specification stage of the problem specification process. On the basis of a model template, scenario knowledge along with other types of knowledge are applied in order to make a detailed problem specification. The application of scenario knowledge in a problem specification process is depicted in figure 3.

C)   Unit knowledge

To each unit applies knowledge about how the unit should be specified in various situations. Such knowledge include:

● Valid parameter combinations.

● Parameter constraints.

● Typical parameter values (may be situation dependent).

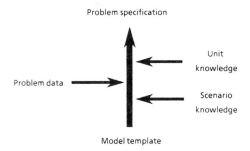

Figure 3:   Problem specification

Frames are useful representations for units. Unit parameters are then represented as slots in the unit frame. Constraints on unit parameters may be represented as rules, but it may also be useful to supply parameter declarations with constraint declarations, e.g. represented as parameter attributes.

D)   Consistency knowledge

A complete problem specification is always subject to a number of constraints, e.g. certain combinations of units may be inconsistent with their specifications.

E)   Handicraft knowledge

A lot of knowledge can only be aquired through practical experience with problem solving. (This knowledge is part of what distinguishes an expert from a novice). Practical knowledge about which mechanisms to use to achieve certain results is labeled *handicraft knowledge*, and consists of heuristics related to program performance and system behaviour.

F)   Knowledge about how to improve simulation results

Simulations must often be rerun because the results are classified as bad, either because the results are inconsistent with data, or because they are inconsistent with the expert's own scenario knowledge. Improving bad results without affecting good results is an important, but complicated expert task, requiring skill.

Knowledge about how to improve simulation results is often handicraft knowledge, but an equally important component of this knowledge is the expert's deep understanding of physical, causal relationships.

G)   Causal models

Qualitative, causal models are currently subject to a lot of interest in the AI community [3], mainly because they will let a knowledge system reason about system behaviour in a much more general sense than 'shallow' production rule system could. The reason for this is that in a causal model, there will be no fixed set of rules and, thereby, fixed dependencies within the system. Dependencies within the system will be generated dynamically by means of general causal relations. In order to restrict the number of generated dependencies, the dependency generation must be controlled in a much stricter manner than for traditional rule inference due to a wider state space. Subjected to a proper control mechanism, dependencies will generate a qualitative description of system behaviour, which in turn can be input to a rule inference process.

Reasoning about physical systems often requires the ability to assess the behaviour of the system by reasoning about dependencies and causal relationships. In simulation, this kind of reasoning is used e.g. to improve simulation results and to analyze them. Causal knowledge is an important part of the scenario knowledge.

The extension of the simulation model with qualitative, causal models would make it possible to imbed knowledge about result analysis and improvement in the IFES in a systematic manner. This would enhance the IFES potential significantly. The way this should be done is not clear, mainly because a firm theory on the representation of causal models has not yet been established. The integration of causal reasoning with numerical simulation process is illustrated in figure 4.

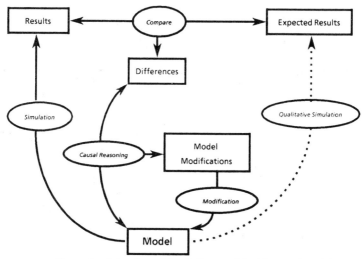

Figure 4:   Extension of simulation model with causal models

5.   IFES Architecture

A general architecture of an IFES is shown in figure 5. The main modules of this architecture are: *User Interface, Knowledge Bases, Simulation Models* and *Simulation Results*.

Interaction between these modules must be mediated by various system functions, such as translators and presentation functions. It should be clear from this architecture that the actual expert system is only a minor part of the IFES, while the rest are system functions providing necessary functionality.

Here follows a descriptions of the main modules:

User Interface. The user interface should support several different modes of input/output, such as graphical input/output, menu-driven input as well as traditional alphanumeric input/output.

Models. One objective of the IFES is to support the construction of simulation models. The Models module of an IFES is a workspace containing one or several simulation models. Model operation functions, i.e. user-inferred model operations or model operations inferred by rules, support model modifications. A model translator translates the model into the input format of the simulation program.

Knowledge Bases. One or several knowledge bases containing the knowledge. The knowledge bases may be accessed directly from the user interface, or via model operations.

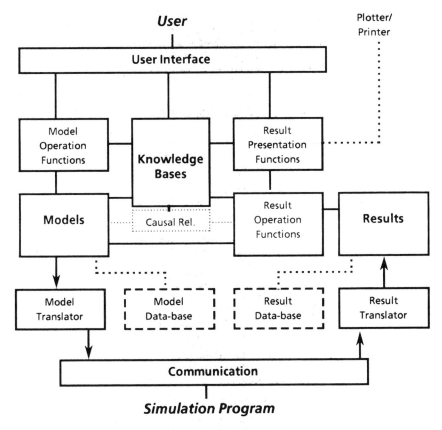

Figure 5: IFES main modules

Results. A workspace containing simulation results . Result operation functions allow access to simulation results from the model and reentry of selected results into the model. The result operation functions may also incorporate post-processing functions as well as functions supporting qualitative analysis based on causal models.

Result presentation functions present results to the user in various forms: On the screen, on plots or on print..

6. A Sample IFES: KIPS

This section describes an IFES system realizing some of the principles outlined above. KIPS (Knowledgebased Interface to Process Simulation) [4] is an intelligent front end to a static process simulation program, PROCESS [5]. While the standard interface to PROCESS is through a text editor and an elaborate command file, the work pattern with KIPS is as follows. The user with some initial design ideas starts by building a flowsheet on the graphics screen of the workstation. The design work is supported by knowledge embedded in the KIPS database, which contains basic building blocks and model (sub)assemblies, as well as design rules. The user is freed from manual handling of drawings, preparation of detailed input files, etc., and instead interacts with the system in terms of familiar process symbols. As soon as the model has been constructed in an interactive session, the corresponding input file is automatically generated and sent to PROCESS for execution. KIPS is being implemented in LOOPS [6] on the XEROX 1109 work station. The project is carried out by Computas Expert Systems in cooperation with Statoil, the norwegian State's Oil company.

The objective of the system is to support design of **Process Models**, which are input from, and displayed to the user graphically as process flow diagrams, and converted to text form for PROCESS.

The process models are created and manipulated through a number of interactive model operation functions, or **Design Functions**. Foremost among these are a graphical editor for flow diagrams and a PROCESS input file generator.

The design work is supported by **Knowledge Bases**, where PROCESS concepts and previously acquired model components, design rules, etc. are encoded.

The user gains access to the system through a uniform **User Interface**, using the familiar window/mouse/icon approach.

The KIPS Knowledge Base

The knowledge base is a major focus for this work. Constructing a PROCESS model is largely seen as copying pieces of information from the knowledge base into the evolving model, then modifying the pieces to suit the current needs. This *instantiation* of general descriptions to particular instances is accompanied by activation of design rules for checking the validity of user actions. Advice is provided upon request. Parts of the model description is filled in automatically based on default information and heuristics.

The "backbone" of the knowledge bases in KIPS is a Loops class hierarchy defining model components, augmented with rule sets as described in more detail below. Figure 6 depicts a central fragment of the class structure:

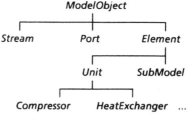

Figure 6. Model object taxonomy

A model contains **ModelObjects**. A ModelObject is either an **Element, a Port** or a **Stream**. Elements constitute what is referred to as *units* in earlier sections. The Element is a general class, with subclasses **SubModel** (i.e. a submodel with its own internal structure), or a basic **Unit**, of which **Compressor, HeatExchanger**, etc. are specific subclasses. The units (e.g. Compressor) may spawn further subclass definitions, corresponding to particular ways of using these units (based on experience). Figure 7 shows some of the currently defined PROCESS units. The inclusion of both SubModel and Unit as building-blocks in models means that fully recursive structures are possible.

A **specification** of a unit is defined as a particular way of using that unit, minimally defined by partitioning the set of parameters for the unit into **required, optional, special, fixed** and **unused** parameters. The specification of a unit can be changed during a session, and the system will change its behaviour with respect to that unit correspondingly.

Each unit parameter description may have associated rulesets and lisp expressions of the following kinds:

check   Method and/or lisp expressions for checking validity of a proposed new value.

advice   Method or lisp expression for advising the user on how to select a new value.

Checks are activated as a side-effect of an attempted update of a parameter value, using the active value mechanisms in LOOPS.

Hierarchical design is a most important aspect of design processes, and is supported by the general model structure shown in the previous section. Functions for creating submodels, zoom in on the internal structure of submodels, etc. are available to the user. We believe this is a fundamental requirement for any system purporting to support design in a complex domain, such as simulation modelling. Existing design knowledge is represented as predefined submodels and advice on their use. After letting the user specify his design goal for a particular part of the model, KIPS will fill in that part of the model automatically.

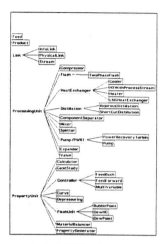

Figure 7: PROCESS unit taxonomy

A snapshot of a typical KIPS screen is shown in figure 8.

KIPS Knowledge Structures

The knowledge in KIPS is encoded in a multitude of ways. Each type of knowledge is implemented in the most efficient way, using the multiple programming paradigms in LOOPS, that is: Object oriented, access oriented, rule oriented and procedure oriented programming.

The KIPS knowledge base is highly modularized. Units and submodels constitute a frame hierarchy organized as a semantic network featuring multiple inheritance. Rules are used for executing checks and giving advice upon request. The rulesets are distributed among the nodes in the hierarchy and attached to the nodes to which they apply. A forward chaining inference mechanism is used to apply these rules. Some predicates for declaring common constraints among units and parameters have been defined as part of the frame system. The LOOPS inheritance mechanisms allow for optimal distribution of knowledge in the knowledge base with respect to fast and easy access to the knowledge.

Although most of the knowledge in KIPS is structured in terms of the above mentioned mechanisms, certain parts of the domain knowledge, such as methods for defining a calculation sequence for units, is heuristic procedural knowledge which is not easily implemented using these constructs. In such cases, it was found nescessary to encode the knowledge in Lisp functions.

Current Status

At present, a prototype of KIPS has been issued to Statoil, mainly for testing' purposes and gaining user experience. KIPS has generated a lot of interest among users of PROCESS, but in

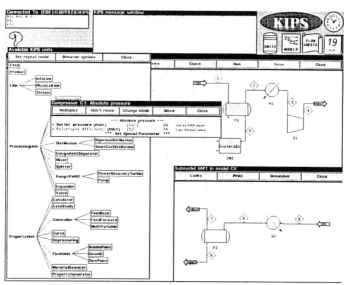

Figure 8:   KIPS screen snapshot

order to become a real engineering tool, a lot of auxiliary functionality must be added to KIPS, such as e.g. plotter interface and interface to component databases.

- The graphical flowsheet editor is operational but further enhancements are under development.

- PROCESS units regarded as relevant for offshore simulations have been incorporated in the knowledge base by "tapping" experienced process engineers.

- A set of submodels relevant for offshore processes has been incorporated in the knowledge base

- A PROCESS input file is automatically generated and transmitted to a host computer (an IBM main-frame) and the simulation results are transmitted back to the Xerox workstation.

Future Work

A major motivation behind the KIPS project is finding ways of including *design knowledge* in the intelligent interface to PROCESS. This is clearly a vast topic, and we have chosen to approach it in an incremental fashion.

Logically, the design should proceed top-down, and the reasons for decisions at different levels should be maintained for later project phases. Unfortunately, this is seldom carried out in practise, thereby losing a major source for making informed model revisions.

Another possible direction for the KIPS project is to extend the present concentration on the model design aspect to also include other phases of simulation projects:

- Planning (sequences of) simulation experiments to achieve given project goals.

- Qualititative/coarse simulation in the frontend to weed out first-line problems.

- Fault diagnosis of simulation if the results are wrong or non-satisfactory.

- Evaluation, interpretation and presentation of the simulation results.

7. Conclusions

Numerical simulation programs is a class of computer programs requiring extensive input in a cumbersome format. Augmenting a numerical simulation program with an IFE would dramatically improve its user interface.

An intelligent front end to a numerical simulation program (IFES) is a knowledge system combining AI techniques with traditional software techniques. The knowledge base plays a central role in an IFES (as in all knowledge systems), because much of the IFES functionality depends on the knowledge put into the system.

Due to the apparent similarities between numerical simulation programs in general, a general knowledge structure of an IFES can be identified and described. Furthermore, similar functional demands on IFES makes it possible to identify a general IFES architecture.

Causal reasoning about physical dependencies constitutes important parts of the expert's reasoning. Qualitative, causal models of physical systems is a vast research area of itself, and it is not at all clear how such models can be incorporated in an IFES.

Intelligent front ends to numerical simulation programs (IFES) bear promise of becoming practical engineering tools. Several leads point in that direction: The increasing power of low-cost engineering work stations makes distributed simulation interesting as a tool for e.g. safety assessments and design work. Furthermore, IFES may provide new, more efficient ways of working with simulation.

As supercomputing becomes common along with the introduction of the new generation of cheap supercomputers, there will be a growing need for new, more interactive ways of working with simulation. In order to fulfill this need, a new user interface technology is required. The IFES concept of simulation interfaces contributes to the development of this technology.

References:

1) J.A. Spriet, G.C. Vansteenkiste: *Computer-aided Modelling and Simulation*. Academic Press, London, 1982.

2) A. Bundy: *Intelligent Front Ends*, in *Expert Systems*, Pergamon Infotech Ltd., 1984.

3) B. Kuipers: *The Limits of Qualitative Simulation*, Proceedings of the Ninth International Joint Conference on Artificial Intelligence, p. 128. Morgan Kaufman Publishers, Los Altos, 1985.

4) R. Fjellheim: *Knowledgebased Interface to Process Simulation*, AI in Simulation Conference Proceedings, Ghent, 1985.

5) N.F. Brannock et al. : *PROCESS^{TM} Simulation Program, A Comprehensive Flowsheeting Tool for Chemical Engineers*, Computers & Chemical Engineering, Vol. 3, pp. 329-352, 1979.

6) D. G. Bobrow et al.: *The LOOPS Manual*, Xerox Corporation, 1983.

M. Stefik et al.: *Knowledge Programming in Loops*, AI Magazine, Fall 1983.

FACTORING OUT INVESTIGATIVE INFERENCE

Robert Macdonald

Intelligent Systems Centre
P A Computers and Telecommunications
Rochester House
33 Greycoat Street
LONDON SW1P 2QF

Abstract

This paper is based on the results of constructing an expert system to assist military personnel in the identification of conventional (i.e. "mass-produced") munitions. The major feature of this work is the separation of the reasoning strategy into logical and investigative inference, which has enabled the adoption of a knowledge-based approach to question selection. Factoring the reasoning strategy gives a clearer picture of the functionality of inference techniques, leading to more natural and transparent reasoning and encouraging the explicit representation of both domain and control knowledge.

1. Introduction

Logical inference is the reasoning that leads to the advice and conclusions presented by a system. Investigative inference is the reasoning that leads to deciding which goals to investigate, and in what way. The two types of reasoning are often integrated into a single strategy, where the emphasis is placed on the correctness of the logical reasoning process; investigative reasoning being considered as a 'by-product' of the main strategy. Investigative inference can be factored out of the reasoning process by implementing a separate mechanism for propagating investigative knowledge and explicitly representing the control knowledge that this mechanism uses. This facilitates the design of a flexible and robust system with a wide range of explanation and cognitive support facilities. The system's reasoning becomes more transparent, and there is a greater chance that it will reflect the user's own reasoning process as both logical and investigative inference can be tailored, without compromise, to the task at hand. The approach also supports the use of a knowledge-based question selection routine. This enables a variety of question-asking strategies to be designed and evaluated, resulting in a well controlled dialogue, and allowing abstract strategic explanations to be made, benefiting both user and knowledge engineer.

Section 2 describes the implementation of these concepts in the munition identification system. Section 3 discusses the implications of factoring out investigative inference from the viewpoints of reasoning, knowledge engineering and man-machine systems.

2. Implementation of the Model

The model was implemented as an inference network of nodes connected together by links. Each node represents a question or hypothesis, and consists of a statement, together with a measure of truth, and a measure of investigative importance. Each link defines the logical and investigative relationship between a pair of nodes.

2.1 Logical Inference

Decisions regarding control of the dialogue and question selection can largely be ignored while considering logical inference if a separate method of investigative inference is used. This means that the logical inference mechanisms can be tailored to the way domain experts make decisions or suggestions according to the facts at hand. It also enables knowledge pertaining only to logical inference to be represented explicitly in the system.

In the identification of conventional munitions, safety considerations impose conservatism on decision-making, and thus only definite conclusions are of any value in making an identification (this is not true, however, for decisions about investigative strategy). Therefore, a three-valued logic was adopted (True, False, Don't Know). Propagation of truth values was based on two simple mechanisms, one using necessary and sufficient conditions between nodes, and one using principles of mutual exclusion.

2.2 Investigative Inference

The task of the investigative inference strategy is to work independently of, and in parallel with, logical inference, in order to build up a measure of investigative potential on each node. These measures of potential can then be used to identify those goals most worthy of further investigation, and the most fruitful approach to their investigation. The method described below was adopted because:

-     it is simple, efficient and easy to understand

-     control knowledge can be explicitly represented

-     domain users regarded it as reflecting the way they built up investigative evidence.

Potential

Each node has a measure of <u>potential</u>, which is a number in the range $[-1, 1]$.

Potential can be defined as:

> "A measure of the likelihood of attaining a value which is either wholly true or wholly false given the current (inconclusive) evidence."

The closer the potential of a node is to 1, the greater the likelihood of it being proved true; the closer to -1, the greater the likelihood of being proved false. The potential of all nodes is initialised to 0. It is important to stress that potential in no way affects the truth value of a node.

The level of potential on a node varies as <u>support</u> is 'contributed' by its antecedents.

Support

Support represents the influence that a node has on the investigative importance of its consequents. It determines what proportion of an antecedent's potential is contributed to a consequent's potential. Support for a node is distributed amongst its antecedents; more encouraging evidence being given a greater proportion of the support.

Each antecedent-consequent relationship has two measures of support; one for when the antecedent's potential is positive, and one for when it is negative.

When a node's potential changes, a proportion of this change is added to, or subtracted from, the potential of each of its consequences, according to the respective levels of support. In this way, potential is propagated throughout the network and those nodes with greatest potential can be singled out for investigation.

In the munition identification example, measures of support were assigned numerically, and improved upon by experimentation. However, for future work, the following scheme is anticipated:

. use an algorithmic technique to produce a first cut allocation of support

. use a symbolic mapping function to calculate support from significance judgements, and override automatic allocations

. use machine learning during trials.

The separation of reasoning into a simple scheme for logical inference and investigative inference with explicitly stated control knowledge, has major implications for both the system's ability to express itself, and the design of a mechanism for question selection.

2.3 Knowledge-based Question Selection

One result of the reasoning strategy described is that a large amount of information is explicitly known, and therefore available to the system. For each node:

. the truth value is known
. the potential is known
. the necessity and sufficiency of any antecedents is known
. the strength of the support of any antecedents is known.

The combination of this knowledge has been used to provide a knowledge-based approach to goal and question selection.

The selection of a new goal for investigative purposes is performed after each input of new information by the user. This task is performed by a set of rules, which analyses the potential of the nodes in the inference net and sets two system variables. The first is the selected goal: this could be a node, a list of nodes, or just a 'general' goal representing no particular node. The second is the status variable, which reflects the potential of the node(s) forming the selected goal, relative to the potential of other nodes in the inference net. Another rule set uses this status variable, and the selected goal, to choose a search paradigm to use when selecting the next question.

Three major components make up the approach to question selection:

. Paradigms: a paradigm is selected according to the status of the network and the current goal. It embodies the desired approach to the selection of a question for the selected goal. It contains a list of search primitives to be used in the search ordered by preference.

. Search primitives: these are small LISP functions that take one step backwards along a search path towards a possible question. Each search primitive contains a simple test, which is applied to the antecedents of a node.

. A general purpose routine: this uses the description within a paradigm to apply the search primitives in a mutually recursive fashion.

A list of relevant nodes from which to select a question is constructed by backward chaining from the selected goal. At each stage in the search, each search primitive specified in the chosen paradigm is applied in turn to the current node, producing a set of antecedents of the node that:

- satisfy the condition of the search primitive

- are not already in the list of relevant nodes

The members of this set are added to the list of relevant nodes, together with a rank, according to the position of the primitive which they satisfied in the chosen paradigm. These, in turn, become the current node.

The list of relevant nodes is then filtered to remove those that are not direct questions and sorted according to rank. It is then used to select which question, or mutually exclusive set of questions, is to become the default next question.

Examples of paradigms are:

. "the selected goal has high potential - select the most direct question in an attempt to prove it as quickly as possible".

. "the selected goal has low potential - select a question that affects as many other goals as possible".

. "the top few goals have nearly the same potential - select a question to distinguish between them".

2.4 The Munition Identification System

The identification and safe disposal of conventional munitions (e.g. grenades, mortars, incendiary devices) is a routine but hazardous operation performed by teams of Explosive Ordnance Disposal (EOD) operators located around the country. Reports, usually from the general public, are handled by the police who call on the expert assistance of EOD operators. The objects reported (generally left over from wars or training exercises) are often corroded. This fact, coupled with the large number of munition types, leads to the difficulty of making precise identifications.

The identification task is performed without disturbing the object, even if it is only partly visible. Identifying features include shape, size, fitments, and, where possible, colour and markings. If there is any doubt as to the safety of the object, it is detonated on site.

The system referred to in this paper is a demonstrator commissioned to explore the feasibility and potential benefits of providing EOD operators with computerised support.

The demonstrator was developed using a Xerox AI workstation running Interlisp-D and LOOPS. Its operation is controlled entirely by the use of a mouse. Figures 1 and 2 are extracts of conversations with the system concerning the identification of two inch mortar bombs. Some screens have been omitted for sake of brevity. The system uses standard EOD terminology, and all text has been verified as being consistent and meaningful to intended users. Rather than present an exhaustive display of the system's capability, figures 1 and 2 are intended just to give a flavour of its performance.

Figure 1

A bomb that has been fired generally has its nose buried, with only the base and part of the body visible. It will not be disturbed until proved safe.

There are no flash holes visible in this case. If the bomb is badly corroded, an EOD operator may play safe and elect to answer 'Don't know'.

Which of the following aspects of the UXO are visible?	Objective
☐ the nose of the UXO only	Question
☑ the base of the UXO only	Expand
☐ the entire UXO, but NOT any markings	Check
☐ the entire UXO, and any markings	Conclusions
☐ Negate	Revise
☐ Don't know	Restart

It has now been shown that... the UXO is a two inch mortar	Objective
How many flash holes are present in the base? Select from the following:	Question
☐ none	Expand
☐ four	Check
☐ two	Conclusions
☐ Negate	Revise
☑ Don't know	Restart

Arrows in the left hand corners indicate further options on other pages. In this case, however, the answer is on the first page.

The user decides to investigate the system's current objective. There are options to change or directly satisfy the current objecive, but the user chooses to question the system's selection.

Which one of the following statements concerning the shape of the base of the bomb is true: ▲	Objective
☐ the base is conical	Question
	Expand
☐ the base has ridged shoulders	Check
	Conclusions
☑ the base is flat, with square shoulders	Revise
▼	Restart

It has now been shown that... the UXO is an Anti-Trip Wire Bomb Remove and keep safely - UXO is valuable	Objective
Does the body of the bomb consist of a grapnel device ?	Question
☐ Yes	Expand
☐ No	Check
☐ Don't know	Conclusions
	Revise
	Restart

Satisfied with the explanation, the user returns to the 'Grapnel' question and answers 'No'.

The only remaining alternative is the 'Projectile Cordtex' bomb. However, with the nose invisible, it is impossible to prove categorically that this is the bomb's correct classification.

The system is primarily interested in determining whether... Grapnel	Objective
The aim is to distinguish between Grapnel Projectile Cordtex	Question
as these are equally promising because... the UXO is an Anti-Trip Wire Bomb the base is flat, with square shoulders	Expand
☑ Continue	Check
	Conclusions
	Revise
	Restart

The disposal method is... Remove and keep safely - UXO is valuable	**Objective**
It has been shown that... the UXO is an Anti-Trip Wire Bomb the UXO is a two inch mortar	Question
The munition could be... Projectile Cordtex	Expand
There are no more questions to ask.	Check
	Conclusions
	Revise
	Restart

Figure 2

Bombs, when discovered, are generally old and rusty. By saying that no markings are visible, the system avoids asking annoying questions about colouring, lettering etc.

Which of the following aspects of the UXO are visible?	Objective
☐ the nose of the UXO only	Question
☐ the base of the UXO only	Expand
☑ the entire UXO, but NOT any markings	Check
☐ the entire UXO, and any markings	Conclusions
☐ Negate	Revise
☐ Don't know	Restart

The initial questions that determine that the device is a two inch mortar have already been asked. The user observes that there are two flash holes.

It has now been shown that... the UXO is a two inch mortar	Objective
How many flash holes are present in the base? Select from the following	Question
☐ none	Expand
☐ four	Check
☑ two	Conclusions
☐ Negate	Revise
☐ Don't know	Restart

Before asking the next question, the user decides to check the conclusion that the bomb type is 'Signal or Illumination'.

It has now been shown that... the UXO is a Signal or Illumination Bomb Remove UXO for later disposal	Objective
Which one of the following statements concerning the nose is true	Question
	Expand
☐ the nose has a centrally positioned eye bolt	Check
☐ a nose cap is present, secured to the body by three rivets or by welding	Conclusions
☐ the nose is open, revealing body interior	Revise
☐ an embossed closing cap (lid) is in position	Restart

Selecting 'Check' for the 'Signal or Illumination' hypothesis produces a checklist of features. The user returns to the current question and selects the fourth option.

For Sig or Illum	Objective
it is always the case that... there are two flash holes present in the base the base is conical	Question
	Expand
and can be identified by one of... the nose is open, revealing body interior an embossed closing cap (lid) is in position there are two flash holes present in the base the base is conical	**Check**
	Conclusions
☑ Continue	Revise
	Restart

Having established that the bomb possesses an embossed closing cap, the system can ask about its markings. It is embossed with the letter 'P'.

Which of the following statements concerning the closing cap (lid) is true:	Objective
☐ the closing cap is embossed with special markings	Question
☐ the closing cap is embossed with the letter S	Expand
☑ the closing cap is embossed with the letter P	Check
☐ Negate	Conclusions
☐ Don't know	Revise
	Restart

Both the specific device and its disposal method have been identified. The system presents its conclusions but can be interrogated further if required.

The device has been identified The munition is... Illumination with parachute	Objective
The disposal method is... Remove UXO for later disposal	Question
It has been shown that... the UXO is a two inch mortar the UXO is a Signal or Illumination Bomb	Expand
	Check
There are no more questions to ask.	Conclusions
	Revise
	Restart

3. Implications of the Model

The model described in this paper was developed to solve a particular problem: that of assisting military personnel in the identification of conventional munitions. Although the initially perceived need was for a probabilistic diagnostic system, early in the knowledge engineering phase it became apparent that conclusions were either definite, or of no use. However, the task consisted of using observations of an unidentified object to successively narrow the solution space until firm conclusions about how to classify or at least dispose of the object could be made. In contrast to the identification procedure, the investigation procedure required informed guesswork to identify the most promising path of investigation. In light of this it seemed natural to adopt separate mechanisms for logical and investigate inference.

Having described the implementation, the lessons learnt and the insights made will now be explored.

3.1 Reasoning

The fundamental feature of the model was the factoring of the reasoning mechanism into logical inference and investigative inference. This lead to a greater understanding of the role and functionality of the reasoning. The two parts, though both conceptually simple (even naive) perform together as a sophisticated whole, the virtue of their component simplicity being transparency and understandability.

Logical inference was further factored into conditional reasoning based on sufficiency and necessity considerations, and mutually exclusive reasoning based on set membership, each part being performed by a simple set of rules.

Reasoning based on three-valued logic was particularly suited to the problem of munition identification, and is applicable to other fields where classification and/or safety are key issues. It is however an over-simplification for those fields of expertise where more subtle reasoning is required. This does not undermine the principle of striving for clarity and explicitness, and replacing algorithmic with rule or knowledge-based control wherever possible.

The scheme described by Dodson and Rector (1984) is similar to that described here in that they have factored out investigative inference. However, their method favours more sophisticated mathematical algorithms instead of simple heuristic control.

It also uses distributed control to overcome the limitations of using a single goal as a basis for question selection. The power of the knowledge-based approach is that it allows the flexibility to use a variety of search paradigms to select a question. A paradigm can be selected which takes into account the status of the whole inference net while selecting a question for an identified goal.

The advantage of using knowledge-based control is two-fold. Firstly, the transparency of the reasoning benefits both the user, in understanding and manipulating the system, and the knowledge engineer, in designing and evaluating the system. Secondly, both paradigms and search primitives are explicitly represented, enabling abstract explanations of strategy (see 3.3).

Keravnou and Johnson (1984) emphasise the importance of explicitly represented knowledge, and explicit reasoning strategies in order to build 'competent' expert systems stating that:

"A model of competence is . . . a model of the relationships between the structural (domain dependent) knowledge and the uses made of it (i.e. the reasoning processes that manipulate it). To every component of the structural knowledge there corresponds some reasoning process that manipulates it and vice versa. The result of this manipulation is competent behaviour."

Clearly, the separation of logical and investigative inference, and the one-to-one mapping between these processes and the components of knowledge they manipulate, constitute a step in the direction of competent expert systems.

3.2 Knowledge Engineering

Four types of knowledge were required:

. deductive knowledge
. support knowledge
. question-finding knowledge
. background knowledge.

Deductive knowledge consists of the concrete rules of the problem domain. Eliciting deductive knowledge involves defining the nodes (as statements), attaching the necessary text to the nodes, and defining the sufficiency and necessity relationships between them, or alternatively, writing a set of rules which can be compiled into a network structure.

As this is 'hard and fast' knowledge, it was easy to accumulate and manipulate, and was the main concern of the domain expert. Knowledge concerning mutual exclusion was added separately.

Allocation of support proved to be the most difficult of the knowledge engineering tasks. This appeared to be due to confusion arising when making decisions between what were and were not relevant factors. In order to overcome this confusion, a more automated approach was adopted. First, approximate measures of support were produced algorithmically, which were sufficient to result in a working system. The expert was then able to make 'significance judgements' about which factors most affected which other factors. These were mapped onto new measures of support by the knowledge engineer.

As the 'fine tuning' of support is essentially based on empirical knowledge, machine learning techniques could be used to successively improve allocations of support as the system is used. This could be done without endangering the correctness of the advice given, as support and potential have no affect on truth values.

Constructing the question-finding knowledge base involves writing a rule set to determine the system 'status', and then defining the search primitives and constructing the paradigms. This was very much the concern of the knowledge engineer, using his feel for the problem, and understanding of the search system.

Of considerable assistance while constructing the question-finding knowledge base was the ease with which search primitives and paradigms could be created and modified. This encouraged experimentation with a variety of configurations. Furthermore, with control knowledge explicitly stated, more thorough evaluation of the system's behaviour can be made.

Background knowledge was provided entirely by the domain expert. By tailoring it to educational needs, the system's role as a teaching aid was enhanced.

3.3 The Man-Machine System

The munition identification system was intrinsically designed to be one part of an effective man-machine system. One way of achieving this is by concentrating design and evaluation on the performance of the conversational system produced (resulting from the interaction of an intelligent human expert and the computer-based expert), rather than just on the performance of the automated subsystem (Keravnou and Johnson 1984). The performance of such a system should be greater than that possible by either man or machine alone (Woods 1986).

When an automated decision aid is introduced into a decision-making process it needs to be remembered that it is the human component who is responsible for the outcome of any decisions made. The responsibility-laden human must be in complete control of the decision aid and fully understand its behaviour, in order to avoid stressful, or even impossible situations. That is, there must be a high degree of 'cognitive coupling' between the human and machine sub-systems (Fitter & Sime 1980).

The munition identification system was designed to form part of a man-machine system with high cognitive coupling by attention to the following:

. natural and transparent reasoning
. subservience to the user
. cognitive support and explanation.

Human experts do not use the same reasoning to make deductions as they do to drive their investigations. It is thus natural that an automated decision maker should reflect this dichotemy. This not only introduces the advantage of being able to consider the two types of reasoning separately, but makes each type more explicit and understandable. The way in which potential is accrued evolved not from theoretical or mathematical considerations, but rather from an intuitive feel for how investigative inference is naturally performed. As potential has no affect on truth values, logical integrity is in no way endangered by adopting a model of investigative inference with no formal theoretical basis. The benefit of this intuitive approach has been the surprising degree to which domain users have understood and accepted as natural, this type of reasoning, and also its operational effectiveness.

As the human element of a man-machine system is the responsibility bearer he/she must have dominion over the machine element (Fitter & Sime 1980). This requirement has been catered for in a number of ways.

Firstly, the user is never committed to any particular action. The machine recommends objectives to explore and questions to answer, but these are only default assumptions; users are free to select their own objectives and questions at any time. Alternatively, they are free to revise a previous answer, or make use of the cognitive support or explanation facilities described below. This kind of flexibility is made easy by the explicit representation of logic and control information. The system has access to knowledge about its own workings.

Secondly, attention has been paid to the distribution of functions across the man-machine system (Hollnagel & Woods 1983). It is not sufficient to make an a priori assignment of functions between man and machine, using the machine to perform those functions that the human finds difficult, precisely because this takes control away from the user, introducing the perils of low cognitive coupling. This is overcome by providing a high degree of redundancy in the functionality of sub-components of the joint cognitive system. The main division being that the human is expected to provide the semantic and common sense, or "tacit" (Collins, Green & Draper 1985) knowledge, while the machine contributes its ability to store and manipulate large quantities of articulable knowledge. Redundant functionality means that the user can choose how to distribute the tasks between himself and the machine as he so wishes, provided he can understand the machine's behaviour.

Thirdly, all the information is available all of the time, so that, although for convenience the machine tries to make the most relevant information most immediately available, the user can find any of the information, or select any objective or question, to suit his own needs.

As much of the control knowledge in the system is explicitly accessible, it is possible to provide meaningful explanations and a variety of cognitive support facilities.

For the munition identification application, the following were implemented:

(a)   Why a question has been selected
(b)   Why a goal has been selected
(c)   Why or how a conclusion has been made
(d)   How to further substantiate a conclusion
(e)   What must be done to prove a goal/conclusion
(f)   Why information provided is contradictory
(g)   What information has been provided so far
(h)   What answering a question will achieve
(i) What background information pertains to the current situation.

These facilities are designed to support the cognitive activities of the user. For instance, by producing a list of unproved facts that should be true given a certain conclusion, a user can confirm his belief in that conclusion, or be reminded of facts that may have been overlooked. Similarly, by providing background information about a given situation, a user can improve his broad understanding of a problem area, and expand his reasoning capabilities.

By providing different types of knowledge and support, a system can adopt the role of a guidance program, increasing its usefulness and acceptability (Coombes & Alty 1984). Experience with the munition identification system showed that users enjoyed the enhanced professionalism afforded by a system that supported their decision making.

For any question, the paradigm used to reach it gives a high level insight into why it was selected, and a trace of specific search primitives gives a detailed explanation. These correspond to the abstract and concrete explanations discussed by Clancey (1983) which can result from explicit representation of control knowledge. With suitable text attached to each paradigm and search primitive, the following kind of explanation can be constructed:

What is the current objective?

The objective is to identify which of A and B
  are true: (from the status).

This is because A and B are both very promising as:

   I is true   (from the antecedents)
   J is true   (from the antecedents)
   and K is slightly promising. (from the antecedents)

Why is the current question being asked?

As A and B are both very promising (from the status)

A question has been selected with
the aim of distinguishing between
A and B(from the paradigm)

Question X is being asked because:

X will prove whether Y   (from the search primitive)
which will distinguish between (from the search primitive)
A and B.

The role of the interface as a two-way medium for conversation cannot be overstated. Just as it is important to design an interface with the user's model of the system in mind, the importance of developing a system's model of the user, or the system's conversational "grammar" of the user (Keravnou and Johnson 1984) is becoming increasingly recognised. Interface design should be taken seriously as an independent and important problem (Norman 1986).

4. Conclusions

Human experts do not use the same reasoning to make deductions as they do to drive their investigations. As such, it seems prudent for consultative expert systems to use a separate method of investigative inference, even when the deductive mechanism is rich enough to support it.

It is imperative that a user of an automated decision tool fully understands the behaviour of such a tool, and remains in control of it, and not vice versa. Both these aims are more easily met when deductive and control knowledge are explicitly and separately represented.

Regarding the function of a consultative expert system as a conclusion-maker, with explanation and cognitive support facilities merely by-products of the reasoning strategy, is contrary to the real needs of many expert system users.

Amongst the practical benefits observed as a consequence of using the strategy described in this paper are:

- paradigms and question selection primitives are easy to create and experiment with, promoting optimal question selection in a variety of circumstances

- meaningful explanations of why goals and questions are chosen can be provided (for instance, using the high level 'statement of intent' embodied by a search paradigm)

- a high degree of cognitive support (e.g. verification, justification) is afforded

- empirically based machine learning can enhance the investigative inference without endangering logical consistency;

- knowledge-based control increases the flexibility and transparency of the system;

- non-technical users readily understand and accept the system's line of reasoning.

Acknowledgements

I would like to thank Major Joe Hastings of the DLSA for granting clearance to discuss the EOD project, PA Computers and Telecommunications for giving me time to write this paper and, in particular, Andy Paterson, Paul Sachs and Mike Turner for their encouragement and guidance.

References

1.	Clancey WJ (1983). The Advantages of Abstract Control Knowledge in Expert System Design: AAAI 83, pp 74-78.

2.	Collins HM, Green RH & Draper RC (1985). "Where's the Expertise?" Expert systems as a medium of knowledge transfer: Expert Systems 85: Proceedings of the 5th Technical Conference of the BCS Specialist Group on Expert Systems pp. 323-334.

3.	Coombes M & Alty J (1984). Expert Systems - an alternative paradigm: International Journal of Man-Machine Studies 20, pp. 21-43.

4.	Dodson DC & Rector AL (1984). Importance-Driven Distributed Control of Diagnostic Inference: Research and Development in Expert Systems: Proceedings of the 4th Technical Conference of the BCS Specialist Group on Expert Systems, pp. 51, 60.

5.	Fitter M & Sime M (1980). Creating Responsive Computers: Responsibility and shared decision making. In HT Smith and TRG Green: Human Interaction with Computers, pp 39-66 London Academic Press

6.	Hollnagel E & Woods D (1983). Cognitive Systems Engineering: New wine in new bottles: International Journal of Man Machine Studies 18 pp. 583-600.

7.	Keravnou ET & Johnson L (1984). Design of Expert Systems from the perspective of Conversation Theory Methodology: Cybernetics and Systems Research pp 651-54; Elsevier.

8.	Norman DA (1986). Cognitive Engineering. In User Centred Systems Design: New Perspectives on Human Computer Interaction. ed. DA Norman & SW Draper pp 31-61. Lawrence Erlbaum Associates.

9.	Woods DD (1986) Cognitive Technologies. The Design of Joint Human-Machine Cognitive Systems: The AI Magazine Winter 1986, pp. 86-92